Style & Status

Style & Status

Selling Beauty to African American Women, 1920–1975

Susannah Walker

THE UNIVERSITY PRESS OF KENTUCKY

Publication of this volume was made possible in part by a grant
from the National Endowment for the Humanities.

Scholarly publisher for the Commonwealth,
serving Bellarmine University, Berea College, Centre College of Kentucky, Eastern
Kentucky University, The Filson Historical Society, Georgetown College,
Kentucky Historical Society, Kentucky State University, Morehead State University,
Murray State University, Northern Kentucky University, Transylvania University,
University of Kentucky, University of Louisville, and Western Kentucky University.
All rights reserved.

Editorial and Sales Offices: The University Press of Kentucky
663 South Limestone Street, Lexington, Kentucky 40508-4008
www.kentuckypress.com

11 10 09 08 07   5 4 3 2 1

Library of Congress Cataloging-in-Publication Data

Walker, Susannah, 1970-
  Style and status : selling beauty to African American women, 1920-1975 / Susannah
Walker.
     p. cm.
  Includes bibliographical references and index.
  ISBN-13: 978-0-8131-2433-9 (hardcover : alk. paper)
  ISBN-10: 0-8131-2433-6 (hardcover : alk. paper) 1. African American women—
Social conditions—20th century. 2. African American women—Race identity.
3. Beauty, Personal—Social aspects—United States—History—20th century. 4. Beauty,
Personal—Economic aspects—United States—History—20th century. 5. Beauty
culture—Social aspects—United States—History—20th century. 6. Beauty culture—
Economic aspects—United States—History—20th century. 7. Popular culture—United
States—History—20th century. 8. African Americans in popular culture—History—
20th century. 9. United States—Race relations—History—20th century. I. Title.
  E185.86.W338 2007
  306.4'613--dc22   2006033478

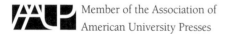

For my grandparents

Dorothy Brigstock (1916–2005)
Robert Brigstock (1910–2003)
Marion Duell (1917–1999)
Charles Walker (1915–2004)

Contents

Illustrations

Acknowledgments

It is probably cliché to mention that I never would have guessed, when I started this project, that ten years would pass between the graduate research seminar paper that inspired it and the completion of this manuscript. Then again, the acknowledgments section is as good a place as any for clichés! I decided to write my dissertation on African American women's beauty culture during my second year as a doctoral student in history at Carnegie Mellon University. I entered that research seminar in the fall of 1995 with a variety of interests, including African American history, cultural and gender analysis, and the history of consumer culture, but with little idea of what I wanted to research for the seminar paper, let alone for my dissertation. Finally I settled on a project that examined African American consumer culture during the 1920s and 1930s, primarily using black newspaper advertising and the records of marketing professionals interested in African American consumers. The preponderance of beauty product and service advertising stood out, and the outlines of my doctoral project, which is the basis of this book, began to take shape.

Therefore, I must first and foremost recognize the director of that seminar, David Hounshell, for helping me to develop my thinking on this topic at its earliest stages. I would also like to thank the members of that seminar, especially John Jensen, Julia Roos, Jon Silver, Jeff Suzik, and Carl Zimring, for contributing to the supportive and intellectually stimulating experience of our coursework years. Other seminars that shaped my intellectual development that I would like to particularly recognize are Joe Trotter's seminars in U.S. and African American history, Mary Lindemann's seminars in European and cultural history, Kate Lynch's seminar in historical methods, and Judith Modell's seminar in ethnographic methods. In addition to my particular grad student cohort, I shared classes, office spaces, and teaching assistant experiences with many others who became good colleagues, sounding boards, and social companions at various points over the years, including Trent Alexander, Jennifer Bannister, Tom Buchanan, Tim Haggerty, Rebecca

Kluchin, Jim Longhurst, Robin Jenkins, Jennifer Trost, Lisa Sigel, Matt Weiss, and David Wolcott. In particular, I want to thank those friends who have continued to offer their support, advice, and guidance as I have moved through graduate school, the job market, first jobs, and the manuscript writing and revision process. In addition to being a dear friend, Jeff Suzik is one of the people I most count on for good input on my research as well as my teaching. Tom Buchanan was a good person to talk history with or avoid work with while in grad school, and he continues to be a good friend. As I embarked on my first teaching jobs, old grad school friends Jennifer Trost and Jim Longhurst, themselves at various stages of their post-Pittsburgh lives, became wonderful people to lend moral support and compare notes with. Finally, Lisa Sigel has not only been a great friend, she has also given me incredibly useful advice and guidance—on the portions of my work she has read and critiqued, on teaching, on the academic profession, and particularly on the harrowing process of turning one's dissertation into a book and getting that book published.

I would also like to thank my advisor, Joe Trotter. No graduate student could ask for a more patient and generous person to supervise her dissertation. Joe has been unfailingly kind and supportive throughout the process. As I was researching and writing my dissertation, he gave me plenty of space to do the work the way that I wanted to do it, but he provided me with excellent advice and feedback at each stage. In recent years, when I moved away from (and briefly back to) Pittsburgh, Joe continued to provide moral and professional support both for this project and for my professional development as a whole. In addition, I want to thank the other members of my committee, Tera Hunter and Scott Sandage. Both have been good, critical readers of my work and have offered sound advice on everything from my research and writing to the job search and publishing process. Kathy Peiss read an early version of chapter 6 for a conference and subsequent publication. I am thrilled to have had such useful input from one of the pioneering scholars in the history of beauty culture. In addition, I would like to thank all those readers and commentators, known and anonymous, who have critiqued my work in various forms and at various stages over the years. Their observations and advice have certainly made this a better book. In particular, I would like to thank the people who read this manuscript for the University Press of Kentucky for their positive reviews and invaluable suggestions. I would also like to thank Ann Malcolm at the press for being such an enthusiastic advocate for the publication of this work. It has been a long road to make this project a book, and I am thankful to have such a supportive editor and publisher involved. Finally, I would like to express my appreciation to my copyeditor Anna Laura Bennett, whose attention to detail and ear for clear, logical prose have made this book more readable, more consistent, and less repetitive than it might have been without her help.

I have been fortunate to receive considerable financial support for my research and writing over the years. I would like to recognize the Department of History at Carnegie Mellon University for the graduate fellowship and stipend that made becoming a historian possible for me. I would like to thank the Center for African American Urban Studies and the Economy at CMU for writing and travel grants that helped me to finish my dissertation and present pieces of it at various conferences. A research grant from the Hagley Museum and Library allowed me to do research within the Avon Collection there, as well as to deliver my first paper at a professional meeting, the Hagley's Beauty and Business conference in 1999. Finally, a New Scholar's Grant and travel grant from the University of Prince Edward Island helped me to do additional research as I was developing the dissertation into a manuscript.

I must certainly acknowledge all of the people at libraries and archives that helped me as I was doing my research. In particular, the archivists at the Chicago Historical Society, home to the Claude A. Barnett Collection, and at the Indiana Historical Society, where the Madam C. J. Walker Collection is housed, helped me through the bulk of my archival research. In addition, I could not have completed this project so efficiently without the extensive collections of African American newspapers and magazines at the Schomburg Center for Research in Black Culture. In addition, I conducted briefer research trips to work with the Marjorie Stewart Joyner Papers, part of the Vivian G. Harsh Research Collection at the Chicago Public Library; the Avon Collection at the Hagley Museum and Library; the Caroline Jones and Nathaniel Mathis collections at the Smithsonian's National Museum of American History; and the Women's Bureau records at the National Archives. All of these trips were made more efficient and fruitful by the help of librarians, archivists, and support staff. Finally, I would like to thank the interlibrary loan office at CMU.

Friends and colleagues have been essential to my sanity, my emotional well-being, and my survival over the past ten years. In my first job at the University of Prince Edward Island, Ann Braithwaite, Susan Brown, Lisa Chilton, James Moran, and Fiona Papps were supportive friends who helped to create an uncommonly collegial atmosphere during those tough first teaching years. Now at Virginia Wesleyan College, I am again lucky to have fantastic colleagues, and I would like to mention in particular Rich Bond, Laura Landolt, Dan Margolies, Olena Prokopovych, and Sara Sewell for their advice, comradeship, and encouragement as I began a new job and prepared this manuscript for publication in the same year. In the summer of 2006, as I completed the final round of revisions on this project, I was fortunate to participate in a National Endowment for the Humanities summer institute, African American Civil Rights Struggles in the Twentieth Century, at the W. E. B. Du Bois Institute at Harvard University. I am grateful to my fellow participants, the institute directors, and the faculty, not only for inspiring crucial refinements in my thinking about this work but also for reinvigorating my life as a scholar in ways that will certainly influence my future research, writing, and teaching.

I also need to express gratitude to the friends and networks outside of work that have sustained me and given me such joy over the years. Thanks to the Ultimate community in Pittsburgh, particularly to Josie Fisher and Erica and Tim Lloyd, who remain friends far beyond the Frisbee fields. Thanks also to the members of the Masters Rowing Team at Three Rivers Rowing Association, who have been teammates, competitors, and some of the closest friends of my life. Thanks especially to Mary and Eric Fisher, Susan Lawrence, Jill Markl, Elizabeth and Derrick Pitard, Tracy Thompson, and Toby Yanowitz.

Finally, and most important, there is my family. My parents and Grandpa Walker provided much-needed financial help throughout this process. Aunts, uncles, and cousins have always shown kind interest in this odd project of mine. I lost all four of my grandparents during the long period of working on this project, but I know that they were all proud of me and my then-unfinished work. Thanks to my brother, Noah and sister, Rebecca, who were small children when I left home as an undergraduate and have therefore probably never associated me with anything but academia. I am appreciating them more and more both as adults and friends. Finally, I can't adequately express my appreciation for my mother and father (and don't do so nearly enough). I have heard so many of my colleagues, in graduate school and beyond, complain that their parents just don't get what they do. My parents not only get it, but they are almost embarrassingly proud of me. I have to keep telling my father that Oprah probably isn't going to invite me on to her show! Beyond all of the support that parents give to their children, my parents instilled in me a love of books and of history. They never pressured me to pursue a more "practical" profession than that of an academic (although perhaps they should have), but rather, they wanted only for me to follow my passions and do something that I really cared about. If any one factor can be said to have made this book, and my career as a historian, possible, it is certainly that.

Introduction

Why Hair Is Political

In 1988, Andrea Benton Rushing, professor of English and black studies at Amherst College, wrote an essay for *Feminist Studies* that deftly wove together personal stories about hair, race, femininity, and family, while illuminating the cultural significance of hair in African American history. Rushing recalled that, before having children, "back in the glory days of black being beautiful, I'd vowed that no daughter of mine would have her hair straightened." Rushing described past mother-daughter trips to New York City to get their Afros shaped and styled, and present reactions to her and her girls' African-style braids, before revealing her own complex hair history. Amid the resurgence of relaxed hair in the 1980s and despite a daughter's complaint that "everyone in the world but us had straight hair," Rushing wrote, she stood firm on the straightening issue. But then she admitted, "I've betrayed my heritage after all. I am, you see, a beautician's daughter." Rushing mentioned a slew of relatives—aunts, grandmothers, and other extended family members—in Harlem and South Carolina who were "in the guild." She described the skill these women had in using "the same Apex pressing oil," hot combs, and curling irons to convert African American women's hair into glossy styles, and the social relationships formed in the homes and beauty shops where women did hair and got their hair done. Rushing's memories revealed the centrality of commercial beauty culture in the lives of black women of her mother's and earlier generations, and she mused that, perhaps, her daughters missed out on an important part of their

1

heritage. "Busily being true to the African part of my ancestry," Rushing wrote, "I've been false to all this other." Perhaps, she concluded, it was time to introduce her daughters to this history "and weave hair stories into the hours we spend getting our hair done."[1]

One does not have to look hard to find evidence of the cultural and political significance of hair for black women in American society. "Hair is the be-all and end-all," wrote *Village Voice* staff writer Lisa Jones in 1991. "Everything I know about American history I learned from looking at black people's hair. It's the perfect metaphor for the African experiment here; the price of the ticket (for a journey no one elected to take), the toll of slavery, and the costs of remaining. It's all in the hair." Observers on this subject routinely comment that hair looms larger for African American women than it does for white women in assessments of appearance, self-image, and social status. Sociologist Ingrid Banks articulates this idea well in her ethnographic study of contemporary black women's thoughts and feelings on "hair matters." "Certainly white women have concerns with their hair," she admits, "but their concerns do not involve the actual alteration of hair texture to the extent that it is an expression of their cultural consciousness. . . . They do not," Banks contends, "have to deal with cultural and political constructions of hair that intersect with race and gender in relationship to mainstream notions of beauty." As Banks and others observe, African American hair has historically symbolized and continues to reflect struggles over race and gender in the United States. This has been shown in recent years by African American critiques of white-owned businesses engaged in the "ethnic" beauty trade. It has been demonstrated in news stories about black women being fired from their jobs, or girls being sent home from school, for wearing braids, dreadlocks, or other hairstyles deemed "extreme" by employers and principals. It is revealed by the fact that, forty years after Stokely Carmichael declared that "black is beautiful," the phrases "good hair" and "bad hair" still have meaning for African Americans. But of course the fact that hair, and other appearance issues, matter in particular ways for black women is nothing new—it has a history that reflects and informs the history of race and gender relations in the United States.[2]

History, Politics, and Black Women's Beauty Culture

The phrase "beauty culture," in common usage throughout most of the twentieth century, refers to the tools, methods, and business practices of altering and caring for women's appearance. Beauty culture encompasses treatments for women's hair, skin, and bodies along with the training and employment of women who work as beauty culturists. It includes the cosmetic and hair products sold to and used by women as well as the advertising and marketing of those products. "Beauty culturist" was the term people in the industry most often used to describe themselves in the twentieth century, although "beautician" and "cosmetologist" gained popularity after World War II. In this study, "beauty culture" and "beauty industry" are roughly equivalent, and terms like "beauty culturist," "beautician," and "hairdresser" are used more or less interchangeably.

Scholars have recently begun to explore in depth the history of American beauty culture and commercialized beauty standards for women, both as a broad topic and with a focus on African Americans. The present work seeks to examine the African American beauty culture industry, and shifting and contested notions of what beauty meant for black women, in the context of African American social, political, and economic history. Although black women's beauty culture mirrored white women's beauty culture in important ways during the period examined here, African American beauty culture was distinctive because it explicitly reflected and articulated twentieth-century racial politics in the United States, especially as it was emerging in the context of black migration and community formation in American cities. Of course the politics of appearance was salient for women across racial lines in the twentieth century, but I argue that beauty culture was uniquely so for African American women, in large part because they confronted popular images of feminine beauty that perpetually used a white ideal. White beauty culture, as Kathy Peiss has observed, certainly associated whiteness with beauty but always did so implicitly, and often unconsciously, as a fact too obvious to require declaration. Ordinary black women, as well as African American hairdressers, entrepreneurs, models, entertainers, and others designated as beauty experts, struggled, often quite openly, throughout the twentieth century to define a broader and more diverse ideal of beauty for themselves despite mainstream beauty standards that tended to exclude or demean them. At the same time, beauty was a controversial issue among African Americans, one that highlighted racial inequities in the United States and revealed social tensions within black communities.[3]

This study examines several aspects of the politics of African American beauty culture. First, the images and rhetoric about African American beauty standards in print advertising, in newspaper and magazine articles, and from beauticians themselves directly and indirectly characterized black women's beauty as a social issue. Second, beauty culture reveals the participation of blacks in American consumer culture. Although major white advertisers mostly ignored black consumers in this period, the success of the beauty industry among African Americans helped to bolster black market researchers' calls for white recognition of black consumers. Third, black women were prominent in the black beauty industry in the early to mid-twentieth century. Efforts by these women to build their businesses, to provide jobs for black women independent of white employers, and to compete with white-owned beauty companies should be understood as a distinctive version of black economic nationalism that sometimes meshed with, and at other times conflicted with, African American efforts to promote the economic power of black consumers to white companies.

My study begins in 1920 for two reasons. First, two fine studies exist on African American beauty culture before 1920. Both Noliwe Rooks's *Hair Raising: Beauty, Culture, and African American Women* and Gwendolyn Robinson's doctoral dissertation, "Class, Race, and Gender: A Transcultural, Theoretical, and Sociohistorical Analysis of Cosmetic Institutions and Practices to 1920," examine the significance of the beauty culture industry for black women in the Progressive Era. Both scholars examine African American beauty in the context of the migration of black people to northern cities, the focus of African American social activists on racial progress, and the role of grooming in the project of racial uplift. Both studies place racial identity, the struggle for African American economic independence, and class dynamics within black communities as central themes in the story of black beauty culture. My own work picks up on many of these themes, as I carry the study of African American commercial beauty culture through the peak years of black migration and urbanization. I begin in the 1920s also because I am specifically interested in examining black women's beauty culture in the context of mass consumer culture and mass advertising, which became centrally important in American life during the 1920s. In continuing my study through the 1970s, I trace the relationship of black women to commercial beauty culture as African Americans became increasingly urban and consumer culture grew increasingly pervasive in the United States after World War II. More important, carrying this study to the 1970s lets me address the impact of the civil rights movement of the 1950s and 1960s and the Black Power movement of the 1960s and 1970s on African American beauty culture.

For me, the subject of African American women's beauty culture opens up all kinds of important historical questions. What role did beauty culture play in the making of black women's racial and feminine identities? How does African American beauty culture fit in with the changing social, economic, and political contexts of black people's lives in the twentieth century? What was the role of black-owned beauty culture businesses in African American communities? What were the differences between black-owned and white-owned manufacturers of beauty products for black women? How does African American beauty culture affect our historical understanding of the rise of consumer culture in the twentieth century, the development of African American ideas about racial progress, the Great Migration, and post–World War II freedom struggles?

African American beauty culture is a good subject for exploring the interplay of race, class, and gender, including how this interplay shaped power relationships in the United States. This has been an important historical project for scholars in the last fifteen or twenty years. Evelyn Brooks Higginbotham has posited that black women are unique subjects for exploring the relationship between categories of race, class, and gender, because black women show us how all three have been inextricably linked throughout American history. Race as an ideological concept has fundamentally influenced and shaped power relationships in the United States, and Higginbotham argues that studying African American women allows historians to make connections between the ideological rhetoric of race and gender on the one hand, and the concrete material conditions, social contexts, and political actions of groups and individuals on the other. In *Race Rebels*, Robin D. G. Kelley reveals the political power of dress, appearance, and public behavior in African American communities. In *Stylin': African American Expressive Culture from Its Beginnings to the Zoot Suit*, Shane White and Graham White explore the roles of African American dress, dance, parades, and hairstyles in forming black communities and resisting racism.[4] These and other scholars challenge us to understand the complex operation of race, gender, and power in American society. This study seeks to contribute further to this scholarship by examining African American beauty culture through its marketing images and rhetoric, through the words and experiences of black beauticians and their customers, and through commentary on the "issue" of beauty in the African American media.

Beauty Culture, Consumer Culture, and African Americans

African American beauty culture exemplified the extensive participation of black people in mass consumer culture as it emerged in the last century. This is important because, as recent historians have observed, twentieth-century culture in the United States was in large part defined by consumerism. Advertisers, according to Roland Marchand, prepared Americans for "consumer citizenship," and consumption became the mechanism by which Americans could express and fulfill their dreams and desires. Commercial beauty culture, in particular, revealed the complex and multifaceted roles consumerism could play in people's lives. Consumption in this case was far more than simply purchasing beauty products. Advertisements, to begin with, attached deep emotional and social meanings to female appearance and, at base, claimed that intangibles like love, popularity, and beauty themselves could be bought. African American women did not just encounter commercial beauty culture in the pages of newspapers or on drugstore shelves. Consuming beauty was often a very personal and interactive relationship—between a beauty company sales agent and her door-to-door contacts, between a home salon operator and her neighborhood patrons, and between beauty shop operators and their customers. Going to get one's hair done was an act of consumption, of course, but it was also, like so many other acts of consumption, a social activity. Furthermore, the popular media bolstered commercial beauty culture though its coverage of female celebrities and discussions on the topic of beauty. Thus, every time a black woman went to the beauty parlor, applied some lipstick, chatted with her neighborhood Madam C. J. Walker agent, or read an article on the beauty regimen of Lena Horne, she was acting, on some level, as a consumer of beauty culture.[5]

African Americans' involvement in consumer culture often highlighted racial discrimination in American society. Social and economic inequities and segregation are obvious examples of this phenomenon, but it also manifested itself in the world of marketing. For much of the twentieth century, white advertisers of products, from foods and household products to televisions and cars, did not view African Americans as worthy of their attention. Most did not see black people as affluent enough to warrant special advertising attention or sophisticated enough to respond to product marketing. African American marketing experts, however, believed it was vital that black consumers be recognized. For them, it was a civil rights issue. Several market research studies of black consumer habits emerged between 1935 and the 1970s; they sought to show that African Americans were worthy of advertisers' attention. The studies stressed that black people were savvy consumers who recognized brand names and bought high-quality items when they could. In particular, all of these studies pointed out that African Americans spent more money on personal care products, including women's hair and cosmetic products, than did whites. African American marketing experts insisted throughout these decades that black consumers were affluent enough, urban enough, and sophisticated enough to warrant attention from white advertisers. African American business leaders fought to promote black spending power, claiming that big business's recognition of black consumer citizenship was a requirement of full racial equality. Beauty culture was one industry that flourished in black communities, and it was an industry dominated by black businesswomen. Nevertheless, some white-owned beauty product companies did develop goods that were marketed specifically to African American women. Black business promoters cited this vibrant industry as one indication that black consumers were significant, but, paradoxically, they also warned against white companies' entering what they saw as a uniquely African American business. Thus black business nationalism competed with the desire for black consumer citizenship in rhetoric about the African American beauty industry.[6]

Race, Beauty Culture, and African American Women

Historian Jackson Lears and feminist scholar Susan Bordo both argue, albeit in different contexts and from different disciplinary perspectives, that advertising and consumer culture have presented the human body as malleable and always in need of improvement. At the same time, advertisements have offered people a narrow body ideal to strive for, and a limited route to achieve it: through the purchase of specific goods and services. The African American beauty industry told black women they could be beautiful, but considerations of race and color shaped the beauty standard promoted and the methods needed to achieve it. African American women could not fail to notice that mainstream commercial beauty culture promoted an ideal that invariably excluded them. It wasn't that race was absent from the selling of beauty to white women, or that white beauty ideals were monolithic. White women's beauty culture in the early to mid-twentieth century managed to constantly invoke race without specifically featuring African American women. Peiss notes, for example, that skin-bleaching creams were promoted to white women as well as black women at least through the 1920s, but for whites, the creams were sold as a way to reverse the effects of time spent in outdoor leisure pursuits. Some manufacturers played on the assumption that a white woman with a tan feared being mistaken for a light-skinned black woman. Even as tans became fashionable and tanning creams abounded, white women were advised to use bleaches once summer ended, so as to reaffirm their racial identity. In addition, white cosmetics companies paid lip service to America's diversity, offering women the prospect of looking like Cleopatra, an Indian princess, or a Mediterranean beauty, but these various celebrated types of beauty were sold to white women as looks that could easily be put on and taken off. "Skin tone was a matter of fashion," Peiss explains; "a dark complexion was one choice among many—as long as the boundary between black and white was secure." It was a hypocrisy that African Americans constantly noted, but the fact that white commercial beauty culture did not promote a truly diverse beauty ideal did not change. Nor did the mainstream industry have real black women in mind when it created its advertising—unless it was creating segregated marketing campaigns for products aimed at African Americans.[7]

Nevertheless, beauty culture was big business in African American communities. Black-owned companies, many founded by African American women, like Madam C. J. Walker, Annie Turnbo Malone, and Sara Washington, as well as some white-owned companies, vied to sell beauty to African American women. But commercial beauty culture was controversial among African Americans from the start. Overwhelmingly in the 1920s and 1930s, advertisements, along with beauty contest winners, celebrities, and models, promoted straight or wavy hair and light complexions as the desirable beauty standard. Some black observers roundly condemned this beauty ideal and accused those who used hair straighteners and skin bleaches of wanting to look white. But it was not that simple. African American beauty culturists continually insisted that their products and methods were not about accepting a white beauty ideal but about treating damaged hair, healing scalp disease, and helping hair to grow. They straightened hair too, but they portrayed their method of shampooing and using pressing oil and a hot comb as a modern, healthy, progressive way for black women to care for their hair. Furthermore, although advertisements aimed at black women in the 1920s and 1930s increasingly stressed the glamour and sexual attractiveness imparted by hair and cosmetic products, many advertisements used an older pitch that promoted personal grooming, including hair straightening, as a route to racial uplift—as a way for African American women to use their appearance to help raise the collective and individual fortunes of black people. Whereas white-owned companies often described African American hair and skin color in derogatory ways, assuming that darker skin and kinky hair were defects that needed to be "fixed," black-owned companies strove to counter negative images of African American women's appearance and to glorify black womanhood.

Although hair straightening might have been somewhat controversial early in the twentieth century, by the 1940s, most African American women frequently straightened their hair. The ideal of glossy, wavy hair changed only in terms of specific styles that were in vogue from year to year. Meanwhile, icons of African American beauty in popular culture, from models and beauty contestants to singers and actresses, continued, for the most part, to possess medium to light brown complexions. After World War II, however, the social and political dimension of black beauty culture deepened, as the emerging civil rights movement influenced the structure and rhetoric of the beauty culture industry. In the 1950s and 1960s, integration emerged as a dominant theme for black-owned beauty businesses. Black beauty culturists no longer felt the need, as many had in earlier decades, to defend their businesses against accusations that they were not respectable, or that they followed a white beauty standard. Instead, they stressed the variety of ways in which commercial beauty products and methods could help any woman, regardless of race, to become beautiful.

Also, starting in the 1930s and continuing after the end of the war, professional black beauticians fought to win positions on the state cosmetology boards that were being set up to regulate the industry. They succeeded in getting boards to require that methods for doing black women's hair be included in curriculums. In some states the law eventually required that, just as black women had to learn to use the permanent wave machine, white women had to learn to use the straightening comb. This was an important symbolic victory in an industry that was essentially segregated throughout the twentieth century. In a similar vein, black-owned cosmetics companies increasingly portrayed a multiracial beauty ideal, even though the industry was still segregated, by using African American, white, and sometimes Asian models together in hair and cosmetics product advertising. Even though these products were marketed exclusively to black women, such ads were meant to symbolically desegregate American beauty standards. These developments demonstrated the continuing politicization of African American beauty culture at the same time that they exemplified the commodification of a centrally important social and political movement in African American history.

The emergence of the Afro in the mid-1960s seemed to defy commodification, offering a radical rejection of straightened hair and a clear affirmation of black pride. The "natural" began as a fringe style for artistic and intellectual black women in the early 1960s, but it quickly evolved into a political statement by mid-decade and became a commercial fashion statement in less than ten years. As Afros gained in popularity, some beauticians worried that natural hair would ruin their business, while others rushed to offer Afro styling to their customers. In the late 1960s and into the 1970s, the Afro's political significance was complicated by its emergence as a hairstyle that was fashionable with all kinds of women, activist or not. Soon, beauty product companies were offering Afro products to consumers, sometimes invoking black pride and African culture in advertising. Many black women (and some white women) wore Afros without necessarily identifying with the Black Power movement. By the 1970s, no one could deny that black women's hair was political, but the consequences of the commodification of "political" hairstyles were only beginning to be considered.

Chapter 1

"The Beauty Industry
Is Ours"

Developing African American Consumer
Citizenship in the 1920s and 1930s

Early in 1929, Claude Barnett, an African American newspaperman and founder of the first black-owned advertising agency, wrote letters to two of the most successful female-headed African American beauty product companies in the United States. To Freeman B. Ransom, general manager of the Madam C. J. Walker Manufacturing Company, Barnett pitched his advertising services and closed by asking whether Ransom thought "it possible to get together on a program of occupying enough space in the papers to overshadow the white firms, gradually excluding them?" Writing to his client Annie Malone of the Poro Company, Barnett warned, "Competition from white firms is constantly becoming keener," and he advised more advertising. Having "watched the trend of events for the past few years," he was "convinced that Poro will get a still smaller share of business unless a new impetus is given to making sales." But Barnett wanted Malone to do more than just buy more advertising space; he also urged her to change her marketing strategy. Rather than running their usual style of ads highlighting the history and achievements of the company, Poro needed a glamorous new campaign that linked its products to beauty, prestige, and happiness for the women who used them. "Make the ads so tempting that every woman who does not use Poro will think she is missing something," Barnett urged.[1]

Claude Barnett had much to gain, of course, if Poro and the Madam C. J. Walker Company decided to put more advertising in black newspapers. Barnett's Chicago-based news distribution company, the Associated Negro Press, depended on the subscriptions of small African American newspapers throughout the country, while those newspapers struggled to secure enough advertising revenue to stay afloat. In his role as an advertising executive, Barnett sought clients, created ads, and sold advertising space in black newspapers. He encouraged those newspapers, in turn, to subscribe to his news service. This was more than just a smart business strategy in which he could profit at several stages of the newspaper publishing process. Barnett was passionate about promoting African American businesses in general; he saw consumerism as a key to the social and political advancement of black people. Barnett hoped to change the attitudes of national-brand advertisers, who mostly underestimated the spending power of black consumers and generally did not bother to advertise in African American publications. As Roland Marchand explains, mainstream advertising of the 1920s and 1930s did not target African Americans because advertisers, who tended to model their audiences from personal experience, envisioned the average "consumer citizen" as white and middle class.[2]

Barnett, along with a handful of other marketing professionals, worked hard to claim consumer citizenship for black Americans. At the turn of the century, Booker T. Washington had encouraged African Americans to focus on becoming effective participants in America's capitalist economy before attempting to gain social or political equality with whites. By the 1920s and 1930s, however, vocational training, steady work habits, and entrepreneurial spirit were not the sole measures of capitalist involvement or success. Participation in American capitalism required consumption of mass-produced goods and, perhaps more important, recognition of this consumption by advertisers and marketing executives. Barnett hoped that market research (then barely in its infancy) might prove the worth of black consumers to white-owned businesses. At the same time, Barnett was a keen observer of new trends in advertising and believed that African American businesses needed to adopt a more modern approach to marketing their goods and services if they wanted to succeed, particularly if they were to compete with white-owned businesses.

Where the beauty industry was concerned, as in many industries with a significant African American presence, promoting black consumer citizenship within the increasingly complex and pervasive American marketplace clashed with economic nationalist concerns over protecting African American–owned businesses. By the 1920s and 1930s, a large proportion of beauty product advertising in black publications came from white-owned companies, which claimed an ever-increasing share of sales. Rather than welcome this trend as a rare example of white businesses' recognition of a lucrative black consumer market, many observers saw it as a threat to one of the most vibrant and profitable of black enterprises. Thus beauty culture both demonstrated the possibilities and revealed the limits of black consumer citizenship in the context of segregation, racial discrimination, and economic inequality—all of which curtailed the ability of African Americans, be they consumers or entrepreneurs, to compete on equal terms with whites. Certainly Barnett himself must have been aware of this problem as he exhorted Malone and Walker to increase their advertising budgets. After all, this was a man who thought big when it came to business: in addition to his newspaper and advertising activities, he had, over the years, attempted to run his own beauty product company and started a literary magazine. Nevertheless, Barnett's ambitious plans were always limited by racial prejudice and lack of capital. Companies like Poro and Madam C. J. Walker could rarely afford to increase their advertising budgets to match those of their biggest white competitors, as Barnett encouraged them to do. The very circumstances that created opportunities for black entrepreneurs nevertheless limited their businesses' ability to grow and left them ill equipped to contend with white competition when it came. The Great Depression left smaller and less financially stable black companies even more vulnerable to this competition. Thus, in Jim Crow America in the 1920s and 1930s, economic nationalism was often the best option, but ultimately a precarious path for black businesses to take.

This is clearly illustrated in the case of commercial beauty culture. The commodification of beauty in the early twentieth century affected black women and white women alike, as the sheer volume of beauty goods and services available mushroomed and advertising itself became more emotional and didactic in tone. Selling beauty to black women created lucrative opportunities for white companies as well as for African American entrepreneurs. When Barnett urged women like Malone to advertise more and to modernize their advertising, he meant for African American commercial beauty enterprises to beat out the white competition, which was using modernized pitches and which, many African Americans seemed to agree, had no rightful place in the field. As noted above, such a position stood awkwardly juxtaposed with campaigns to get more advertising dollars from white companies into black publications, but it made sense for a number of reasons. Beauty culture was one business in which African Americans, especially women, had gained considerable success by the 1920s, and it had brought employment and money into black communities. White-owned cosmetics companies, which had considerably more resources to spend on marketing and often practiced racial discrimination in hiring, threatened the achievements of women like Malone and Walker and the thousands of black women their companies employed. Many African American beauty industry leaders also accused the white-owned companies of racism and insensitivity in their advertising, claiming that their ads encouraged black women to hate their appearance and seek a white beauty ideal. Although this was true to some extent, by the 1920s and 1930s the advertising messages of the most prominent white- and black-owned companies were quite similar. The accusation that the white companies were usurpers that promoted self-hatred in black women reflected deeper anxieties and conflicts within African American communities over whether and how they could shape black female beauty ideals and carve out some level of economic power in the context of mass consumer culture.

African Americans in a Consumer Society

Aside from cosmetics companies, few white advertisers recognized the growing participation of blacks in the consumer economy in the 1920s and 1930s. Most white marketing experts ignored African Americans, and the few analyses of black consumers that were conducted seldom moved beyond crude racial stereotypes. H. A. Haring, a contributing editor for the trade magazine *Advertising and Selling*, expressed a typical attitude in 1930 when he wrote, "What of the American Negro as a buyer and user of goods? Is he worth taking seriously? Is the traditional happy-go-lucky plantation life of the South still a measure of the race's standard of living?" Haring maintained that, indeed, southern rural blacks were too poor to buy anything but "bare necessities" and were so "low" intellectually that "no form of advertising can whet the desire of possession." But he went on to observe that the Great Migration had brought large numbers of African Americans to better-paying northern jobs and thus opened up a whole new consumer market. And what of this market? Haring noted that African Americans were enthusiastic purchasers of records, phonographs, and musical instruments and that black tastes in groceries ran to high-end brands. In an earlier article, Haring wrote that African Americans in Harlem liked to spend extra cash on luxury clothing and accessories. In short, black people were logical targets for advertisers of the luxuries and household items that filled the shelves of modern grocery, drug, and department stores. Haring argued that advertising campaigns directed at African Americans should be visual because, as he put it, blacks were "short on abstract thinking." Despite the racist assumptions undergirding his writing, Haring did recognize the potential of the African American market and realized that it needed to be courted deliberately and directly in African American newspapers and magazines.[3]

The Great Migration had resulted in a steady rise in the proportion of African Americans living in cities, from 27 percent in 1916 to 35 percent in 1920 and 44 percent in 1930. By 1940, nearly half of all African Americans were urban. These wage-earning urban blacks generally had more expendable income than their rural counterparts. Even for families who could afford little more than the bare necessities, life in the city required a greater engagement with consumer culture than did life in the country. Food items that once could be grown were now bought, and nearby stores and commercial amusements were attractive to those with even a little extra money. Furthermore, advertisements in widely circulating black magazines and newspapers, publications that were produced in African American urban communities but read throughout black America, along with the prevalence of mail-order catalogs, ensured that rural and small-town African Americans were not necessarily excluded from consumer culture. By the late 1920s and early 1930s, a few marketing experts, including Claude Barnett, advertising executive William Ziff, and market researcher Paul Edwards, were busily trying to convince national-brand-name advertisers to take black consumers more seriously.[4]

They met with little success. With rare exceptions, companies underestimated the African American market and showed little interest in targeting it directly. In a 1930 letter to the president of the National Negro Business League, Claude Barnett complained that black newspapers got far too little advertising revenue compared with "the millions of dollars poured out into white publications for the necessities that white people buy." To Barnett, this was not an honest oversight but a result of the racist assumption that black consumers were not worth courting. He commented that white advertisers had "built up a defense mechanism against using Negro newspapers which is marvelous and indicates concerted thinking and agreement." An examination of African American newspapers from the 1920s and 1930s seems to confirm Barnett's opinion. Advertisements for cars, radios, appliances, packaged foods, cleaning products, and clothing, common in white newspapers at this time, were rare in African American publications. The pages of black newspapers were instead filled with advertisements for patent medicines, "race records," mail-order novelties, and cosmetic products. Surveys of black newspapers at the time revealed that ads for such products took up 80 to 90 percent of advertising space.[5]

Barnett, Ziff, and Edwards constantly stressed that the recognition of what they called the Negro market was an essential step on the road to racial equality. They represented the African American market as affluent, sophisticated, and discerning. They argued that advertisers needed to make special appeals to black consumers because they led segregated lives and were not reached effectively by mainstream advertising. In the late 1920s, Barnett founded an advertising agency in Chicago to secure advertising for the African American newspapers published weekly in dozens of U.S. cities. Barnett's appeals to potential advertisers demonstrate his belief that recognition of the African American market by white advertisers was tantamount to recognition of black economic, social, and political progress. In a 1930 promotional letter sent to dozens of potential clients, Barnett claimed that African Americans spent a billion dollars a year on manufactured goods, "a market larger than a majority of foreign countries." He stressed that black consumers were "affected by considerations of racial pride and sentiment as well as by price and quality" and that the magazines he represented, such as *Opportunity* and the *Crisis*, were "read by that progressive ten per cent which determines the attitude of all colored America."[6]

Barnett's "talented tenth" theory of consumption, which echoed W. E. B. DuBois' ideas about elite black influence over the African American masses, is unsubstantiated. However, his desire to put a middle-class face on the African American market is understandable. After all, Barnett had dealt with many white companies that undervalued black consumers, and he wanted to counter images such as Haring's "short on abstract thinking" black consumer. When asked in 1930 whether a Cincinnati-based toiletries company could successfully market a special line for African Americans, he was ambivalent. One of the company's executives, he said, had once told him "he thought their line . . . was too expensive for Negroes." Barnett continued, "They seem to have an idea in the back of their minds that colored people are not users of high-class products." The attitude reminded Barnett of "Kotex, who wrote that their products were too high for colored women to buy." For Barnett, the solution was to convince advertisers of black consumer significance through market research and a concerted public relations campaign against prevailing stereotypes. His comments reveal a somewhat self-interested attempt to promote the black press, but he sincerely believed in economic strength and unity as key pillars of racial progress. "We must find a way to marshal our buying power so as to force [national advertisers] to realize our value," he wrote in 1930. "If we are to have segregated institutions, we ought to get whatever economic values go with such forced solidarity."[7]

Most people concerned with promoting African American consumerism agreed that more market research was needed. In 1932, Fisk University economist Paul Edwards published the results of a 1928 survey of African American buying habits and consumer attitudes in four southern cities: Nashville, Birmingham, Atlanta, and Richmond. *The Southern Urban Negro as a Consumer* was exactly the sort of study people like Barnett were calling for. Edwards found that, across class lines, and in spite of their earning average incomes significantly lower than those of whites in the same cities, the black consumers he surveyed favored top-quality, more expensive brands of staple foods, household products, and clothing. For his part, Barnett argued that similar consumer habits prevailed among black Chicagoans, many of whom were, of course, recent migrants from the South. As Lizabeth Cohen has observed, this sort of brand loyalty was somewhat unique among working-class people in Chicago. Most notably, white eastern and southern European Americans tended to shop in small neighborhood stores rather than in chain stores (which did not extend credit) and to buy bulk dry goods rather than packaged foods, which were more expensive. Citing various marketing experts, including Barnett and Edwards, Cohen explains that African Americans preferred brand-name packaged goods and chain stores in part because they felt less likely to be cheated when shopping for prepackaged goods with clearly marked prices. They also felt less prone to racial discrimination in chain stores, which could more easily and effectively be targeted by civil rights activists in areas where they did discriminate, as in the Don't Buy Where You Can't Work protests conducted in several northern cities in the 1930s. Edwards found not only that African Americans bought brand-name goods but that they also paid attention to advertising and had definite ideas about what sorts of images of black people they wanted to see in ads. Ads featuring black people as servants, such as those for Aunt Jemima Pancake Mix, received a negative reaction because they portrayed the "slavery type of Negro." Meanwhile, cosmetics advertisements showing glamorous black models were viewed favorably because in them, as one survey respondent put it, "the Negro was dignified and made to look as he is striving to look."[8]

The Edwards study provided men like Claude Barnett and William Ziff with concrete data supporting claims they had long made about the significance of the African American market. Ziff was a white advertising executive whose Chicago agency represented African American and foreign language newspapers. He was also the chairman of the Interracial Council, a group of foreign language and black newspaper editors that sought "to better the economic and social conditions of alien-born and Negro peoples in America." In 1932, Ziff published *The Negro Market*, a pamphlet for distribution to potential advertisers. Drawing primarily on the information in Edwards's book, Ziff presented African American life as affluent, unique, and largely separate from white society. Ziff asserted that "the originality and difference of Negro Life will be found a source of mystification and difficulty on all sales charts, unless when merchandising to these people, particular attention is paid to their peculiar and secluded position in American Life."[9]

The pamphlet was lavish, printed on heavy paper featuring glossy photographs of African American hospitals, schools, colleges, banks, homes, sports teams, social clubs, and businesses. "Starting with birth," the text read, "the Negro is isolated, treated and handled as a separate complete portion of American civilization." The pamphlet stressed that African Americans were well educated, took good care of their homes, went to church, and participated in a large variety of activities that went unnoticed by white America. Surely this was a desirable market for advertisers, and the only 100 percent effective way to reach it was through the black press, which alone covered African American social, political, and cultural life. In effect, Ziff used racial discrimination and segregation as reasons that advertisers needed to make use of the black press: in order to "speak to the Negro alone—in particular to the best part of the Negro group." Warning that "Negroes have a certain amount of race pride which asserts itself in rebellion against advertisements which make comedy at their expense," Ziff offered the services of his company in providing information and advice on targeting the African American consumer.[10]

Like Ziff, Barnett was an enthusiastic supporter of the Edwards study. Barnett and Edwards maintained a regular and friendly correspondence throughout the 1930s, and Barnett helped to promote *The Southern Urban Negro as a Consumer* through his newspaper service. A promotional letter Barnett sent out to various advertising firms and product manufacturers asked, "Do you know what proportion of your sales are made to Negroes? Have you ever investigated this market of 12,000,000 people?" Edwards's book, the letter continued, "gives the picture of the field. It is just off the press and will prove a valuable addition to your library, perhaps revamping entirely your ideas regarding the worthwhileness of the Negro from a customer standpoint." Barnett also hoped to use Edwards's book as a model for a study in Chicago, a city that by 1930 had a black population of more than two hundred thousand. He sent out dozens of letters about the proposed study to advertising and manufacturing associations, but few organizations responded, and none offered any financial support to the project. In 1932, Barnett wrote that he was "bitterly disappointed" that so few advertising companies had shown interest in the Edwards study. In 1933, Edwards himself complained that "the Negro field as a real market is too new, and the ignorance of its import on the part of the national advertiser is pathetic."[11]

Edwards, Barnett, and Ziff continued trying to convince American manufacturers that advertising to black consumers was worthwhile. Although their own research indicated that working-class African Americans were savvy consumers too, the image of deserving black consumer citizenship they promoted was a middle-class one. In this respect, they differed little from the white advertising executives Roland Marchand describes. They hoped to appeal to national-brand-name advertisers, but those companies expressed little interest in black consumerism. Edwards and Barnett both blamed this on the ignorance and prejudice of white businessmen. Although they were probably right that many white advertisers unfairly dismissed the importance of black consumers, their claims of African American affluence forced them to downplay, and in some cases put a positive face on, the obvious economic and social barriers black people faced. Relatively low wages, legal and extralegal segregation, and social and cultural discrimination all meant that African Americans could not always consume on the same terms with whites. In the end, these men could not get segregation and racial exclusion to work in their favor. That they were trying to promote African American consumer power in the midst of the Great Depression did not help matters. White-owned companies that had never before advertised in African American publications would not easily be encouraged to do so while black unemployment rates were running at twice the national average. Campaigns to convince advertisers to entice black consumers would not begin to succeed until the more prosperous post–World War II era.[12]

White-Owned Companies and the Black Beauty Industry

African American newspapers and magazines saw little advertising revenue from most national-brand companies; black women's cosmetics and hair product advertising was a striking exception. White- and black-owned companies, with national distribution of their products and services, frequently advertised in black publications throughout the 1920s and 1930s. Whereas Claude Barnett bemoaned the lack of prominent white advertisers for other products, he had the opposite complaint when it came to the beauty culture industry. For Barnett, the power of big, white-run companies like Plough's, Golden Brown,

Dr. Fred Palmer, and the National Toilet Company represented a threat to venerable black business institutions. Barnett and other black observers maintained that African American beauty culture was the rightful province of black entrepreneurs and that white-owned companies were usurpers. Wearing his advertising agent cap, Barnett urged African American firms to publicize their businesses. Lack of advertising was, according to Barnett, threatening to erase the names of black-owned companies like Poro, Walker, Apex, and Overton Hygienic from black consumers' minds. This created a contradiction. Barnett wanted most national-brand-name advertisers to recognize and target African American consumers as distinctive and separate from white consumers, but when it came to beauty culture, he was among those who adopted a tone of black economic nationalism.

Concern over white ownership of black cosmetics businesses was a recurring theme in discussions about the industry. In her study of beauty culture before 1920, Gwendolyn Robinson points out that black entrepreneurship was based on segregation. African Americans provided goods and services almost exclusively to black consumers because they were not served by white businesses and because whites, particularly after the Civil War, tended not to patronize black businesses. Robinson argues that the black cosmetics industry was significant because it exemplified the salient characteristics of black entrepreneurship in Jim Crow America. Robinson's observation helps explain how someone like Barnett could call on white-owned producers of food products, radios, cars, and other items to spend more money on advertising to African Americans while criticizing white-owned producers for marketing beauty products to black women. Black businesspeople and community leaders consistently claimed that African American beauty culture was and ought to remain an industry dominated by black people. When white entrepreneurs began to enter the African American beauty market around the turn of the century, many African Americans recognized the development as a threat to the survival of one of the few enterprises that offered African Americans economic independence and success.[13]

In 1920, Barnett was himself running a beauty culture company, Kashmir Chemical Company, in addition to his other business interests. That year, he received a letter from F. B. Ransom of the Madam C. J. Walker Company. Ransom complained that Barnett's sales representatives in the field were claiming that, in the wake of Walker's death in

1919, whites had bought out the company. It is difficult to know what to make of the representatives' false claim. Was it an honest mistake? In his response to Ransom, Barnett defended his salesmen and denied any unethical behavior on his part and the part of his staff. Whether Barnett's salesmen believed their story to be true or were maliciously spreading rumors, it is certainly possible that they hoped to win new customers for their black-owned business by questioning the racial credentials of the Madam C. J. Walker Company. Barnett ended his letter by agreeing that the presence of whites in the beauty industry was a problem and suggesting that black company owners ought to develop a "mutual understanding" to contain "this particular business within our own group." Ransom responded immediately, writing that he was "completely in accord" with Barnett that "organizations such as ours should co-operate fully with each other so as to force such firms as the Plough's Chemical Company and other unscrupulous white concerns off the market." In short, the men agreed that whites had no place in the African American beauty culture industry.[14]

As we have seen, Barnett continued to take an interest in this issue even after his cosmetics company failed. In his 1929 letter to Malone, Barnett noted that Plough's, a beauty product company with "not a black face to be seen" in their offices, was by far the largest advertiser in black newspapers. "That is one reason," Barnett added, "it is impossible to get papers to print attacks upon them because of their failure to employ Negro boys and girls." A few years later, in the midst of the Depression, Barnett wrote to the financially troubled Poro Company to try to convince Malone to resume advertising: "Are you following what your competitors are doing? Do you know that while for a time Plough was the big advertiser in the Negro field, that now Godefroy, Excellento, Nadinola, Palmer's and one or two others are also occupying big space? Do you know that all of the colored firms are being crowded out?"[15]

Barnett wasn't the only person critical of white companies' infiltrating the black beauty industry. A 1935 article in *Apex News*, a trade magazine for another African American cosmetics company, likened the influx of whites into the black beauty trade to Mussolini's invasion of Ethiopia. The article referred to the white presence as a "sinister 'penetration' which is designed to usurp Negro business in its most profitable field—beauty products and beauty parlors." African American pioneers in the field, like Walker and Sara Washington (founder of Apex), had "provided for hundreds," the article continued, and created goodwill and prosperity in black communities. Meanwhile, white "usurpers" ridiculed black consumers by suggesting they wanted to look white, rarely hired black employees, and did little to support the communities from which they gleaned their profits. In a 1938 speech to Apex College of Beauty Culture graduates in New York, African American educator Nannie Burroughs added to the voices that condemned white entry into the African American beauty industry. After applauding the achievements of female leaders in the field, Burroughs accused people of "other races" of "trying to chisel in. The beauty industry is ours," she asserted, "and we should keep it ours." Fears of white dominance in the black beauty trade had some foundation. In 1933, Claude Barnett reported to Albon Holsey of the National Negro Business League that Plough's had done $5 million in business to blacks in 1929 (out of $12 million total), and a couple of other white companies had done $1 million each. At the same time, the four top African American companies—Poro, Madam C. J. Walker, Murray's Superior Products, and Apex—had done a combined business of only $1 million. Although Madam C. J. Walker was probably one of the most recognized names in the field, the company's sales reached just under $600,000 in 1920, its biggest year. By 1929, Walker sales were down to $213,000, and in 1933, in the midst of the Depression, the company did only $48,000 in business.[16]

Despite Barnett's efforts, white-owned companies' advertisements in African American newspapers throughout the nation were more frequent and larger in size than those of black-owned companies. Competition from richer white companies certainly played a big part in the declining fortunes of black-owned companies in these years, but the Depression also put pressure on smaller, more financially precarious African American companies. Advertising by black-owned companies did not disappear during the Depression, and in fact cosmetics advertising was as prominent in black publications during the 1930s as it had been in the 1920s. Nevertheless, African American firms did not have the resources to match the promotional efforts of white companies.[17]

In this context, African American business leaders accused white-owned beauty product manufacturers of illegitimately reaping profits from a well-established African American industry. The same 1935 article in *Apex News* that compared white beauty businesses to Mussolini observed that, whereas "at first white people ridiculed the efforts" of black cosmetics businesses, the economic success of such enterprises provoked white competition "with the courageous colored men and women who had ventured their all as pioneers." Claude Barnett, too, claimed that white companies had entered the black beauty culture field only after black entrepreneurs had established the market. In 1933, he wrote that the concept of using straightening irons on black women's hair was "discovered thirty-five years before, and that Madam Walker and Mrs. Malone were the first to successfully commercialize the idea." Claims that white businesses had entered the field only recently, after they discovered how profitable it was, were not, strictly speaking, accurate. Since at least the turn of the century, white firms had marketed hair and skin products to black women along with Poro, Walker, and the other African American "pioneers" in the industry. Still, Barnett rightly observed a new intensity of advertising by white firms during the 1920s. This might well have been the result of the discovery of a new and profitable African American market by some companies, but it also reflected an overall expansion of the cosmetics industry in the United States at the time.[18]

When Barnett's Kashmir agents spread rumors in 1920 that the Madam C. J. Walker Company had been bought out by whites, they highlighted the significance of race and reputation in the industry, as well how difficult it could be to maintain an authentic racial identity in the new mass marketplace. White companies were well aware of the prestige and respect African American businesses enjoyed in their communities. Many went so far as to represent themselves as black-run companies in their advertising. A 1923 Plough's advertisement for Black and White Beauty Creations promised happiness and success to those who would "just follow the example of so many of the girls and boys of *our* race who are using the Black and White Beauty Creations" (my emphasis). An advertisement for Plough's Pluko Hair Dressing similarly referred to "thousands of men and women of *our* group" (my emphasis). Plough's was the company that Barnett had observed employed no African Americans at all. An advertisement by another white company, Hi-Ja, promised that its hair dressing was effective, "as thousands of the Race's leading men and women have proved." Hi-Ja did not explicitly state that it was black-owned, but the use of African American testimonials and references to black people as "the Race" were certainly meant to suggest that this was the case.[19]

The Golden Brown Chemical Company was even more blatant. This white-owned company, headquartered in Memphis, fabricated an African American female company founder named Madame Mamie Hightower. A 1926 advertisement with the caption "From Obscurity to Fame and Fortune" recounted the life of Mamie from "her girlhood in Macon, Georgia, to her forays into beauty chemistry as a young woman." Here was a clear attempt to profit from the popularity of women like Walker, Malone, and Washington, whose rags-to-riches stories were well known to readers of African American newspapers. Echoing familiar advertising slogans proclaiming, for example, that Walker had started out with only "two dollars and a dream," and lauding her as the "greatest benefactor of our race," the Golden Brown advertisement claimed Hightower had begun with "no capital except her knowledge of hair dressing and cosmetics and indomitable pluck." It continued that Hightower was "known by hundreds of thousands of men and women of our Group who bless her name." Advertisements for Golden Brown assured potential customers that "Golden Brown Beauty Preparations are for the Race" and quoted Hightower herself, stating that she had "spent the better part of [her] life studying the treatment of our hair and skin." Declared one advertisement, "Golden Brown Beauty Preparations are the result of [Hightower's] lifelong ambition to help in the progress of our group." Hightower was a real person, but she was not the company founder; she was the wife of a porter employed by Golden Brown's owner. Barnett suggested that the company got away with this in part because the products were sold somewhat anonymously in drugstores, rather than by neighborhood agents. At any rate, such advertising campaigns indicate just how cleverly white companies could invoke race pride to sell their products.[20]

These sorts of promotional ploys prompted observers like Barnett to label white marketers of black beauty products as dishonest and unscrupulous. Massive advertising campaigns by white companies certainly did not reveal the racial backgrounds of their ownership or employees, and many were downright misleading. Some of these businesses did not employ African Americans at all or employed them only in menial positions. As was the case with Golden Brown, however, it was difficult to tell when a company was lying about its racial identity because cosmetics were increasingly being sold in drugstores and marketed through newspaper advertising instead of primarily being sold by door-to-door sales agents. Whereas African Americans were familiar with names like Walker and Malone, they would not necessarily have recognized the claims of Golden Brown and Plough's as fraudulent. The solution, as far as Barnett was concerned, was for black companies to maintain a high profile in African American communities through massive advertising campaigns, in addition to philanthropic and community-building efforts.

Claude Barnett, Poro, and "Modern" Advertising

Claude Barnett was an important advocate of black companies' using the new mass advertising strategies that dominated newspaper and magazine pages by the 1920s. Though he does not deserve all the credit for the change in black beauty advertisers' tone—he himself cited major advertising industry trade journals like *Printer's Ink* as creative influences—his ideas, particularly those he developed for Poro Company, exemplified the new advertising style many African American firms adopted. Barnett's advertising agency sought to represent many black cosmetics firms, but his only client was Malone's Poro Company.

During the 1920s, Barnett placed Poro ads in African American newspapers and helped Malone to design two promotional pamphlets: *Poro Hair and Beauty Culture* and *Poro in Pictures*. These pamphlets, like most Poro advertising in the 1920s, focused on Poro as an educational and philanthropic institution. This early advertising either promoted Poro's beauty college, telling black women that a career in beauty culture was their "big opportunity . . . to make big money," or described the products and services of the company and its agents. An advertisement placed in several black newspapers in 1924, for example, contained a picture of the Poro building and the inspiring headline "Service: The Keynote of This Great Business Institution."[21]

In 1929, however, Barnett urged Malone to alter Poro's marketing image. He suggested that Poro move beyond promoting the beauty college and focus instead on creating demand for the company's products, as white-owned companies were doing for theirs. "More and more," he wrote, doubtless echoing the sentiments of countless advertising executives during the same era, "the virtues of Poro products must be pounded into the public mind." Poro was an "institution" and not just a business, but Poro College's philanthropic activities, though good for public relations, did not touch enough people. For Barnett, brand recognition of Poro as a black-owned producer of desirable beauty products was the key to success. To achieve this recognition, he suggested that Malone move Poro's headquarters to a location in the central commercial district of black Chicago and that she mount a "smart up-to-the-minute" advertising campaign. Barnett advised separating Poro College activities from product sales and urged using massive advertising to put the name of Poro on everyone's lips.[22]

Malone apparently took Barnett's advice seriously. By 1930, Poro had moved its headquarters to 4415 South Parkway in Chicago, the very street Barnett had suggested. Furthermore, there was a striking change in Poro advertising—a new focus on attracting customers. Agent recruitment advertisements did not disappear, but they were joined by prominent promotions of Poro products and their ability to make women look and feel beautiful. One 1929 advertisement that pictured an elegant woman promised to keep users of Poro deodorant "as sweet and fresh as though you just stepped out of your bath" and offered the product in "new art jars." A 1931 advertisement declared, "For lustrous hair and flower like complexion," Poro hair and skin preparations were just the thing. "Particular women all over America have become intimate friends with these beauty aids," the copy continued. "To be really smart and chic, you too, must use Poro Products." Another 1931 advertisement, perhaps evoking the Depression, featured the following caption: "Chasing the Blues Away! Nothing so lifts one out of the 'dumps' as a nice, warm bath . . . hair properly dressed . . . and a few minutes attention to the skin."[23]

Poro advertising was now more modern in that it linked the purchase and use of beauty products to luxury, indulgence, and female success at being beautiful. The focus was now on products, and not just hair dressings, but also soaps, deodorants, face creams, and powders. Though Poro had long offered these items, women were now encouraged to buy them in drugstores and use them in the comfort of their own homes. The new advertisements encouraged women to be "smart and chic." Advertising portrayed Poro products as pleasurable to use and essential for women who wanted to be beautiful and feel good about themselves. Unfortunately, the new advertising campaigns could not save Poro from financial disaster. As a result of the Depression and competition from bigger, white-owned companies, Poro could not afford to continue advertising after 1932 and did not resume full-scale advertising until after World War II. Nevertheless, Poro offers a good example of how, in the 1920s and 1930s, the promotion of beauty culture to black women increasingly focused on beauty itself as a commodity.[24]

Advertising and the Commodification of Black Beauty Culture

Kathy Peiss argues that, by the 1920s, beauty advertising had begun to align cosmetics use with modern womanhood, hedonistic pleasure, true love, and the "democratic" notion that any woman could achieve beauty if only she worked hard enough and bought the right products. Black women's commercial beauty culture shared in this transformation, but in doing so, it exposed and often supported racially limited definitions of ideal feminine beauty. Nevertheless, African American beauty advertising also used ideals of racial uplift and community building to promote hair and cosmetic products. Black women's relationship to commercial beauty culture was complex, and definitions of ideal beauty were shaped within African American society as much as they were influenced by the white beauty standards promoted incessantly in American popular culture.[25]

By the 1920s and 1930s, selling beauty was an integral part of the consumer society that had come to dominate American culture. According to Susan Porter Benson, cosmetics manufacturers ranked second only to food companies in money spent on advertising in the 1920s. Advertisements for black women's cosmetics and hair products filled the pages of African American weekly newspapers like the *Pittsburgh Courier*, the *Chicago Defender*, and the *New York Amsterdam News* during the 1920s and 1930s. The African American beauty culture industry defied white advertising and marketing experts' assumptions that black people were not worth selling to because they were too poor to be a significant market and too ignorant to understand modern advertising. Sophisticated appeals to black women by black- and white-owned beauty companies were ubiquitous in African American publications.[26]

Across racial lines, advertisers stressed the ideas that beauty was the natural goal of women and that female success was defined through appearance. These notions were part of a twentieth-century beauty industry that "offered a sex-specific definition of success and a sex-specific means to attain it." By the 1920s, cosmetics advertisements routinely suggested that women needed to worry about their appearance, their chances for social success, and their attractiveness to men. At the same time, these ads offered women the chance to change their appearance and solve all their problems through consumption and a little extra effort. Cosmetics advertising from the 1920s onward reveals that, in general, beauty was promoted both as a commodity and as a primary female occupation. In the case of African American advertisements, this new rhetoric differed from earlier beauty product advertising that had stressed good grooming as a route to racial uplift and respectability rather than beauty as a route to popularity and love. The rhetoric of respectability continued but was less common in black cosmetics advertising by the 1920s. Still, African American beauty advertising continued to promote race pride in other ways: by celebrating black female beauty, by lauding the successes and charitable activities of black beauty entrepreneurs, and by advocating beauty culture as a desirable occupation for African American women.[27]

Thus, although African American women's beauty culture shared some important features with white women's beauty culture, particularly in its promotional rhetoric, black commercial beauty culture was socially and politically meaningful in very different ways than white beauty culture was. Black women's beauty was in itself a social and cultural issue in African American communities. For the most part, white-controlled mass media and popular culture in the United States denied that black women could be beautiful. In response, African American newspapers, magazines, and beauty advertisements insisted that black women were the most beautiful women in the world. At the same time, however, the presumed desirability of long, straight hair and a light brown complexion, along with the corresponding beauty products sold to black women (especially hair straighteners and skin lighteners), was controversial within African American society. For black women, personal appearance had contentious, racially charged implications even in an era when few challenged the notion that it was a woman's duty to be beautiful. But African American beauty culture was never entirely about creating glamour and beauty. The beauty industry was a profitable one in black communities, and black women who succeeded in the business became social, philanthropic, and political leaders in African

American society. The African American beauty industry as it developed in the 1920s and 1930s invoked questions of black independence and economic power; provided a base for ambitious black women to create personal wealth and social and political influence in black communities; and highlighted deep problems with racially limited standards of feminine beauty.[28]

Beauty culture also strikingly illustrates the lively participation of African Americans in mass consumer culture in the 1920s and 1930s. African American cosmetics advertising contained many conventions that were familiar during this era in which advertising, according to Roland Marchand, became modern. As Marchand explains in *Advertising the American Dream: Making Way for Modernity, 1920–1940,* "modern" advertising personalized and rationalized the huge marketplace of the twentieth century. Addressing anxieties about the impersonal nature of contemporary urban America, advertising rhetorically divorced itself from its economic function of imparting information about a product—its availability, its function, and its quality. In the case of cosmetics advertising, this meant that instead of describing beauty products, ads promoted beauty itself as a natural goal for women, focusing on romance and exploiting women's fears about public image. Kathy Peiss argues that modern beauty culture "popularized the democratic idea that beauty could be achieved by all women if only they used the correct products and treatment." This "led to the assertion that every woman should be beautiful . . . and those who were not beautiful had only themselves to blame." Furthermore, observes Peiss, modernity presented women with particular dilemmas, since they were increasingly visible in the public sphere as "workers, citizens, consumers and pleasure seekers." Throughout the nineteenth century and into the early twentieth century, wearing makeup was hardly ever considered respectable, but by the 1920s, this was beginning to change. The market and mass media often expressed questions about women's roles, sexual appeal, and respectability in terms of their appearance. Advertising frequently sought to assure women that cosmetics use was not only acceptable but also desirable and necessary.[29]

That beauty culture and its promotion reflected tensions in early-twentieth-century society over women's new, more public presence was significant for black women. The increased urbanization of black women and their extensive public participation as wage workers, churchgoers, club members, and leisure seekers ensured that, like white women, they would have to decide what sort of public image they wanted to convey. For many African American women, the question of respectability had a particular urgency. Darlene Clark Hine has pointed out that, from Reconstruction to the early twentieth century, African American women sought to combat the prevailing stereotype of hypersexualized and promiscuous black womanhood by emphasizing respectability in their activities, public behavior, and appearance. Before 1920, black-owned cosmetics companies, sensitive to potential accusations that their products were immoral, promoted African American women's beauty culture as part of an aesthetic of respectability and racial progress. After 1920, however, African American cosmetics advertising increasingly promoted sexual attractiveness, not just a neat appearance, as a desirable goal. Hazel Carby has observed that tensions emerged in some early-twentieth-century black communities between "respectable" and "sexual" images of black women. This was, in part, the result of urbanization and of the emergence of new types of prominent African American women such as blues singers. Like Hine, Carby is concerned with determining the degree to which black women could define their own public image given the negative white representations of black female sexuality. Carby typically presents respectability as a middle-class concern, one that often came into conflict with the more open sexuality of working-class black women. However, the work of Evelyn Brooks Higginbotham on African American Baptist women complicates this picture, indicating that devoutly religious women of all classes were deeply committed to promoting self-esteem and demanded public respect by following mutually agreed upon codes of decorous behavior.[30]

In 1920s cosmetics advertising for black women, the tension between sexuality and respectability was played out in the realm of personal appearance, but it was a conflict that increasingly favored the more sexually open and socially adventurous flapper image popular during that decade. For example, many ads used glamorous celebrity endorsers from the world of black entertainment and asserted that women needed to be beautiful to attract men. Nevertheless, the respectability message did not completely disappear from black beauty product advertising, as it nearly had by this time in advertising for white women. A 1931 advertisement for Madam C. J. Walker's Wonderful Hair Grower pictured a "Prominent Minister's Wife" as a model. An advertisement for Plough's

Black and White Complexion Powder, also from 1931, featured an endorsement by a Mrs. Clara Robinson, a beauty parlor owner and "special nurse for crippled children in the public school system." The use of these women as models for African American hair and cosmetic products emphasized not just respectability but also middle-class status. That well-educated and community-minded women such as these used commercial preparations on their hair and faces lent an air of bourgeois legitimacy to products that still suffered from a shady reputation in certain circles of African American society. The Madam C. J. Walker Company's 1931 ad mentioned above, for example, could be interpreted as an attempt to counter statements by some church ministers who railed against the use of hair oils, straightening irons, and face powders. At the same time, stage entertainers from popular black-cast shows of the day and blues singers like Ethel Waters were also common models in beauty product advertising. Most of these women were not of the African American middle class, and they worked in occupations whose respectability was at times still questioned. But to promote products as broadly as possible, African American beauty advertising featured these high-profile celebrities in addition to middle-class female "pillars of the community." In doing so, African American women's beauty culture in the 1920s and 1930s invoked, but did not always take a clear stand on, longstanding debates about black women's public image, upholding traditional ideals of hardworking and moral Christian womanhood while promoting a new image of fun, modern femininity.[31]

African American observers recognized that most beauty products had been considered immoral but asserted that they were now essential and desired by all women. In 1921, *Half-Century Magazine's* beauty columnist observed that there were "those who condemn the modern woman as frivolous, immoral and disgusting," but she countered this view, asserting that the woman who coifed her hair and rouged her face made herself and her family happier and more contented. Writing in *Apex News* in 1938, a columnist assured readers that whereas "a few decades ago, a woman who painted her nails or her face was considered immoral," it was now common and acceptable to have tinted nails and a made-up face. In her address to Apex graduates, Nannie Burroughs declared that women should "not be apologetic or feel ashamed of the desire to make ourselves more presentable and beautiful." In these ways, black women were told to link cosmetics use with enlightened modern womanhood.[32]

African American cosmetics advertising in the 1920s and 1930s mirrored many trends in mainstream beauty advertising at the time. For example, advertisers assured women that their products and methods were modern and scientific. Beauty culture was always presented in a positive light, as innovative, up-to-date, and progressive. A 1925 advertisement for Madam C. J. Walker products declared, "What a Change a Few Years Make. Remember way back there when lard, tallow, petroleum and a spool of thread were the accepted articles to improve the appearance of the hair? . . . Today there are Madam C. J. Walker agents, thousands of them, in your city, everywhere, skillful, well trained and willing to serve you in the most advanced methods." Here was an appeal to modernity, but with a specifically African American dimension. By mentioning items like thread and lard, the advertisement evoked methods of African American hair care that dated back to slavery. In contrast, Walker products were presented as modern, emblematic of the progress African Americans had made since emancipation. The Madam C. J. Walker Company appealed specifically to migrants and those still living in rural areas, who were perhaps not so far removed from these traditional home beauty treatments. Walker and other companies were portraying the hair-straightening combs, pomades, and pressing oils employed by trained "beauty culturists" in a well-appointed beauty shop as emblems of urban sophistication. Taking a trip to the hairdresser was one way a black female migrant to the urban North could demonstrate her acclimation to city life. At the same time, African American women from small towns and rural areas throughout the country could purchase beauty products, become sales agents, or train to be beauty culturists through Walker, Poro, Apex, and other companies. By the 1920s and 1930s, most black women had access to these "modern" hair care methods and products.[33]

Advertising presented beauty products as the results of scientific innovations. Skin bleaches, though hardly progressive in terms of racial consciousness, were promoted as modern and scientifically produced. Plough's Black and White advertisements asserted, "Now . . . science shows you the way to LIGHTEN and WHITEN your skin," and Nadinola promised that its bleach was "extra-powerful, double-quick, yet so scientifically blended it cannot harm your skin." The Kashmir Chemical Company combined claims of modernity with another popular motif: the ancient and exotic beauty secrets of famous, beautiful women like

Madam C. J. Walker advertisement, 1925: "What a Change a Few Years Make" (*Chicago Defender*)

Cleopatra. A pamphlet promoting Kashmir's Nile Queen line stated that the preparations were "based upon those ancient Egyptian Formulas and improved by the modern and scientific methods of the Kashmir Chemical Company Laboratories." White companies commonly evoked

Egyptian beauty secrets, but Kashmir made a distinctive appeal to race pride by lauding Cleopatra as "the World's famous Brown Beauty." In twentieth-century African American beauty culture advertising generally, "new" was modern, progressive, and therefore desirable.[34]

Modern beauty culture advertising and advice literature insisted that beauty was the natural prerogative of women. Cosmetics advertisements, whether aimed at black or white women, agreed with Kashmir's assertion in a 1919 pamphlet: "Women everywhere want to be beautiful." A beauty columnist for the Chicago-based African American magazine *Abbott's Monthly* wrote in 1933 that, since "all women have that innate desire for beauty, they should take advantage of every asset and enlarge upon it." An article titled "The Business of Becoming Beautiful" in the same magazine asserted that, "to become beautiful, if you are not born so, you must give time, thought and have a strong inward urge." The writer, an admitted "ugly duckling," reported spending the sizeable sum of five dollars a week on beauty products and considerable time on her beauty regimen. Promotional literature insisted that beauty was necessary for popularity and sexual attractiveness. "When men's glances linger, then frankly admire . . . what feminine heart doesn't thrill," declared a 1931 advertisement for Dr. Fred Palmer's Skin Whitener. One advertisement for Plough's Pluko Hair Dressing asserted, "Everyone admires the woman who has beautiful hair!" Another Pluko advertisement was more specific, promising that "men prefer girls who have beautiful hair." An advertisement for Hi-Ja hair dressing asked, "Why do Men Fall in Love? . . . Because of beauty of course! . . . Beauty is the only charm that never fails." In the rhetoric of beauty culture, then, beauty was the main desire of all women, their business and their obligation, if they expected ever to find romance. "Ugly ducklings" could hope to become beautiful only if they bought the right products and worked constantly on their appearance.[35]

Cosmetics advertising emphasized that women were constantly on public display, that their looks were continually being judged, and that beauty was necessary for success in life. In her address to Apex graduates, Burroughs said, "We must look our best and less than our years at all times in order to hold our husbands if we have one, or our jobs if we haven't." African American celebrity endorsers reminded readers of the standards they ought to aspire to. "Vaudeville Star and Famous Phonograph Record Artist" Esther Bigeou is quoted in a Hi-Ja advertisement: "Beauty is priceless, because with beauty there will come every-thing else you desire in life—friends, admirers, social leadership, and great success." A Madam C. J. Walker advertisement invited women to "look closely at the next beautiful lady you see. . . . To be beau-tiful when looked at closely, you should use Madam C. J. Walker's Superfine Preparations for the Hair and Skin." Plough's told readers, "Leading actresses of the stage and screen, whose popularity depends so much on their personal appearance, as well as thousands of the leading women in all walks of life, praise the exquisite texture and the marvelous effectiveness of the Black and White Beauty Creations." Advertisements like these seemed to suggest not only that it was de-sirable to look like a glamorous entertainer but that a person could expect to be scrutinized like one when she ventured out into public. Some advertisements blatantly sought to provoke anxiety in women about their appearance. A Plough's advertisement appeared in 1933 with the headline "She longed to be at the party but she was ashamed to go!" The copy continued, "No wonder she was ashamed to go. No wonder no man had even asked her to go. Her face was a mass of bumps and pimples." An advertisement for Hi-Ja Quinine Hair Fix pictured a fashionably coiffed young woman with the headline "Could This Girl 'Vamp' Your 'Sweetie'?" It continued, "Your sweetheart—your husband is not blind. If you have short, ugly hair he knows it." Such advertisements used messages of shame and fear of competition from more beautiful women to convince readers that they needed to buy more beauty products.[36]

Advertising, Femininity, and Racial Identity

Although beauty advertising for both white and black women shared some rhetorical themes, African American beauty culture advertising often explicitly invoked racial issues. Questions of racial identity were embedded in appeals that promoted sexual attractiveness and feminine success through appearance. A central feature of beauty culture rhetoric across racial lines was the idea that any woman could be beautiful given the right products and a little time and effort. But what did this mean for black women? In the context of 1920s and 1930s America, when images of white women dominated popular depictions of beauty, much of African American cosmetics advertising took pains to assert that

Could
This Girl "Vamp"
Your "Sweetie"?

Your sweetheart—your husband is not blind. If you have short, ugly hair he knows it.

Suppose that the girl whose picture is above should take a fancy to your sweetheart. Could she get him away? Would he fall for that long, wavy, beautiful hair?

Why take chances? Why not have hair as charming as hers? If you have won his love with short hair, think of how much more he would adore you if your hair was long and straight.

Start now to make your hair a shimmering, shining crown of beauty. Begin using Hi-Ja Quinine Hair Fix today. This product costs 50c but is worth the extra price, many times over. It is made from the finest materials and rarest perfumes. It cannot be compared with any hair dressing you have ever used because it is superior to them all.

It's white; it's quick in action; positive in results. Order from your druggist, from one of our agents or accept our low-priced trial offer.

Special Introductory Offer

If your druggist does not carry Hi-Ja Quinine Hair Fix refuse all imitations and send $1.00 to-day for our Bargain Assortment, consisting of 2 boxes of Hi-Ja Quinine Hair Fix and 1 cake of Hi-Ja Beauty Soap sent postpaid (value $1.25). Ask for Assortment B.

Dream Book Free

To each buyer of the assortment above we will send FREE a copy of the Hi-Ja 1928 Dream Book— a beautiful book you will find laden with useful information.

HI-JA
Chemical
Company
Box 598
Atlanta, Ga.
Dept. D-3

Free Gifts
to
New Agents.

We have openings for a few live Agents. If you are interested in making some extra money and in winning valuable and beautiful prizes. Write to-day.

Hi-Ja advertisement, 1928: "Could This Girl 'Vamp' Your 'Sweetie'?" (*Chicago Defender*) black women could be beautiful in the first place. Some advertising, primarily that of white companies, crudely portrayed black hair and skin as defects that needed to be corrected through the use of hair straighteners and skin whiteners. Other companies, white- and black-owned, celebrated black beauty. Many of these firms sold hair-straightening products and skin bleaches too, but their subtler sales techniques invited women to improve their looks and denied that their customers wanted to look white. Nevertheless, advertisements consistently promoted a beauty standard of smooth, glossy hair and a light complexion. In this way, black beauty culture advertising contained intrinsic contradictions that revealed the complexities of class, color, and racial identity within African American society.

Many cosmetics advertisements offered black women the chance to fundamentally change their appearance. They can be viewed as part of what Kathy Peiss terms the "democratic" nature of commercial beauty culture that was ubiquitous by the 1920s. At the same time, most of these advertisements offered African American women an even narrower choice of looks to strive for than white women encountered. Many white-owned companies did not hesitate to depict African American skin tones and hair textures as undesirable. A 1929 advertisement for Dr. Fred Palmer's Skin Whitener invited women to "Choose Your Own Complexion . . . make it like you want it with these beauty preparations." A 1932 Palmer advertisement claimed Skin Success soap would make skin "1 stage lighter, Overnight!" Nadinola, a consistent advertiser of skin bleaches throughout the twentieth century, told "girls who are craving a whiter skin" to use their bleaching cream. "Quickly," the advertisement promised, "the dark, ugly tones of the skin give way, shade by shade, to light-toned beauty." It added, "Lighter skin makes you more popular." Golden Peacock, using white models, offered to "Lighten Your Skin 4 or 5 Shades Almost Overnight." The crudest ads showed "before and after" pictures, or even a picture of a face split down the middle, one half dark and one half light. Advertisements for hair preparations were often little better than the bleaching cream ads. A 1928 Hi-Ja advertisement declared baldly, "Kinky nappy hair—don't have it!" Plough's ads for Pluko and Black and White hair products promised to transform hair "from stiff, wiry and tightly curled to long, soft and straight" and declared that "Ugly Stubborn Hair Quickly Changes to Beautiful Easy-To-Dress Hair." An advertisement for Zura Kinkout stated, "No matter

Dr. Fred Palmer advertisement, ca. 1929: "Choose Your Own Complexion" (*Chicago Defender*)

how nappy, dull and crinkly your hair may be, a simple application of this new discovery will show you immediate, startling results."[37]

These ads implicitly assumed that black women, deep down, believed they were ugly; the white companies that produced them took for granted that beauty was all about looking white. A closer look at the broader spectrum of African American cosmetics advertising shows that this was a miscalculation. The history of color consciousness in African American culture complicates our understanding of black women's beauty standards. In some segments of African American society, a light brown complexion and straight hair were indeed associated with social and economic success. This link undoubtedly had its roots in the history of racial injustice and inequity in the United States, but the popularity of this beauty standard very likely had more to do with the color hierarchy within African American society than with the desire for whiteness. Many African Americans criticized this hierarchy, and few would have accepted the portrayal of African American features as ugly, but the straight hair and light skin ideal held prominence well into the twentieth century. The advertising of African American–owned companies and the more savvy white companies, therefore, had a more nuanced approach to selling beauty to black women.

The advertising of black-owned companies and some white-owned companies told black women that they were beautiful. They did this within the context of American popular and beauty culture, which routinely ignored or belittled black women. Referring to white women's beauty advertising, Peiss points out that, although a multitude of types existed for white women to choose from, these choices were almost always European. Even when "exotic" types like Sheba and Cleopatra were featured as suntans became fashionable, such choices were just that—fun looks white women could choose at will. Peiss reminds us that "underlying the celebration of ethnic variety was the belief that the true American face was still a white face. Mass marketers consciously avoided black imagery in beauty advertising." In contrast, African American beauty advertisers consciously emphasized that black women were glamorous and beautiful. The black media celebrated types of beauty too, but they did so in order to promote the beauty of black women of various skin and hair types, not to offer them a variety of looks to choose from. Advertisements celebrated beautiful black women and assured readers that, with a little attention to themselves, they could be beautiful too. Nevertheless, like their more insensitive white competitors, these companies sold hair-straightening products. Some promoted skin-bleaching creams, and most favored fair-skinned, wavy-haired models in their advertising imagery even as they praised intraracial variety in their text.[38]

Cosmetics advertisements often focused on the beauty of African American women. A full-page Madam C. J. Walker advertisement from the 1920s pictured several attractive women (all of fair complexion) with the caption "Beauty is your Birthright. You, too, can win the charm of these colored beauties." In this case, black women were told not only that they had the means and the duty to be beautiful, but that they had the right to be beautiful as well. Another Walker advertisement had the headline "Glorifying Our Womanhood." The copy continued, "No greater force is working to glorify the womanhood of our Race than Madam C. J. Walker's Wonderful Hair and Skin Preparations." The advertisement went on to say that "Madam C. J. Walker through her preparations, if for no other reason, remains yet, the greatest benefactress of our race." A 1925 advertisement for the Madam C. J. Walker Beauty Shoppe in New York promised, "Beauty . . . It's Made in Our Shop!" A 1935 Apex advertisement declared, "You Too can Have Beautiful Hair." Plough's, the most prominent white-owned company, did not rely on negative advertising to promote its products. Instead of invoking shame and anxiety, a 1926 Pluko Hair Dressing advertisement exhorted black women to "Be Proud of Your Hair!" Ads for the Pluko line as well as those for the Black and White line commonly featured beautiful celebrity endorsers, particularly singers and dancers from black musical theater. The most prominent of these was Josephine Baker, but there were many others. Golden Brown, another white-owned company, used Ethel Waters, "the most famous and beautiful of Our Race Stars," as a spokeswoman. In 1925, Golden Brown ran a nationwide beauty contest to "prove once and for all that we [African Americans] have here in America some of the most beautiful women of the world." Although promising beauty, using comely models, and featuring celebrity endorsers were common in white cosmetics advertising, the ads directed at black women explicitly or implicitly reassured black women of their beauty when so much of American popular culture told them they were unattractive.[39]

Similarly, African American beauty culture advertising elaborated

Madam C. J. Walker advertisement, 1925: "Glorifying Our Womanhood" (Madam C. J. Walker Collection, Indiana Historical Society)

on familiar marketing claims that stressed that beauty was the result of using the right products and not a function of having the good fortune to be born beautiful, adding the message that being beautiful did not require belonging to any one race. Rather, beauty was created through time and effort and the use of products made expressly for black women. An advertisement run repeatedly by Madam C. J. Walker asserted, "Constant Care—Not Luck . . . Many persons believe that a head of naturally long and beautiful hair, a healthy scalp and a lovely smooth complexion come from luck, but they do not. Constant care and the frequent use of preparations of proven merit are the secrets." Excellento, a white-owned company in Atlanta, presented a "Renowned Atlanta Girl" who stated that any woman could "have supreme beauty of face, and hair that will give her that proudest delight" by spending a "small sum of money" to buy Excellento products and "a small amount of time each day" to use them. Golden Brown ads promised beauty to black women who paid attention to their appearance. "Our type of beauty rivals that of all other peoples," declared an advertisement announcing the company's 1925 beauty contest. "Our girls and women are endowed with beauty—but too many of them have been neglecting their heritage." African Americans responded to similar advertising positively. In his survey of black customers, Paul Edwards asked respondents to evaluate images of African Americans in advertising. Across class lines, those surveyed responded positively to the illustrations of black women in advertisements for both Madam C. J. Walker's and Dr. Fred Palmer's products, observing that "here were illustrations which pictured the Negro as he really is, not caricatured, degraded or made fun of."[40]

Many companies emphasized that their products were made especially for black skin and hair. A Golden Brown advertisement quoted Mamie Hightower: "In my study of the skin I have found that our skin is of a different texture than the other Race—it requires different treatment." In naming its line High Brown, Overton Hygienic made it clear that its products were intended for African Americans. White-owned McBrady and Company marketed "Brown Talcum Powder for Brown Skin People." Lavish pictures of young black women adorned the boxes of this product "Made Specially for the Race." Meanwhile, a Plough's Black and White advertisement warned that so-called beauty experts did not "know the needs of our race" the way Plough's did. In this way, many companies, black and white, took pains to assure African American women that they had their specific beauty interests at heart.[41]

African American beauty culture businesses may have worried about the presence of white companies in their industry, but by the 1920s and 1930s, it was becoming more difficult for the average black female consumer to tell whether a product was made by a black company or not. This was a testament to the success of beauty culture, as well as to the general growth of African American consumerism. At the turn of the

Golden Brown advertisement, 1923: "Pride in Our Race" (*Chicago Defender*)

century, most African American women bought their beauty products, if they bought any at all, from an African American sales agent, perhaps even a neighbor. Thirty years later, not only were black women more likely to buy products, but they were also more likely to buy them in stores, perhaps settling on brand names familiar from billboards or newspaper advertisements. This transition was a result of social changes that many African Americans were experiencing, such as migration and urbanization, but it also stemmed from the explosion in retailing, marketing, and advertising that was transforming how Americans chose and purchased all sorts of goods. African Americans were caught in a paradox of sorts. Not recognized as consumer citizens by most white advertisers, blacks nevertheless lived and shopped in an ever-expanding consuming nation. Economic nationalism, however, was a precarious refuge for all kinds of reasons, not least that it was now easier for white beauty product manufacturers to pose as black-owned companies to promote and sell goods to black consumers.

The most successful white beauty companies became adept at developing ad campaigns designed not to offend African American women. Race was always present in beauty product advertising, whether it was aimed at white women or black women. White cosmetics advertising never featured black women, but as Kathy Peiss suggests, "blackness" was present in much of it—as an undesirable quality. Some advertisements, without picturing or mentioning African Americans, told white women to use skin bleaches if their fashionable tans got "too dark"; others presented a "melting pot" of diverse American beauty while conspicuously leaving the darkest beauties out. Meanwhile, "whiteness" was present in most beauty product advertising aimed at black women. Sometimes it was explicit, as when ads assured women that using certain products did not amount to a desire to look white. More often, however, the connection was subtle, in the declarations that African American women were beautiful and in the promotion of beauty standards that were certainly complex but were, at least in part, influenced by white America.

Chapter 2

"Everyone Admires the Woman Who Has Beautiful Hair"

Mediating African American Beauty Standards in the 1920s and 1930s

In a 1920s Madam C. J. Walker Company advertisement, a dreamy woman clad in an evening gown sits at her dressing table applying cosmetics. She is a light-complexioned black woman with wavy hair pinned up in an elaborate style. "You, too, may be a fascinating beauty," promises the caption. "Perhaps you envy the girl with irresistible beauty, whose skin is flawless and velvety, whose hair has a beautiful silky sheen, the girl who receives glances of undoubted admiration. You need not envy her. Create new beauty for yourself by using Madam C. J. Walker's famous preparations." In 1929, a young woman wrote a letter to the Lonesome Hearts column of the *New York Interstate Tattler*, an African American newspaper. Referring to another letter writer who had described herself as "a black girl," the writer commented, "I venture to say that she is not as black or as unattractive as I. . . . I don't expect anyone to want to take me places, or to become interested in me, but oh, how I should love to receive a letter now and then. . . . I am black, have short hair, very unattractive, a typical Negro type." Earlier that year, a male correspondent to the same column wrote of the girl he sought, "No, she doesn't have to be good looking but she must be dark. In other words, a real Negro is what I wish better than anything else in the world. . . . I'm a Negro and I want a Negro pal." These examples help illustrate the complex role race and color consciousness played in the African American beauty industry as it evolved during the 1920s and 1930s. The Madam C. J. Walker advertisement contains many elements that became familiar in cosmetics advertising during the twentieth century: the illustration of a woman absorbed in the business of becoming beautiful; the suggestion that women compete with each other over who can be more attractive; the assertion that women are always on public display and crave "glances of admiration." Specifically, the advertisement promises beauty to any woman who buys and uses Madam C. J. Walker products. The first Lonesome Hearts letter heart-wrenchingly illustrates the emotional toll the beauty ideal of long, wavy hair and a lighter complexion took on some black women. The second letter suggests that not all African Americans accepted this beauty ideal uncritically.[1]

At the center of the story of African American beauty culture were the black women who dominated the industry. These women were the mediators between commercialized beauty culture's standards and the African American women who were supposed to be buying the products and visiting salons. African American beauty professionals embodied the contradictions their business presented within black communities. On the one hand, they were businesswomen who wanted to make money, who shared the consumerist ethos that beauty could be bought, and who sincerely believed that the products and services they provided helped black women. On the other hand, in promoting beauty culture, these women faced challenges from within African American society even as they fought discrimination and racism outside it.

Selling commercialized beauty culture to African American women was problematic on many levels. The products and services were expensive for most working-class black women, even though the profit margins of most African American beauty entrepreneurs remained narrow. Hair straightening and use of complexion creams and powders were, moreover, extremely controversial in African American society: they received criticism from various corners, including those (especially ministers) who scolded women for tampering with God's handiwork, those who regarded the practices as frivolous, and those who accused

Madam C. J. Walker advertisement, ca. 1920: "You, too, may be a fascinating beauty" (Madam C. J. Walker Collection, Indiana Historical Society)

product users of wanting to look white. It did not help matters that white media and beauty product manufacturers sometimes assumed that African Americans accepted white beauty standards. From this perspective, African American beauty professionals were in an awkward position. They were financially, intellectually, and emotionally invested in a business that, one could argue, black women did not particularly need, that many could not afford, and that, according to some, did them considerable harm. In various ways, black beauticians responded to these problems, even if they did not completely solve them. African American beauty professionals lived in black communities and knew firsthand the social and economic challenges black women faced. As a business and an occupation, they argued, beauty culture offered black women relief from financial stress rather than an unnecessary expense. Black beauty culturists also fought accusations that their business eroded race pride. They encouraged advertising and marketing rhetoric that celebrated the beauty of black womanhood rather than portraying African American skin and hair as "problems" that needed to be fixed. Still, black beauticians failed to escape this issue entirely. Assertions that hair straightening was not about emulating a white beauty standard, for example, did not always ring true, and beauticians themselves did not speak as one voice on the issue.

Female Entrepreneurs in African American Beauty Culture

By the 1920s, the names Madam C. J. Walker and Annie Malone were very familiar in black communities. In the next decade, Sara Washington would be added to the list of prominent African American female beauty business leaders. These women were not admired merely for their economic success. Again and again, company promotions and outside observers alike described in heroic terms the work of helping black women "become beautiful." Furthermore, Walker, Malone, and Washington always stressed that they provided employment for black men and women and contributed generously to a multitude of African American philanthropic institutions. In particular, these woman-headed companies highlighted female economic independence as a primary function of their enterprises. Beauty industry entrepreneurs frequently insisted that their companies were as much in the business of helping "the race" as they were concerned with marketing beauty products. Race pride was a common theme in company advertising and other promotional materials during the 1920s. Appeals that urged women to buy their beauty products from "race" businesses stood in direct opposition to the advertising of white-owned companies. Thus, in addition to defining beauty standards for African American women, black beauty culture addressed issues of racial identity, authenticity, and independence.

A 1922 promotional pamphlet for Poro College, the beauty school and production factory founded by Annie Malone, described the institution as "an heroic achievement in the economic life of Our Group." Asserting that the success of Poro was something all black people could be proud of, the pamphlet followed a narrative familiar in African American beauty culture rhetoric. It told the history of Malone's business, from her childhood interest in hairdressing to the invention of her "hair grower" and the subsequent growth of her enterprise. Photographs of ever-larger company buildings illustrated Poro's success. Among the stated "Aims and Purposes" of Poro were "To contribute to the economic betterment of Race Women. To train to useful lives. To develop proficiency" and to inculcate "ideals of personal neatness and pride, self-respect, physical and mental cleanliness." Pictures of the Poro plant in St. Louis showed an opulent lobby, spacious classrooms, an auditorium, modern offices and manufacturing facilities, comfortable guestrooms, and a luxurious dining room. The plant was meant to be not only a beauty college and factory but also a center for Poro's philanthropic and public relations endeavors. Alongside the pictures and descriptions of Poro products, the text assured readers that Poro was "intensely interested in religious progress and in those institutions and movements which, sanely directed, have for their purpose human uplift and community betterment." Racial uplift, training, and employment of black women, and selling beauty products, seemingly in that order, were the main goals of the company.[2]

Promotional materials for the Madam C. J. Walker Company followed much the same pattern as those for Poro. From the beginning, Walker used her own rags-to-riches story to promote her business. Born in 1867 to former slaves, orphaned at seven, married at fourteen, and widowed at eighteen, Walker had to work hard from an early age. As a single mother in St. Louis, Walker toiled as a laundress and a cook, but

poverty and stress caused her health to fail and her hair to thin. Searching for a hair and scalp remedy, Walker discovered her future calling.
Starting out as a Poro representative, Walker soon developed her own
formulas and hairstyling methods and, by 1900, was busily promoting
both to African American women throughout the United States. Madam
C. J. Walker Company products and methods would improve black
women's appearance, advertisements promised, and, if they chose,
women could become Walker Company representatives and free themselves forever from back-breaking, low-paying jobs. Walker traveled the
country extensively, lecturing on the "Negro Woman in Business" and
urging women to become Walker Company representatives.

Walker died in 1919, but her name was well known to African
Americans by the 1920s and 1930s. A 1928 advertisement pictured
the Walker Building in Indianapolis along with a headline that dubbed
the structure "A Haven of Hope for Millions." A promotional newspaper supplement from the early 1920s told Walker's life story, which
was repeated in countless other company publications, advertisements,
and press releases over the decades. "From slave cabin to palatial mansion," the copy read. (Other versions showed an artist's depiction of
Walker's childhood sharecropper's home juxtaposed with a picture of
Villa Lewaro, her lavish estate on the Hudson River.) "From obscurity to
fame . . . Madam C. J. Walker's rise reads like a fairy tale . . . yet withal,
it was service to the race that prompted her every decision and action." This two-page advertisement put the Madam C. J. Walker Company squarely in the context of racial progress since emancipation, with
pictures of Walker products and the Indianapolis headquarters inter-
spersed with photos of African American churches, banks, businesses,
and colleges. Company promotions also highlighted Walker's legacy as
a philanthropist, routinely referring to her as the "Greatest Benefactress
of Her Race." Marketing materials frequently mentioned Walker's charitable contributions to African American schools, orphanages, the YMCA
and YWCA, and other black organizations. The role of the company in
furthering the fortunes of the "race" was often just as prominent in such
publications as the quality and effectiveness of its products.[3]

Furthering the fortunes of the race was not conceived solely in terms
of the economic success and philanthropy of the Madam C. J. Walker
Company. The company represented Walker products and methods as,
in themselves, partially responsible for the progress of African Americans.

A HAVEN OF HOPE FOR MILLIONS

In these times, when we are so greatly concerned about jobs, it is refreshing to know that here is one company where the color of one's skin is not a bar to employment. Countless women have availed themselves of the ever widening opportunity as Walker agents, and have learned what it means to be economically free and financially independent.

MADAM C.J.WALKER'S PREPARATIONS
Made by Colored People · · · *for* Colored People

By their secret formulae, especially conceived for the peculiar texture of Race hair and skin, Mme. C. J. Walker's preparations have renewed the hopes, brightened the future and increased the self respect of our entire Race.

Do you want a good job?

Have you short, thin unsightly hair?
If your scalp itches, you have dandruff, tetter or scalp eczema —if your hair is brittle, thin and falling out, use—
TETTER SALVE

You owe it to yourself to prepare now for any emergency in life. Become a Beauty Culturist —a Mme. C. J. Walker Agent. Earn your own money. Be independent. We show you how.

Is your skin sallow, splotched and ugly?
Nothing counts against one so much as rough, pore clogged, pimply skin. Rid yourself of surface skin disfigurements. Use—
TAN-OFF

SEND FOR FREE CATALOGUE

The MADAM C. J. WALKER MANUFACTURING CO. *Inc.*
WALKER BUILDING · INDIANAPOLIS

Madam C. J. Walker advertisement, 1920s: "A Haven of Hope for Millions" (Madam C. J. Walker Collection, Indiana Historical Society)

The same 1920s newspaper supplement that highlighted Walker's philanthropy also asserted, "Attractive Faces and Beautiful Hair—these are the symbols of our success! . . . More than any other one element in the rise of our race is our bettered appearance, now at its zenith because of Mme. Walker's assistance and preparations." Declaring that Madam C. J. Walker products were made "By Colored People—For Colored People," Walker advertising stressed that these products were "made for you" and exhorted readers to "look your best. . . . You owe it to your race." In some respects, such statements reflected middle-class concerns about public appearance, which had reached new heights. Certainly they echoed the advice of African American groups, like the National Urban League, which were urging recent migrants to pay more attention to their appearance and hygiene in order to land jobs and earn respectability. But this advertisement did not simply parrot bourgeois values. It expressed the importance of hard work and racial pride that Walker, herself the daughter of sharecroppers, had introduced to the company thirty years earlier.[4]

Walker's agents and hairdressers, many of whom came from humble roots themselves, repeated similar sentiments. In a 1980 interview, Marjorie Stewart Joyner, who was a teacher, demonstrator, and spokesperson for the Madam C. J. Walker Company for fifty-seven years, described the company's preparations as miraculous for black people in the early twentieth century. "You have no idea how unruly colored people's hair was at this time," she said; any product developed to solve this "problem" must be seen as a miracle. Just before her death in 1919, Walker had traveled throughout the United States, lecturing to women's groups and promoting her company. Women who saw her speak and became Madam C. J. Walker agents remember Walker as an impressive and inspiring example. She would tell of how she began as a laundress and, with "two dollars and a dream," built up a business worth $2 million. One southern black beautician recalls being impressed by Walker's appearance (she was always well dressed and often wore a mink coat) and manner (observers described her as elegant, but also gracious and easygoing). Walker employees Joyner and Violet Reynolds both spoke about how respected Walker was for developing an effective hairdressing system and for creating a means for respectable, independent employment for black women.[5]

Madam C. J. Walker and Poro were only the most prominent of the black companies that stressed race pride and progress as primary functions and selling points of their beauty products. A 1922 advertisement for Overton Hygienic, a Chicago company founded by Anthony Overton, featured an imposing picture of the Overton Building. "We have erected a monument," Overton's advertising copy began, "a building inside and outside that will stand as a memorial to Negro enterprise and thrift." Claude Barnett's Kashmir Chemical Company advertising prompted women to buy their products so as to look good for their men returning from World War I, but it also encouraged them to become Kashmir agents. "Kashmir is a colored concern," a promotional letter declared. "We are looking out for our Race. YOU must not fail us." Sara Washington of Apex was another entrepreneur, touted in promotional literature as a "cosmetics mogul and philanthropist." Washington founded a home for girls and a camp for black youths. She also funded several scholarships and gave money to many African American philanthropic institutions. Her company's trade magazine, *Apex News,* never failed to feature elegant photos of her and stately pictures of her Atlantic City headquarters. Particularly in the 1920s, African American beauty culture businesses portrayed the purchase and use of their preparations as progressive acts of racial solidarity and connected their enterprises to the economic independence of black people.[6]

Black Beauticians

African American beauty culture businesses asserted that one of their most important contributions to black communities was the jobs they created, particularly for African American women. A 1924 advertisement for Poro asked, "How can I, a woman without training and experience, earn the money so necessary to the welfare and happiness of myself and those I love?" Poro offered the solution: as a representative of Poro, a woman might earn a fine living selling products, providing beauty services, and training other women to be Poro agents. "You can have a profitable occupation right in your own home and build for yourself a permanent income by serving your neighbors, friends, acquaintances and others," the advertisement promised, asserting furthermore that the company had solved the economic woes of "thousands of Race Women, who make nice profits through PORO." Poro presented

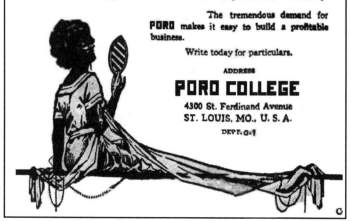

Poro College advertisement, 1924: "Your Question . . . Our Answer" (*Chicago Defender*)

beauty culture as a respectable business that contributed to the racial uplift and social betterment of African American women.[7]

In the 1920s and 1930s, black-owned companies like Apex, Poro, and Walker promoted their "beauty systems" as routes to economic prosperity and independence. As agents for these companies, black

Madam C. J. Walker hairstyling demonstration booth, Chicago, 1920s (Madam C. J. Walker Collection, Indiana Historical Society)

women would learn the skills of beauty culture and make their living as hairdressers, sales representatives, and teachers. Companies assured women that, as beauty culturists, they could earn more money and enjoy greater freedom than they could in domestic service. Moreover, beauty culture training required less education, time, and money than training for professions did. Beauty culture was a real option for some black women in an era of very few occupational choices, but in the 1920s and 1930s it claimed only a tiny fraction, less than 2 percent, of black women employed in the U.S. Census Bureau's personal and domestic service category. Although the census likely undercounted the real numbers of black female beauticians, many of whom worked as freelancers out of their homes, it is not likely that the proportion of employed black women who were beauty culturists was significantly larger than the official figures indicate.[8]

Still, promotional materials for Walker, Poro, and Apex offered beauty culture as the solution to the poor employment conditions many African American women faced. A 1917 company press release praised

Walker's interest in "race women," announcing that she helped "deserving girls" who could not otherwise afford to get started in the beauty business. Walker's correspondence with the home office in Indianapolis confirms this. Writing in 1918, Walker informed company general manager F. B. Ransom that she was "making the offer of fifteen [dollars for training and a supply kit] to Agents where ever I go and if they can't pay that, take what they can pay you until they can," explaining that she wanted to have fifty-eight thousand agents. More agents meant more profits, of course, but the opportunity Walker's success afforded her to help other black women lift themselves out of poverty was one of her proudest accomplishments. A 1928 Madam C. J. Walker College of Beauty Culture textbook urged students to follow the example of the company founder: just as "Madam Walker struggled against adversity, fear, and worry, so must every woman struggle." "Independent Livings Made," proclaimed a 1926 Walker advertisement, observing that Walker agents were "supporting families, educating children, buying houses, cars, and even luxuries from their handsome profits." Marjorie Stewart Joyner commented in the early 1980s that, even in retirement, she still ran into people who told her they had been able to buy homes and educate their children because they had become Walker agents.[9]

These companies knew well that most black women had to do wage work to help support their families. A 1928 Madam C. J. Walker College of Beauty Culture brochure called beauty culture "the most profitable business in which a woman can engage"; it portrayed a laundress, a cook, and a nanny as vivid reminders to readers of the less lucrative alternatives. Similarly, Poro assured women that, finally, they could give their "full time or spare time and be handsomely paid for it." Not only would Poro agents receive fair and generous rewards for their labor, but they would also have rare flexibility to work full- or part-time. "It may be conservatively stated," Poro proclaimed in 1924, "that PORO COLLEGE is affording a more far-reaching economic opportunity to a greater number of race women than is any other one commercial enterprise." Apex aggressively promoted its beauty schools in the pages of its monthly magazine, Apex News. One advertisement asked, "Are you capable of making enough money whereby you can soon become financially independent—Or—Are you a 'wage slave' who works hard making others rich and happy?" In selling the Apex beauty culture program, Apex News advertisements and articles spoke to black women's financial con-

Madam C. J. Walker College of Beauty Culture graduating class, Chicago, 1934
(Madam C. J. Walker Collection, Indiana Historical Society)

cerns and their desire for economic independence. Apex alumnae "are now literally making money hand over fist," proclaimed one editorial in 1929. "Race women" could be trained in eight to twelve weeks as beauty operators, allowing them finally to meet weekly expenses and answer the bill collectors' "doorbell ring without a quavering heart." During the 1930s, Apex billed beauty culture as the "Depression-proof business" and intensified its promotional rhetoric. Stressing the need for skills in a time of economic crisis, one 1930 article claimed that "no matter how hard times are, people must do four things—eat, be housed, clothed, and look well. The harder times are, the more people stress looks and appearance." Thus, claimed Apex promoters, beauticians would always be in demand. Certainly Apex, along with Poro and Walker, was primarily concerned with selling its courses, increasing sales, and widening the distribution of its products. In doing so, however, all three companies addressed economic challenges many African American women faced.[10]

Promoters of beauty culture as a an occupational field for black women claimed that the work was easy, fun, creative, and clean, particularly in comparison with domestic service and laundry work. African American beauty culturists were supposedly prosperous, independent, and free from exploitation by white employers. Those women who secured full-time employment as beauticians sometimes did well for themselves in comparison with African American women in other occupations. A few were successful enough to start their own salons, becoming independent businesswomen rather than waged operators. The pages of company newsletters were full of reports from successful beauty school graduates. *Apex News* ran a regular feature titled "What the Rambling Grads are Doing" in the late 1920s and throughout the 1930s. Typical entries included pictures of successful salon owners with short updates: "Miss Thompson, a graduate of the Chicago School . . . is the owner of a smart, modernistic shop in Detroit, where she says there is great demand for Apex products." "Rosa Lee Edwards is the youngest shop owner in Suffolk [Virginia] and has gained the large patronage she enjoys by studying her customers' needs and trying to please them with first class service." "A sensation is being created in North Philly by Mrs. Kate Taylor, a recent graduate, whose splendid work and becoming hair-dos make her invaluable." "Mme. Lillian Fernandez [of Brooklyn] . . . enjoys a wonderful clientele of fastidious femme on the other side of the East River." Such reports attested to the successes of some black beauticians, as well as the popularity of beauty services among black women, in the 1920s and 1930s.[11]

Beauty shop working conditions compared favorably with conditions in other occupations available to black women. A 1935 U.S. Department of Labor Women's Bureau study of beauty shops in four cities found that working conditions in most salons tended to be safe and clean and that the work environments were generally comfortable. Nevertheless, hours were long and irregular, and rates of payment varied wildly. A diploma from a beauty college did not guarantee full-time employment in a prosperous beauty salon, and many women were forced to work part-time or independently. In fact, most black beauticians worked without independent unions, wage standards, and other labor protections. The reality of beauty culture work often failed to live up to beauty school brochure promises. In 1939, beauty shop workers observed by Federal Writers Project writer Vivian Morris in several Harlem salons identified long hours and tiresome customers as the primary disadvantages of their occupation. "It's sure no bed of roses," said an operator in a typical Harlem shop. "We learned beauty culture to get away from sweating and scrubbing other people's floors," she complained, "and ran into something just as bad—scrubbing people's scalps, straightening, and curling their hair with a hot iron all day, and smelling frying hair." Another woman agreed, adding that "you sweat just as much [as domestic workers] or a damn sight more." Still, she admitted, beauty work was "cleaner and you don't have no white folks goin' around behind you trying to find a spec of dirt." But serving a clientele made up primarily of domestic servants was no picnic. "Well it's Thursday again," said an operator in the same shop. (Maids in New York often had half days off on Thursdays.) "Soon the place will be so crowded with 'kitchen mechanics' you can't move." Another woman observed that they would be in the shop until two in the morning and added, "One of these days, when this place is full of people who come in just before closing time, without an appointment, I'm gonna jump

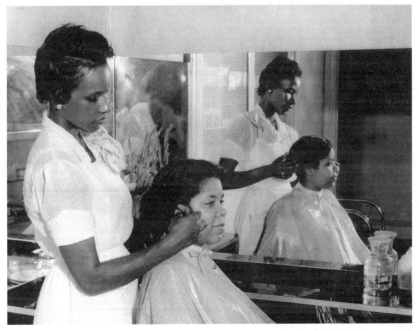

Ru-Lo Academy beauty salon, Washington, D.C., 1940s (Women's Bureau, U.S. Department of Labor, National Archives)

salty [fly off the handle] and throw up my hands and holler." Fixing the hair of domestic servants also meant that beauticians had to listen to their customers complain about their white employers. "You'd think on their day off they'd forget their madams," commented the first beautician, but one customer had barely opened the door before launching into a story about "what my madam said." Beauty parlors were notorious as places where black women could let off steam, gossip, and speak their minds. The comments of these beauty workers suggest how exhausting it could be to lend a sympathetic ear hour after hour in a hot, overcrowded shop.[12]

Advertisements for Walker, Poro, and Apex beauty schools claimed that African American beauty culturists could make a lot more money than they could in other occupations. In 1928, for example, the Madam C. J. Walker Company promised earnings of ten to one hundred dollars a week for Walker graduates. Poro and Apex also assured women throughout the 1920s and 1930s that they could earn up to one hundred dollars a week as beauticians. These high estimates were based on the assumption that agents could get top dollar for their services and that they would make a large portion of their income selling their companies' products to their customers. In reality, most women did not earn anywhere near a hundred dollars a week. The Women's Bureau found that, in 1935, the median income of African American beauty operators in the four cities studied was only eight dollars a week.[13]

In 1938, journalist LeRoy Jeffries decried the poor labor situation of beauticians in Harlem. He blamed the prevalence of home beauty salons and booth renting for beauty workers' poor wages and long, inconsistent hours. Women who worked out of their homes (nearly a third of all African American beauticians in Harlem) could not be regulated, Jeffries argued. Home operators worked in potentially dangerous and unsanitary conditions, he maintained, and they could afford to undercut "legitimate shop owners" who had to pay rent and licensing fees. Booth renters worked in salons but rented the space from the shop owner and charged clients individually, rather than working for a wage. Jeffries estimated that booth renters made up 65 percent of salon-based beauticians in Harlem in 1938. Because they were essentially self-employed, booth renters rarely worked steady hours for regular wages. Jeffries also blamed them for the price gouging that was rampant in the industry.[14]

Economic and social circumstances played a huge role in shaping the working conditions and the income of black beauticians. The beauty industry claimed that beauty culture was a reliably profitable business because women would always spend money to be beautiful. Still, African American beauticians were dependent on other black women for their financial survival. Domestic servants, laundry workers, and unskilled and semiskilled factory operatives were their bread and butter. Black hairdressers served women with limited income and time, forcing them, even in the best of times, to keep their hours flexible and profit margins close to the bone. Few black hairdressers commanded wages much better than what they would have earned as domestic servants. Fewer still could expect to own and run their own shops with staffs of salaried beauticians. Booth renting, despite Jeffries's criticisms, was beneficial to small salon owners and women who otherwise might have worked out of their homes to survive and maintain their own businesses. Booth renters also viewed themselves as independent businesswomen who could choose when they worked and keep a consistent group of customers. Whether they owned their own shop, rented a booth, or worked for a wage, though, black hairdressers depended on black female customers for their livelihoods.

The Depression only magnified the precarious economic situation of African American hairdressers. In the four cities studied by the Women's Bureau in 1935, prices charged for services had decreased since the late 1920s, while the number of hours worked had increased or remained the same. Despite claims that beauty culture was a "Depression-proof" business, declining demand led many salon owners to cut staff and slash prices, just as beauty product companies like Poro and Walker had to cut their advertising budgets (see chapter 1). New Deal efforts to stabilize spiraling deflation and unemployment in this period were not always effective for African American beauty businesses. The National Recovery Administration attempted to establish standard wages and price floors for services in beauty shops. Later on, minimum wage legislation did stabilize the incomes of some African American beauty workers, but only those who worked in the most affluent shops, serving a middle-class clientele. In 1938, Harlem beauticians, who were the best paid in the country, made only sixteen dollars a week, two dollars less than the minimum wage standard set for beauty workers that year. In fact, many shop owners complained that they could not afford to pay minimum wage. Washington, D.C., salon owners surveyed by the Women's Bureau in 1939 frequently cited inability to pay the minimum wage as the reason they rented booths rather than hired beauticians. Booth renters, along with those women who worked independently out of their homes, could not easily be regulated, and some (like Jeffries) blamed them for price gouging and otherwise degrading the industry. In the context of the Depression, however, it is hardly surprising that the African American beauty business would respond in such ways to the serious economic constraints of its customer base.[15]

Beauticians and Black Beauty Standards

Part of the work of beauty culture included advocating the products and processes available to African American women. Although beauty services, especially hair straightening and styling, were popular with customers, black hairdressers constantly faced accusations that they promoted a white beauty standard. Claims that black beauty culture facilitated economic independence for "the race" could only go so far. African American beauticians often had to address troubling questions about race and the beauty ideals they helped to develop. African American beauty culturists believed they were helping black women to look good and feel better about themselves, but they encountered challenges to this assumption from many fronts. African American critics condemned the beauty business from a variety of ideological perspectives. In the 1920s, editorials on the Woman's Page of Marcus Garvey's *Negro World* denounced the "class of 'want-to-be-white' Negroes who peal [sic] their skins off and straighten their hair" so that "they may be admitted into better jobs, moneyed circles, and . . . share the blessings of the prosperous white race." One editorial accused black women, who once treasured long hair, of embracing the "boyish bob" because white women said it was beautiful. *Negro World* credited the Garvey movement with educating African Americans and causing the "would-be white" minority to fade in prominence, but the paper did run advertisements for beauty products—not just those of black-owned companies like Madam C. J. Walker but also those of white companies like Golden Brown and Dr. Fred Palmer. Like so many financially strapped African American newspapers, *Negro World* could not be as selective as it might have liked when trying to earn advertising revenue.[16]

The black church could also be quite critical of beauty culture. In a 1993 interview, Marjorie Stewart Joyner recalled that black ministers used to tell their female parishioners, "God made your hair like that and it's a sin to straighten your hair . . . and you must be interested in a red light district or you wouldn't be putting that rouge and lipstick on you and powdering up your face to look like white people." Such accusations linked cosmetics and hair products not only to race betrayal but also to prostitution and sinfulness. It is hardly surprising that companies like Madam C. J. Walker sometimes featured ministers' wives in advertising. It is possible that, although leaders in the black church opposed cosmetics and intricate bobbed hairstyles, they did not object to the simpler hairdressing methods many black women were employing by the 1910s and 1920s. After all, Walker routinely gave agent recruitment speeches in African American churches, presumably with the ministers' permission. As Noliwe Rooks observes, Walker spoke at church functions in part to "dignify hairdressing as a career." Evelyn Brooks Higginbotham points out that Baptist women in the early twentieth century were discouraged from wearing gaudy or revealing fashions but were urged to present a "respectable" public appearance that may well have included straightened hair as long as it was put up or covered by a hat.[17]

African American beauticians and product manufacturers did at times put out contradictory messages about what their goods and services were for. Many scholars have emphasized, for example, that before Walker died in 1919, her company completely denied that it in any way promoted a white beauty ideal. Walker refused to produce a skin bleach while she was alive; by the 1920s, however, the bleach Tan-Off had become part of the Walker line. In 1928 a brochure promoting the Walker beauty colleges primly stated that skin bleaching was "a recognized part of beauty work and the really expert operator will be called upon to practice it." Walker had also continually insisted that she did not sell hair straighteners, and this claim did not end with her death. Company policy stated that saleswomen and beauty culturists were not to use the word "straightener" or say that they "straightened" hair. A piece in a 1928 issue of the company newsletter, titled "The Newest in Beauty Culture Language," told agents not to ask a customer if "she wants her hair straightened" but to use the word "treated" instead. Nevertheless, the Madam C. J. Walker Company did sell hair-straightening products, and Walker schools taught methods for pressing hair. Joyner was quite open about it in a 1997 interview. African Americans, she said, were "all born with a different type of hair. Some hair is kinky, some is what we call good hair, hair with no kink, some hair is as straight as any white person's hair." But "you couldn't tell our hair from white people's hair when I got through with it." In a 1980s interview, Joyner suggested that, although the Walker method may have made black women's hair shiny and straight like that of some white women, this was not, ultimately, an attempt to make them look more white. Recalling the philosophy of the Madam C. J. Walker Company, Joyner described the hair treatments as "a method to beautify rather than thinking about making a woman look white."[18]

Elizabeth Cardozo Barker, co-owner with her two sisters of a fashionable African American beauty shop in Washington, D.C., from the 1930s to the 1970s, was proud of the services she and her sisters provided to black women. "We used to enjoy it," Barker commented in a 1976 interview, "when girls came up from the South . . . with this hair that had been fried and stewed and boiled and everything," and they could use more modern and refined methods to save this "steel wool" hair. Barker emphasized her ability to dress all textures of hair, pointing out that not all black women had "kinky" hair or needed a "hard press" to get it straight. She related at length how she used lighter hair oils and brushes to minimize the need for harsher pressing techniques, even for women with very tightly curled locks damaged from years of neglect or over-treatment. Barker's sister Catherine Cardozo Lewis straightforwardly described the purpose of her business. "Negro women at that time felt that they should be well groomed. And one of their ways of being well groomed was to have their hair fixed as close as possible to the way white people felt." But Lewis went on to explain that "we just felt that we were contributing to the self-respect of . . . Negro women, and that was the most important thing as far as we were concerned. . . . It was just something that all of us felt was necessary." Good grooming, self-respect, and having hair that behaved "like a white person's" seemed to go together for some black beauticians. African American beauty culturists juggled, sometimes awkwardly, the contradictions between what their products and services actually did and what they wanted them to represent—uplift, independence, and progress for black women.[19]

Contradictions in Advertising
African American Beauty Products

Black women in the beauty industry faced constant challenges to their image and their professed mission from within the industry. Many white-owned beauty companies' advertisements especially lent credibility to black beauty culture critics by using negative stereotypes to sell their products. In her study of African American beauty culture in the late nineteenth and early twentieth centuries, Rooks notices a stark difference between the advertising rhetoric of the Madam C. J. Walker Company and that of various white-owned companies. White advertisers, Rooks observes, portrayed African American women's bodies as "handicapped or imperfect" if they did not exhibit straight, glossy hair and light skin. On the other hand, Walker advertising before 1920 focused on hair and scalp health, along with "biblical references to 'hair as a woman's crown and glory.'" In the 1920s and 1930s, this picture became much more complicated. Without completely abandoning denigrating rhetoric, most of the more prominent white companies introduced narratives about racial pride, black beauty, and choice into their advertising copy. At the same time, black-owned companies increasingly played on black women's anxieties about their appearance. Both white- and black-owned companies, without exception, promoted lighter complexions and softly waved hair as beauty ideals. For their part, African American beauticians promoted the benefits of their services while tiptoeing delicately around the issue of race and beauty standards.[20]

Advertisements that promoted hair and skin products to black women often reflected ambivalence about black women's beauty standards. They presented African American female beauty as light skinned and straight haired, but at the same time they claimed to celebrate a broader range of racial beauty. The more sophisticated white advertisers did not always condemn African American physical characteristics in favor of white ones. Skin bleach advertising consistently stressed improvement of skin texture and promised to remove blemishes. The headline of an advertisement for Golden Peacock Bleach Creme declared "New Discovery Whitens Skin Almost Over Night." The copy, however, did not focus on lightening but instead told women they could get rid of "freckles, pimples, redness, roughness, blotches, muddiness or any blemish." Nadinola advertisements tended to cover all bases, inviting women to "just rub on Nadinola and watch your skin grow lighter every day," while also claiming that its bleaching cream would make "pimples, roughness, enlarged pores," and "eruptions" vanish. Plough's Black and White advertised both a bleaching cream to "Lighten and Whiten your skin" and Peroxide Cream to protect skin from getting "dark and rough from the effects of sun and wind." Rooks argues that this sort of language "positioned [dark skin] as a disease or blemish." Rooks's observation is insightful, but one cannot discount the possibility that black women bought bleaching cream to solve perceived complexion problems that had little to do with color per se, especially since these products were not effective skin lighteners.[21]

Advertisements for hair products were equally ambivalent. A 1933 advertisement for Plough's Black and White hair products declared, "Ugly Stubborn Hair Quickly Changes To Beautiful Easy-to-Dress Hair." The advertisement suggested that women needed to worry about having "ugly" hair but offered no description of ugly hair or beautiful hair. It simply offered to soften the hair and "make it easy to dress in any style." A Golden Brown advertisement promised that its hair dressing "quickly controls unruly, wiry hair" but also emphasized that it "promotes healthy hair growth." In addition, the advertisement invoked African heritage by claiming that the product was perfumed with "Flowers of Liberia." Pluko advertising sometimes referred to "stiff, wiry and tightly curled" hair that ought to be "long, soft and straight," but it always emphasized that its hair dressing made hair "easy to dress in any style you choose." These advertisements clearly portrayed typical African American hair textures as unattractive, but they left open the possibility of choice. A black woman may or may not have opted to have her hair pressed by a beautician (a great many did), but the use of a hair dressing would increase the manageability of her hair and allow her to dress her hair in any way she liked. Again, this was a contradictory message, offering choices even while presenting a limited list of styles that were attractive.[22]

Advertisements produced for the Madam C. J. Walker Company after Walker's death continually wavered between advocating race pride and selling beauty for its own sake. One 1928 advertisement for Madam C. J. Walker's Wonderful Hair Grower (not a straightening product but a hair and scalp conditioner) warned that "surface applications of so-called slickers and straighteners are of no benefit to permanently improve your hair." This pitch seemingly rejected straightening, but it did promise that the product would "grow the hair long and thick, which may then be dressed beautifully correct." It was left up to the reader to determine what "beautifully correct" hair might involve. Another advertisement for Wonderful Hair Grower went so far as to claim that the product would "soften and silken rough, wiry hair." True, it did not use the word "straightener," but its reference to silky, easy-to-dress hair implied that many black women intended to straighten as well as use the hair grower. Elizabeth Cardozo Barker confirmed this, observing that the Walker product line was designed for women who pressed their hair. Models pictured in Walker advertising all have long or fashionably bobbed hair that is straight or wavy, indicating what "beautiful" hair looks like. Similarly, advertisements for Walker's Tan-Off promised to keep skin "clear and unblemished," removing blackheads, pimples, blotches, and freckles and preventing skin from darkening in the sun. In smaller print, the advertisements sometimes mentioned lightening the skin, but Madam C. J. Walker Company's promotions were much

Apex advertisement, 1929: "Don't Fear the Beach" (*Apex News*)

less likely to stress the lightening of the skin than white companies' were.[23]

Other African American companies had similarly complex messages. Murray's Superior Products sold a bleaching cream. Its ads claimed that it was really "pore film" that made skin "dark and unsightly. . . . Remove it and your skin becomes soft, clear and light." Poro and Apex produced both hair-straightening products and bleaching creams. An Apex advertisement declared, "Don't Fear the Beach; Use Apex Bleach." The advertisement promised the cream would lighten the complexion, but it also claimed to be a "skin purifier" that would remove, among other things, "tan, freckles, liver spots, blackheads, pimples, [and] collar marks" and would cause users' "complexion to glow with youthful vitality." Another Apex advertisement, this one for Glossatina hair dressing, declared, "You Too Can Have Beautiful Hair." The copy made it clear what beautiful hair meant: "Regardless of the condition of your hair, you can make it amazingly straight, soft and silky by the regular use of Apex Glossatina. It is the ideal preparation for straightening the hair with the hot comb."[24]

Beauty Standards and African American Entertainers

Popular culture also contributed to this developing beauty standard for black women. At a time when female entertainers were emerging as the new standard-bearers of increasingly sexualized twentieth-century beauty ideals, African American women singers, dancers, and actresses became models of black glamour and beauty within African American popular culture. Whereas the white entertainment industry ignored black women or relegated them to comic and novelty roles, black entertainers strove to portray themselves as glamorous and beautiful stars. In this way, black female celebrities were important representatives of African American attractiveness in an era when mainstream American culture rarely recognized darker shades of beauty. Starting in the early 1920s, the leading ladies and chorus girls of all-black musicals swelled the ranks of African American glamour girls. Noble Sissle and Eubie Blake created *Shuffle Along* in 1921 on a shoestring budget. The show played at first in Harlem for primarily black audiences but soon became a hit with white New Yorkers in Manhattan. The success of *Shuffle Along* led to a string of black musicals on Broadway throughout the 1920s and launched the careers of black performers like Florence Mills and

Josephine Baker. These musicals opened up sensitive issues about race, color, and femininity in American culture. Undoubtedly the all-black revues of the 1920s favored chorus girls with light skin and European features. Early in Josephine Baker's New York career, producers told her she was too dark to be a chorus girl and eventually hired her only because her frenetic, comical dancing style was such a hit with audiences. Daphne Duval Harrison writes that, on Broadway and in nightclubs, light skin "was a badge of beauty blacks valued," and those "who were not born with it used cosmetics to whiten up."[25]

After the crossover success of *Shuffle Along*, producers developed shows with white audiences in mind. (Indeed, the clubs most famous for beautiful, light-skinned black chorus girls, notably the Cotton Club and Connie's Inn in Harlem, allowed white patrons only.) Show producers and club owners assumed that white audiences would not want to see glamorous black women of all shades on the stage. Biographer Phyllis Rose explains Josephine Baker's hurt feelings when Sissle and Blake initially rejected her for *Shuffle Along* in an effort to produce a cast "acceptable" to white audiences. "It rankled," Rose writes, "to be rejected as too dark by the New York show . . . when she was disliked in her Southern vaudeville troupe and in her own family for being too light." At the same time, even the "high yellow" chorus girls of 1920s shows and clubs challenged prevailing ideals of female beauty. In her study of Ziegfeld girls, Linda Mizejewski argues that black revues on Broadway, which featured women who were as attractive as any girl in the Ziegfeld chorus lines, threatened the implicit Ziegfeld dogma that the "glorified American girl" could only be white. Responding to this threat, Ziegfeld girls began to perform racier numbers in "feminine blackface," or "café au lait" makeup, signifying the "naughty sexuality" of black women in contrast to the wholesome beauty of white Ziegfeld girls. The limited range of skin colors among black performers was, of course, controversial among African Americans, but black audiences loved African American musicals, and black newspapers celebrated the glamour and beauty of their bronze-skinned stars more often than they complained about the lack of diversity on the stage.[26]

The African American beauty culture industry was quick to exploit the popularity of female entertainment personalities. Today the use of celebrities to sell makeup and other beauty products is ubiquitous, but in the 1920s and 1930s it was relatively new. Film actresses began to appear in cosmetics advertising around 1916; by the 1920s, the use of stage and screen stars to promote cosmetics was one of the most common tie-ins in beauty advertising. In African American beauty product advertising, the use of beautiful and sexy showgirls and blues singers was part of the larger transition from advertisements that promoted good grooming and stressed the functionality of products to those that emphasized romance and sexual attractiveness. Many beauty product manufacturers had used company founders, agents, black teachers, college students, and wives of prominent professionals as models in early print advertising. As the 1920s progressed, however, advertisers increasingly turned to popular black actresses, singers, and dancers to endorse their hair and skin preparations.[27]

Chorus girls from various Harlem-based musical revues made up the bulk of celebrity endorsers. Advertisers made direct connections between the popularity and beauty of these stage personalities and their use of particular products. White-owned companies seem to be the most frequent producers of this type of advertising. Plough's ran a series of celebrity-centered advertisements for Pluko Hair Dressing throughout the 1920s. A full-page advertisement in the *Chicago Defender* featured the female star of a hit traveling show. "No small part of the popularity of the musical comedy, 'Shufflin' Sam from Alabam,' playing this week at the Booker Washington Theatre in St. Louis, is due to the attractiveness of the prima donna, Baby Hines, whose beautiful hair is only one of her many charms." The advertisement pictured Hines in a floral dress, hat, and heels, posing charmingly for the camera, along with her words: "I use Pluko Hair Dressing because it is so soft and melty, it is a pleasure to use it; and it always keeps my hair soft, straight, and glossy." Another Pluko advertisement featured three young women: "dainty, fascinating Lottie Gea, famous actress of our group who is now winning new triumphs in Europe . . . popular Edith Spencer, leading lady in the original 'Runnin' Wild,'" and Gussie Williams, "whose beautiful hair is one of her many charms."[28]

Some celebrity endorsers' names are well known to us today. Ethel Waters appeared in a Golden Brown advertisement in 1923: "Queen of Blues singers Ethel Waters tells how Madam Mamie Hightower's Golden Brown beauty preparations have made her the most famous and beautiful of Our Race Stars." The face of "Beautiful Josephine Baker" graced a Plough's advertisement in 1926 with a testimonial from Miss Baker her-

Plough's advertisement, 1926: "Beautiful Josephine Baker"
(*Chicago Defender*)

self: "I was so delighted with the way the improved Pluko Hair Dressing smoothed out and straightened my hair, and made it easy to dress any way I wished, that I kept right on using it." Other black celebrities of the 1920s, like Esther Bigeou, the "Vaudeville Star and Famous Phonograph Artist" from New Orleans, and "Miss Gladys Robinson, Stage Star" (both Hi-Ja product endorsers) are less familiar names. Nevertheless, these celebrity advertisements shared common features. All played up the fame and glamour of these performers, banking on their name recognition in an era when celebrities were emerging as prominent public figures. These young starlets were constantly covered in the entertainment pages of black newspapers, and they traveled throughout the country performing for African American audiences. Some were recording artists in the new "race record" industry. It is very likely, therefore, that these women were familiar to African Americans throughout the United States.[29]

In their endorsements, performers stressed the importance of appearance in their chosen profession. Gladys Robinson attested that Hi-Ja Quinine Hair Dressing was "the best thing of its kind I have ever tried and since I am an actress and one who must be as beautiful as possible all the time, I have naturally used many products." Here Robinson cited her "expertise" in being beautiful as a credential for evaluating Hi-Ja products. Similarly Pluko endorser Gussie Williams stated that "realizing the importance of one's hair to their appearance, I never use anything but the best hair dressing." Hi-Ja spokeswoman Esther Bigeou told readers, "I owe my success to Beauty and I owe my Beauty to Hi-Ja Beauty preparations." Bigeou also advised that "beauty is priceless . . . because with beauty will come everything else you desire in life—friends, admirers, social leadership, and great success." Bigeou's "celebrated beauty," which, according to the advertisement's copy, "has won for her the admiration of vaudeville audiences all over the United States," was meant to confirm her authority as an expert on the subject. But celebrities did not hold a monopoly on beauty. "Miss Bigeou is only one of millions who have learned the value of Hi-Ja beauty preparations," continued the same advertisement. In its advertisement featuring vaudeville star Miss Wells, Plough's declared, "Improved Pluko Hair Dressing is fairly taking the country by storm as more and more men and women, like Miss Wells, are finding how easy and pleasant it is to use this delicately fragranced preparation." Pluko's Josephine Baker advertisement asserted, "The experience of Miss Baker and thousands of other men and women of our group proves that YOU can make your hair just as long, straight and glossy as you wish." "Look at her Hair," commanded a 1928 Golden Brown advertisement, referring to a photograph of Cotton Club chorus girl Louise Howard. The ad copy promised, "Yours can be just as beautiful." In the 1920s, at the height of black Broadway's success, African American stage stars were proffered to black women as examples of ideal beauty.[30]

African American Beauty Contestants

Like female entertainers, the beauty contest winner quickly became a highly visible example of ideal female beauty in the early twentieth century. And like all venues for defining beauty standards in the United States, beauty contests were shaped by ideas about race and by race relations within American society. Beauty contests were segregated affairs in the early twentieth century. White-run contests typically barred black participants, but even when African American women were able to enter white-run pageants, they were long shots. The Miss America Pageant, for example, did not begin to see serious black contenders until the 1960s. African American beauties who slipped though the cracks of racially exclusive contests could expect considerable obstacles to success. In 1924, a beauty contest in Flushing, New York, was called off when an African American woman entered and became a favorite to win. The black press was quick to expose this incident as proof of white America's refusal to recognize the beauty of African American women. Black America responded to this situation by staging its own beauty contests. As Maxine Craig and other scholars have demonstrated, African Americans used their pageants to proudly display black womanhood and proclaim that there were indeed many types of racial beauty. African American newspapers, civic groups, fraternal organizations, and colleges all created beauty pageants at one time or another. Beauty contest sponsors in the 1920s and 1930s included the African American publication *Half-Century Magazine*, the beauty product manufacturers Nelson Manufacturing Company and the Apex Company, and Harlem's Savoy Ballroom. Throughout the mid-twentieth century, local contests run by philanthropic and fraternal groups garnered coverage in the black press. The Nelson Manufacturing Company's contest for determining the Nelson Girl drew contestants from thirty states. Apex ran beauty contests in the late 1920s that drew local women from the New York area and that the company promoted extensively in *Apex News*. Apex billed the 1929 contest, held at Manhattan's Rockland Palace, as a glamorous extravaganza, featuring entertainment from the stars of Broadway's *Hot Chocolates* and at least two jazz orchestras. Advertisements for the event informed readers that Broadway producers and stars would judge the contest and that Universal Newsreel would film it so it could be "shown all over the world." In 1925 Golden Brown ran a newspaper beauty contest that attracted 1,400 contestants and three hundred thousand "votes" (readers bought Golden Brown products and sent in proofs of purchase worth fifty to one hundred votes each). In each case, the contests combined business promotion, the celebration of beautiful black womanhood, and the bald-faced exploitation of the public's new interest in viewing young, scantily clad women in competition for the title of most beautiful girl.[31]

In 1921, *Half-Century Magazine* invited readers to send in pictures of black women to answer the question "Who is the Prettiest Colored Girl in the United States?" It was typical, as Craig tells us, for these early African American contests to be put on by a black publication or business enterprise. Usually, she observes, commentary on the contests reflected that their sponsors were middle-class males, mixing self-promotion (of the sponsor) with male voyeurism and expressions of racial pride. *Half-Century Magazine*'s contest was open to "every Colored woman of sixteen years of age or more." Every month, a "blind-folded child" would draw six photographs from those sent in, and the final winner was to be selected by seven judges, including Mrs. Robert Abbott, wife of the Chicago magazine's publisher, Chicago beauty preparation mogul Anthony Overton, and Ida B. Wells-Barnett. The 1921 contest was explicitly framed as a way to "prove" that African American women were beautiful. "Many white people are under the impression that there are no pretty Colored women," explained *Half-Century Magazine*. "We want to show them that there are many Colored beauties of varying types. Let us show them that all beautiful hair is not straight, that all beautiful skin is not white, that all the pretty profiles do not belong to members of the white race." The magazine published the photographs of entrants from throughout the South, Midwest, and East, including Wheeling, West Virginia; Memphis; Cleveland; Texarkana, Arkansas; Chicago; New Orleans; and Washington, D.C. In a reassuring tone, the magazine told women, "Don't hesitate to send in your picture because you do not consider yourself unusually good-looking. There are many types of Colored beauty." Indeed, the pictures of contestants included a reasonably wide variety of facial features and complexions, although all the women had naturally wavy or artificially straightened hair.[32]

A full-page June 1919 tribute, "Types of Racial Beauty," in *Half-Century Magazine* featured many small photos of "beautiful" black women, and the caption stated with pride, "Our race has produced more varieties of beauty than any other race on earth." The author of the article observed, "The Colored man certainly has a wide range of complexion, hair and features to choose from . . . be it the bronze Venus with the mysterious black eyes and crispate hair, . . . or the Indian peach variety with the baby gray eyes and brown curls." Each black woman "is a representative beauty of her own type." This piece and others like it were important because they proclaimed that black women were beautiful when white media ignored them or overtly denied their attractiveness. Nevertheless, even though the article recognized "bronze" skin and "crispate hair" as parts of the pantheon of African American beauty, the photos favored lighter skin and straighter hair. According to Craig, such contradictions were reflected in African American society: although midcentury surveys of African Americans' attitudes reflected criticism of the idea that lighter skin was better, marriage patterns, particularly among middle-class blacks, tended to reflect a bias toward women with lighter complexions.[33]

Still, publicly at least, not all African Americans accepted this standard. Many working-class blacks and, as some of the survey results Craig cites suggests, a good number of middle-class blacks expressed admiration for brown complexions. Blues singer Bessie Smith was popular even though she did not resemble the lithe, light-skinned beauty ideal that black cosmetics advertising and media authorities promoted. Smith drove this point home in her song "Young Woman's Blues," in which she uncompromisingly asserted her sexual attractiveness despite her failure to live up to prevailing beauty standards: "I'm as good as any woman in your town / I ain't no high yella, I'm a deep killer brown." Smith's lyrics highlighted aesthetic and class divisions over color in African American society even as they challenged the notion that light complexions were more beautiful. Still, there is some evidence that the ideal of medium-to-light skin and glossy hair held sway with African Americans from a variety of backgrounds. In her autobiography *I Know Why the Caged Bird Sings*, Maya Angelou recalls growing up in an African American community in rural Arkansas steeped in black pride and independence. Yet Angelou, arguably middle class by virtue of her grandmother's ownership of small grocery store, remembers that, as a young girl, upon seeing her mother for the first time in years, her "beauty literally assailed me. Her red lips . . . split to show even white teeth and her fresh-butter color looked see-through clean." Angelou reports that her mother was "a pretty woman, light-skinned with straight hair."[34]

Beauty Standards and Black Women

Whether African Americans generally accepted the beauty standard so prevalent in cosmetics advertising and in beauty contests is unclear. Certainly the prevalence of African American beauty salons in cities across the country attests to the demand for hair straightening. Black newspapers including the *New York Amsterdam News*, the *Pittsburgh Courier*, the *Baltimore Afro-American*, the *Norfolk (Va.) Journal and Guide*, the *Chicago Defender*, and the *California Eagle* (of Los Angeles) featured dozens of small advertisements for local beauty shops each week alongside larger advertisements for nationally marketed beauty products. Getting one's hair straightened could be expensive, but for adolescent girls, it was an important step to womanhood. Annabelle Baker, a retired New York City nurse who grew up in Florida, recalls that, as a young girl in the 1930s, hair straightening was for special occasions only, and she was not allowed biweekly trips to the beauty parlor until she was thirteen and deemed ready to stop wearing her hair braided. Even so, she points out, female family members saved money by touching up their hair between visits. Hairstyling procedures might cost as much as one or two dollars, a fair chunk of the average black working woman's salary in the 1920s and 1930s. In a Harlem beauty shop frequented by domestic servants, Vivian Morris overheard one woman tell the beautician that her employer had "asked me what I had done to my hair last Friday when she saw it all curly and pretty. I told her I'd been to the hair dresser. She asked me how much it cost and when I told her she just looked funny and started to ask me how I could afford it. She needn't worry 'cause I'm dead sure I'm gonna ask her for a raise." African American domestic servants like this one were willing to spend their one free afternoon a week waiting to get their hair done—shampooing, straightening, and styling took as much as two hours, and because domestics often had the same days off and salons frequently lacked an appointment system, the process could take the entire afternoon. That they were willing to spend a tenth or more of their weekly income on their hair is significant. Getting one's hair done was a source of pleasure and a way of asserting personal pride and independence. It was an essential precursor to a day in church or a night on the town. As another patron overheard by Morris put it, "Got to make time. Me and my boyfriend . . . we're gonna 'dig that new jive' (see the new show) down the Apollo; then we'll 'cut out' (go) to the Savoy and 'beat out a few hoof rift' (dance) till the wee hours then I'll 'fall on back to the mansion' (job) 'dead beat for shut eye' (sleepy) but willing to 'carry on' (work)."[35]

Beauty products for black women were big business, and none were bigger than products designed for hair care. In 1920 Madam C. J. Walker Company's best seller, by far, was the conditioning Wonderful Hair Grower, at $155,790 in total sales for the year. Second in line was Glossine Hair Pressing Oil, at $63,691. In 1925 the Walker Company ran an ad that featured women's letters to the company praising the products. "I have used your Wonderful Hair Grower and it is a great success and help to me," wrote Florence Butler of Philadelphia. Estelle Huie of Cuba wrote, "I have been using your preparations for two months now. The quality of my hair has changed for the better." Walker's face powders seemed less popular, making only $1,728 in 1920. The Walker brand skin bleach Tan-Off, perhaps not yet widely available in 1920, was not mentioned in this report, but by 1928 Walker agents and salon owners were singing the praises of the product. "We had noted with a great deal of interest that Tan-OFF has been in great demand by Mrs. Terry," bragged *Walker News* in the Agent News section of the September 1928 issue; "one cannot visit her shop without having her tell them about Tan-OFF." The trade newsletter quoted Terry herself: "If you are not using Tan-OFF you had better get started at once." She went on to claim that "improved complexions" had even attracted male clients, including "husbands and sweethearts," to learn the secret of "beautifying the skin." The February 1930 edition of *Walker News* quoted Ema Jenkins of Buffalo, who wrote, "As for the Tan-Off my trade is more than delighted and I feel that it is growing." In July the newsletter reminded readers that "Madam C. J. Walker Tan-Off is the most effective bleach on the market today. If you have dark spots on your face or arms, a blotchy, cloudy complexion, use this Tan-Off. You will notice an improvement after each application. Suggest this to your customers. Tan-Off is our best seller in some sections where the agents boost it." Vivian Morris observed the use of such a product herself while visiting a tony beauty salon in the Sugar Hill area of Harlem. A woman wearing "two diamonds and an imported wristwatch" was discussing the latest non-fiction bestseller "from under her application of bleach cream."[36]

Correspondents to the Lonesome Hearts personal column in the *New York Interstate Tattler* offered rare glimpses into how African American women viewed their own appearance and what types of women African American men were attracted to. The *Interstate Tattler* was a gossipy weekly tabloid that focused extensively on the doings of New York's black celebrities, sports figures, and elites. The Lonesome Hearts column appeared in 1929 and ran through the early 1930s. Correspondents could write a short letter describing themselves and the sort of person they hoped to meet. The inclusion of a stamped, self-addressed envelope ensured that hopeful singles would receive any responses to their appeals. It is difficult to get a definite idea of just who these lonesome hearts were. Of those who mentioned education or profession, many seemed to be middle class, but a good number worked as laborers or service employees, and many others did not note their occupation. A few claimed to be musicians, singers, or actors. Although most of the correspondents wrote from the New York area, a good many hailed from other northern cities, and others mentioned that they were recent migrants from the South. Added to this mix were male convicts, who were well represented each week in the column.

The most striking feature of these letters was that virtually all noted skin color, possessed or sought after. This quality was as frequently mentioned as age and more frequently mentioned than height or weight. Most of the letters also mentioned quality of hair. The correspondents described a wide variety of complexions, reflecting the broad range of "types of racial beauty" often lauded in the black popular press. Common adjectives for skin color included "brownskin," "dark," "chocolate brown," "high brown," "light brown," "golden brown," and "yellow." Writers to the column seemed to be honest in describing themselves, implicitly acknowledging the predominant beauty standards of the day and comparing themselves to that standard. A twenty-five-year-old nurse described herself as having "brownskin" and "coarse black hair." A male correspondent noted sardonically, "Of course, I am a Negro—they are not usually white; neither am I a stack of coal." Another man took pains to be precise, writing that he was a "brownskin—one of those things you call chocolate brown—you know what I mean, a sugar brown," and mentioning that he wanted a "nice dark brown girl" but "not too dark." Many correspondents related their physical characteristics with some pride. A few made a point of their Caucasian features. One man described himself as "very bright in color, good hair and can pass for white." A woman mentioned that she was "considered good-looking, able to pass for a . . . blonde of the Caucasian race (although am full Negro blood)." Many other letter writers, however, boasted about their darker-toned skin. "I am a tantalizing brown," wrote a young woman, "about 5 ft. 4 in., straight black hair bobbed, eyes dark brown and charming to look at." A twenty-year-old man wrote that he had a "dark complexion, smooth skin, inbetween hair and a perfect form . . . considered a nice looking dark boy." A young woman described herself as having "dark brown skin, nice hair, considered nice looking." Another woman declared that she was "a brownskin mama, brown eyes, good hair and not bad to look at." As in the survey findings that Maxine Craig relates, the physical ideal most often described in the letters was that of "brown" but not "too dark" skin and "good" (meaning straight or wavy) hair.[37]

When stating their preferences in a mate, few correspondents expressed a desire for persons with lighter complexions than they had themselves. More commonly, letters requested introductions to people of a similar shade. Some correspondents echoed the young man who wrote, "I am not particular about color or grade of hair, as the majority of the beautiful belles have proved to be dumb-bells." Less frequently, writers expressed disdain for those who insisted on lighter complexions in a romantic partner. One man looking for a girl of "any color" asked why the contributors to the Lonesome Hearts column "discriminate on account of color? . . . How in blazes do they expect equality from other races when they don't even practice it among themselves?" A young woman complained, "My mother objects to my boy friend on account of his color. She admits that he is charming in every other way. Would you give him up just to please such a whim?" These lonely hearts typified those urban working- and middle-class blacks who were most likely to be influenced by the commercial beauty and entertainment industries that were in full swing by the 1920s. Their letters indicate at least a recognition of the prevailing beauty standard touted in African American beauty culture advertising, even if not all accepted that standard entirely. The high level of acceptance of, or even preference for, brown skin (which could describe most African American complexions) and straight or wavy hair (which was, after all, achievable with a trip to the beauty parlor) suggests that popular beauty standards for black women were not so narrow, or so "white," as one might suppose by looking at an advertisement, a beauty contest winner, or a chorus girl.[38]

Rhetorically at least, much advertising and beauty literature did stress varieties of black beauty. A Poro advertisement from 1923 declared that Poro products were "For Every Texture of Hair and Skin." The Beauty Hints columnist for *Half-Century Magazine* commented that there were "so many textures, colors, and qualities of hair, especially among our women, that it is almost impossible to give a rule that will cover all cases for the care of the hair." Several companies offered face powders in a variety of shades, a much wider variety than was ever offered by mass-market cosmetics producers. Overton Hygienic sold powder in "four distinct shades: Natural, Flesh-Pink, White and Brunette." Poro manufactured eight shades, including "5 browns, Brunette, Flesh, White." A Chicago company, Marguerita Ward, offered "White, Flesh, Olive, Peach, Seal, Dark and Light Chocolate." Companies like Madam C. J. Walker and Plough's offered similar choices. By providing shades not offered by mass-market companies, whose darkest shades were olive or brunette, these companies were recognizing that black women came in all different shades.[39]

On the other hand, all of these companies, whether black- or white-owned, used terms like "natural" and "flesh" to refer to the lighter shades of powder, apparently recognizing shades of powders marketed to white women as the standard. Although ads suggested variety and choice, models in these ads were, as previously discussed, always light complexioned, and the majority of cosmetics tints offered ran from light brown to white. Still, the following letter from Lelia Walker, Madam C. J. Walker's daughter, to F. B. Ransom suggests that these choices might have been sufficient for most African American women's complexions. Lelia Walker became president of the company after Walker's death in 1919. In 1927 Lelia Walker, herself a brown-complexioned woman, wrote to Ransom that she did not "agree with your idea of darker powder. I think a pink powder for light complexion and a light tan for brown skin people is all the powders we need. That dark brown powder dirties all your clothes around the neck if you wipe your face with a kerchief it ruins the kerchief it is altogether a nasty mess for I have used it."[40]

The narrow range of "types of racial beauty" represented in African American beauty culture advertising and other popular media during the 1920s and 1930s reveals tensions over class and color in black society. Historians who have written on the subject observe that color has been an emotional and divisive issue in black communities since slavery but that it became particularly prominent after emancipation. The offspring of black women slaves and their white owners were widely believed to receive favorable treatment. Mulattos were more likely to gain their freedom, and they made up a disproportionate number of free black people before the Civil War. In the latter half of the nineteenth century, the white preference for more Caucasian features when hiring African Americans perpetuated certain economic advantages for mulattos. Furthermore, as historian Willard B. Gatewood points out, mulatto elites of urban black society sought to use color as a device to exclude new, working-class migrants to the cities. Although color was by no means the only factor for determining African American social status, it was always part of the equation.[41]

Gwendolyn Robinson cites the prominence of the "traditional mulatto elite" as a major factor in the development of the black cosmetics industry. In spite of black commentators' continuing criticism of color prejudice within African American communities, the success of these businesses suggests to Robinson that many black people hoped to improve their fortunes by changing their appearance. Not only was the "industry's clientele . . . based on the black masses," who were less likely to possess mulatto features, but black beauty culture itself provided an avenue for a new entrepreneurial elite to emerge. Before 1920, and to some extent afterward, the connection between appearance and social and economic success was clearly made in black beauty culture advertising. After 1920, as we have seen, advertising also increasingly linked light brown skin and straight hair with beauty and sexual desirability. So by the 1920s and 1930s, black cosmetics advertising reflected a beauty standard that had its origins in African American history and interracial class relations and was influenced by modern ideas connecting beauty with feminine success.[42]

Golden brown skin and shiny black hair were repeatedly offered as the beauty ideal to strive for, and thus African American commercial beauty culture did promote to black women what was still in many ways an urban and middle-class beauty standard. True, hair straightening had been available to rural black women long before the 1920s, and Poro and Madam C. J. Walker agents were to be found in small towns throughout the South and West. As Graham White and Shane White have observed, by the early twentieth century, even poor black women living in cities and rural areas made regular trips to a salon or a neighbor's home for hair treatments. Still, White and White point out that some older, more rural women shunned modern straight styles and the techniques for achieving them. Instead, "these women continued to wrap, braid, and cornrow their hair in the time-honored manner" or to use old-fashioned carding combs to straighten their hair. In fact, not all styles of straightened hair were considered equal. Writing in 1929, Claude Barnett urged Annie Malone to upgrade the Poro image, claiming it was out of date, associated in the public mind with "the humble type of woman, the one who straightens her hair a dead stringy straight." This compared unfavorably with more fashionable women who straightened their hair, then styled it into tidy, waved coiffeurs. Vivian Morris observed that 1930s Harlem beauty shops broke down along class lines into categories that included "Average Harlemite," "Theatrical," "Elite," and "Hometown." So whereas most black women straightened their hair occasionally, if not regularly, by the 1930s, class and region could still influence when, why, and by what method a woman did the job.[43]

Commercial beauty culture had been an important part of many African American women's lives since the turn of the twentieth century, but during the 1920s and 1930s, it became even more prominent. The growth of urban black communities, along with the expansion and maturation of mass consumer culture, brought beauty as a consumer product even more squarely into the consciousness of American women, black and white. Meanwhile, advertising joined with other mass media to powerfully promote a glamorous new set of beauty standards that depended on the purchase of an array of products and services. Whereas the highly racialized nature of this beauty standard was rarely recognized by white America, the looming influence of white ideals of feminine attractiveness made beauty culture a subject of contention in African American communities. Black women confronted beauty ideals in the mass media that could ignore, celebrate, or insult their beauty. Black beauty culture had its critics, but its most vocal advocates, the beauticians themselves, articulated a conscious and complex defense of their industry. Some denied the influence of a white beauty standard while others acknowledged it, but they all sought to serve the needs and desires of their clientele, to help women to feel beautiful, and to make a living for themselves at the same time.

Chapter 3

"An 'Export' Market at Home"

Expanding African American Consumer Culture in the 1940s, 1950s, and 1960s

In the 1920s and 1930s, as mass consumer culture gained prominence in American life, African American marketing professionals worked to promote black consumers to national-brand-name advertisers. At the same time, they sought to protect the African American beauty industry from further encroachment by white product manufacturers. This strategy continued in the 1940s and intensified after World War II, when postwar prosperity and new marketing methods spurred greater interest in African American consumerism. Innovations in consumer research and the launch of several new magazines aimed at African Americans created fresh incentives and appealing venues for national advertisers. More nationally circulating publications and the development of ever-wider distribution and marketing networks for consumer goods made it even more difficult than it had been in the 1920s and 1930s for black-owned businesses to appeal to local or community loyalties. More than ever, women bought beauty products in drugstores and grocery stores, rather than in beauty salons or from agents. African American beauty business leaders and marketing experts still advocated greater recognition of black consumer power while seeking to limit white companies' involvement in the black beauty industry, but the more they succeeded in the former arena, the harder it became to control what happened in the latter. The greater integration of African Americans into the consumer economy after World War II was significant, but it was hardly free of racial discrepancies and did not erase the perception of many black business leaders that it was worthwhile to promote black-owned beauty enterprises. At the same time, many recognized that as African Americans became more visible to white companies as consumer citizens, black-owned businesses might have to change their advertising and marketing rhetoric.

Product advertising throughout the postwar era reflected this shift. African American companies' advertisements invoked race pride and referred to their contributions to black communities less frequently than they had in earlier decades. White-owned companies no longer attempted to pass as African American firms. At the same time, beauty advertising appeals to black women changed in other substantive ways. In the 1920s and 1930s, widespread use of cosmetics and commercially produced hair-straightening products was relatively new. Advertisements and other promotional literature still sought to convince women that buying these products and services was a good idea. By the 1940s and 1950s, this was no longer an issue. Assuming that black women were now using makeup and straightening their hair, advertisers focused instead on what sorts of products were best to use. In particular, hair product manufacturers touted technological and chemical innovations that promised a more natural look for artificially straightened hair.

Postwar Prosperity and the African American Market

During World War II, while factories rushed to keep up with war production and the U.S. Office of Price Administration produced advertisements telling Americans not to buy too much in order to keep wartime inflation down, businesspeople were looking toward postwar markets and worrying that the end of the war would lead to an economic slump. It was assumed that pent-up consumer desires, long denied by the Great Depression and war rationing, would go a long way toward keeping the wheels of industry turning after the war was over. As it turned out, postwar inflation and fears of another depression caused an initial reluctance on the part of American consumers to buy at rates manufacturers hoped for, and as recent scholarship on postwar consumer culture has shown, late 1940s and 1950s advertising that portrayed the suburban "good life" was, at least initially, as much an attempt to seduce wary Americans to buy as it was a reflection of popular desires. Manufacturers and advertisers alike believed that totally new markets would need to be developed to keep production, and prosperity, high. African American market researchers followed these developments and worked to make sure that African American consumers would get attention as a "new" market. Of course the African American market was not new in the postwar era, but it was certainly more affluent and urban than it had been. Although black people continued to face considerable discrimination in the industrial job market, World War II did open up new employment opportunities, and African Americans enjoyed substantial improvements in wages over Depression-era levels. In addition, the earning gap between African American workers and white workers narrowed. Between 1920 and 1943, the annual income of African Americans increased threefold, from $3 billion to more than $10 billion. It was during these years, too, that organized labor, particularly the CIO, began serious efforts to unionize black workers. Black women were generally the last hired and the first fired in war industries, but they nevertheless enjoyed increased job opportunities and wages. As Jacqueline Jones points out, even black women who continued to work in the low-paying occupations traditionally dominated by African Americans (such as domestic service) used low wartime unemployment rates as leverage to demand better pay.[1]

The end of World War II led to some reversals of the progress African Americans had made in employment during the war years. Still, black men and women did share in the postwar prosperity of the 1940s and 1950s, albeit not equally with whites. In the mid-1940s, the average per capita income of African Americans was $779, compared with $1,140 for whites. In many cities, however, black incomes were significantly higher: $949 in New York, $1,081 in Chicago, $1,154 in Washington, D.C., $1,028 in Detroit, $1,100 in St. Louis, and $1,142 in Cleveland. At the same time, residential segregation and housing discrimination, trends that had begun in northern cities earlier in the twentieth century, intensified after World War II. The black population in most urban centers was increasing substantially, but neighborhoods where African Americans could find housing remained static in size or else expanded too slowly to accommodate new residents. Although the intensity of this situation varied from city to city, African Americans were, by the middle of the twentieth century, more urban and more segregated than they had ever been in American history.[2]

African Americans' postwar prosperity, though paltry in comparison with the affluence many whites enjoyed, increased the ranks of the black middle class and boosted the spending power of African Americans generally. Local businesses such as beauty parlors benefited from this situation, as did black marketing experts, whose perennial cries about the importance of the African American market were finally beginning to be heard. Although black people, as we have seen, were closely engaged with American mass consumer culture from its beginning, it was only in the late 1940s and early 1950s that African Americans as consumers gained significant attention from national white-owned companies. During these postwar years, a new generation of marketing experts and advertising executives began fresh efforts to convince big business that the black consumer was worth courting. The launch of several glossy magazines aimed at African Americans provided new nationwide venues for advertisers. As in the case of black newspapers in the 1920s and 1930s, cosmetics and hair product ads were prominent, and they reflected widespread efforts of white- and black-owned beauty companies to attract African American customers.

During the 1930s, as we have seen, media and marketing professionals like Claude Barnett, Paul Edwards, and William Ziff met with little success when they tried to get national advertisers interested in black consumers. White businesses maintained that advertising campaigns directed at African American consumers would not be worth the extra funds required to launch them. Some argued that black consumers were familiar enough with their products though mainstream media advertising and that specialized campaigns were unnecessary. Others assumed that most African Americans were too poor, too rural, and not educated enough to be reached effectively by advertising. Most big companies eschewed black newspapers as venues for advertising, citing low circulation numbers, substandard design, and parochial journalism. At the height of the Depression, it was perhaps too much to ask that advertisers abandon their prejudices and spend the money and effort necessary to court the African American market. This situation began to change during World War II. During the war, as we have seen,

American businesses were already developing plans for maintaining wartime production levels after the fighting ended. Manufacturers felt they had to find new markets, specifically foreign markets in Europe and the developing world. It was in this context that a new group of black advertising executives and market researchers entered the scene. As long as U.S. industries were willing to make up special advertising campaigns for South Americans, Canadians, and Swedes, they asked, why not focus on what one black marketing executive referred to as the "American Negro—an 'export' market at home!"[3]

Notable campaigners for recognition of the "new" Negro market included David Sullivan, founder and president of the Negro Market Organization; Edgar Steele, an African American employee of the Research Company of America, a white-owned marketing firm; and William G. Black, sales manager for Interstate United Newspapers, a group of African American newspapers founded in 1940 by Robert Vann of the *Pittsburgh Courier* that worked to increase advertising revenue for black newspapers. By the mid-1940s, Black had used data on African American income and spending patterns to secure advertisers like Seagram's, Coca-Cola, Pepsi, Ford, and Buick. Sullivan had worked on the advertising staff of black weeklies like the *Los Angeles Defender* and the *Washington Afro-American* before he started his own advertising and marketing firm in the early 1940s. Steele conducted market research surveys of black consumers in several U.S. cities in 1943. The research findings of all three men and their arguments for advertisers to pay attention to black consumers mirrored almost exactly the ideas forwarded by people like Barnett, Ziff, and Edwards in the late 1920s and early 1930s. All the studies from both eras emphasized the size and prosperity of the African American market. All insisted that this market could be reached effectively only by direct advertising appeals to black communities in black media publications. All focused mainly, but not exclusively, on the consumer power of middle-class African Americans.[4]

The front cover of a Negro Market Organization pamphlet sent to businesses in 1945 pictured an illustration of a black person's outstretched hand, holding money, dwarfing a map of Canada. Below this was information on the "U.S. Negro Market" and the Canadian market. In 1943, African Americans outnumbered the population of Canada by 1.4 million and, with a gross income of nearly $9 billion, earned almost $1.5 billion more per year than Canadians did. The Canadian market featured "Tariff Barriers" and a "Bi-lingual Language Market," obstacles that American businesses did not face with African Americans. Inside the pamphlet Sullivan wrote, "The European phase of our two-front war is rapidly drawing to a close. Its ending will result in substantial production cut-backs. . . . Are you prepared to take advantage of every market opportunity . . . do your present or postwar plans provide for action aimed specifically at reaching Negro Consumers? You cannot overlook them." Steele's surveys focused on the buying habits of African Americans in cities across the United States. One such survey estimated the total national income of African Americans in 1947 at $12 billion and stressed to potential white advertisers that black consumers were particularly loyal to standard brands. In an earlier study of Baltimore, Washington, D.C., and Philadelphia on behalf of the Afro-American Newspaper Company of Baltimore, Steele pointed out that blacks made up 13 percent, 19 percent, and 28 percent of those cities' populations. Businesses that wished to succeed in these markets, according to Steele, ignored black consumers at their peril.[5]

Steele and Sullivan both stressed the brand loyalty, high standards, and middle-class status of African American urban consumers. Sullivan pointed out in 1944 that in certain cases, particularly in the areas of toiletries, drugs and over-the-counter medicines, and cosmetics, "Negro per capita expenditures exceed those of white people for the same goods." Steele's 1946 portrait of black consumers in Baltimore, Washington, D.C., and Philadelphia showed blacks in those cities compared favorably to whites in terms of education, employment, and even home ownership. The study suggested that African Americans were increasingly employed in white-collar and skilled jobs and that they were frequent magazine and newspaper readers. In spite of low incomes compared with whites, black people were big spenders, buying new cars and choosing high-end grocery and toiletry products. The black consumer, moreover, could be reached more effectively through specialized advertising campaigns in African American newspapers and magazines. Sullivan promised in his promotional pamphlet that his organization had the resources and marketing information to help businesses sell to "over 45 Negro markets" and that he could create advertising appeals "in language understood by and pleasing to the 13,190,518 Negro consumers." Steele presented black consumers as a monolithic group, distinct in American society because of their "homogeneous in-

Negro Market Organization pamphlet, 1945 (Claude A. Barnett Collection, Chicago Historical Society)

terests and the racial consciousness that has been forced upon them." These factors, he claimed, resulted in African Americans' "collective ambition for improvement" and their desire for the best America had to offer, in everything from education to consumer goods.[6]

Promoters of the African American market argued that blacks shared an interest in consuming on an equal footing with whites, regardless of their class or occupation. They suggested that all African Americans, because of the common experience of racial oppression, shared the aspirations and desires of the black middle class. The idea of a monolithic African American community is simplistic and inaccurate, but in 1945 it was an effective tool to catch the attention of potential advertisers. As in the 1920s and 1930s, black marketing experts used the idea of consumer citizenship to portray the recognition of African American consumers as a question of racial justice. Now, however, as the civil rights movement was emerging, such appeals on behalf of black consumers had a new resonance. Perhaps as a result of this combination of economically and socially based arguments, the "new Negro market" received at least a little more attention from white advertising professionals after World War II than it had before. Advertising and marketing trade magazines like *Printer's Ink*, *Tide*, and *Publishers Weekly* all featured articles on the marketing research efforts of Sullivan and Steele. The March 7, 1947, cover of *Tide*, the "newsmagazine of advertising, marketing, and public relations," pictured a crowd of well-dressed black people superimposed with a large question mark. The article recognized that the war had "improved the Negro market, and made the Negro a more accessible and prospective customer," but it complained that there were too few hard statistics on the size and spending power of African Americans. The 1940 census data were unreliable, the article complained, and the Sullivan and Steele surveys, though they represented a good start, left a lot of questions unanswered. It was hard, for example, for potential advertisers to understand why black people bought high-quality goods when their incomes were so low compared with whites'. The best answers the author of the *Tide* article could offer invoked tired stereotypes: that black domestic servants emulated the tastes of their white employers or that black people, in their ignorance, assumed the most expensive food and toiletry items were the best and bought them without investigating differences in quality between brands. Such statements certainly represented an inaccurate and impoverished view of African Americans and a failure to recognize black people's knowledge and experience of the consumer economy they participated in. Nevertheless, this article and others did recommend that advertisers pay attention to this potentially lucrative new market.[7]

And how to reach this market? White advertisers, according to *Tide*, had in the past shied away from black newspapers, citing unconfirmed circulation figures, low journalistic quality, and a distaste for their likely advertising neighbors (including the ads for hair straighteners, novelties, and patent medicines that were the bread and butter of the black press). After World War II, *Tide* admitted, black newspapers improved in quality and featured more reliable reportage of circulation. More important, several new black magazines had joined these newspapers. The emergence of successful mass-market black magazines after World War II is a crucial factor in the history of African American consumer culture. These photograph-filled periodicals were modeled on magazines like *Life* and *Time* but were aimed primarily at African American readers. The most famous of these, of course, was *Ebony*, a weekly magazine published in Chicago beginning in 1945. With a circulation of more than three hundred thousand in 1947, *Ebony* was the most successful of many magazines founded by black publishing magnate John Johnson. Other Johnson publications included *Negro Digest*, *Jet*, *Hue*, and *Tan*; black magazines produced by other publishers included *Our World*, *Sepia*, *Color*, and *Eyes*. These magazines looked at entertainment, politics, sports, leisure, fashion, and beauty from African American points of view. They celebrated the achievements of prominent black people in a variety of occupations and devoted considerable space to racial issues. Magazines like *Ebony* did draw criticism from some black observers for being too middle class in their subject matter and editorial style. (In 1965, the politically radical publication the *Liberator* went so far as to ask, "Is EBONY a Negro Magazine?") But as Jacqueline Jones points out, *Ebony*, despite its glossy pages and features on fashion, movie stars, and cooking, was no clone of *Better Homes and Gardens* or *Ladies' Home Journal*. In its articles for and about African American women, the magazine consistently recognized that most black women, regardless of class, had to work outside the home. Furthermore, *Ebony* covered race-related social, economic, and political issues that were rarely touched by white-dominated magazines.[8]

The success of publications like *Ebony*, *Jet*, *Our World*, and *Sepia* can be attributed to the increased affluence of African Americans generally and the growth of the black middle class in particular during the 1940s. Earlier in the century, attempts to launch nationwide-circulation magazines did not succeed for long. *Half-Century Magazine* and *Abbott's*

Monthly, both based in Chicago, were published only sporadically, and for only a few years each. Although many of the post-1945 magazines failed within a few years, a good number of them lasted for decades. With their nationwide circulations and standardized formats, the new African American magazines were more attractive to potential national advertisers than city-based black newspapers had been. Although the process was not immediate, by the 1950s, big advertisers such as car manufacturers, makers of home appliances and electronics, and national food producers were regular advertisers in magazines like *Ebony*. Furthermore, the popularity and success of black magazines encouraged these businesses, on the advice of black advertising companies, to use African American models in the advertisements they ran in black magazines. At the same time, black publications continued to feature a great many ads for hair and cosmetic products—advertisements that often complemented feature stories on fashion, beauty, and glamorous black celebrities. Thus the growth of black mass media, occurring in tandem with the increased visibility of African American consumers, fed the expansion of commercial black beauty culture.

The "Arrival" of the Black Consumer in the 1960s

Historian Robert Weems provides a useful overview of the ways in which black consumers were courted (or not) throughout the 1960s. Early in the decade, white corporations' advertising "catered to African Americans' perceived interest in racial desegregation," whereas by 1970, it had turned to promotion of the "soul" market. These businesses' increased interest in black consumers was a significant phenomenon in itself. Throughout this period, African American market researchers pushed a model of a separate African American market—affluent, tasteful, and yearning to be recognized and treated with respect—to try to attract white advertising to black publications. (The postwar integrationist theme that white advertisers picked up on in the 1960s will be explored further in chapter 5.) Weems attributes white advertisers' increased interest in the African American consumer to urbanization, occupational improvements, and the efforts of African American marketing consultants. Between 1940 and 1965, the urban black population increased from 48.6 percent to 73.2 percent. Furthermore, during the 1960s, African Americans continued to enjoy increasing incomes, while the civil rights movement created significantly better educational and employment opportunities for many blacks. John Johnson, founder of *Ebony*, was a tireless promoter of black consumerism. Like Claude Barnett earlier in the century, Johnson mixed promotion of his own business interests with the larger causes of civil rights and equal economic opportunity. Placement of white companies' ads using black models in African American magazines not only helped to break down racial barriers, argued Johnson, but also made good economic sense for all parties involved. In fact, *Ebony* advertising revenue tripled between 1962 and 1969—but not without cost. Johnson's attempts to attract white advertisers included publication of *The Negro Handbook* in 1965, which highlighted lingering tensions between integrationist and economic nationalist views on black business. In it, Johnson clearly demonstrated his sympathy for the former, deriding black businesses for being unwilling to compete with whites. "As the barriers of race are hurdled," Johnson wrote, black consumers who had been "the *private property*" of black businesses were eager to give their business to "white establishments which offer, in many cases, extra services, luxury atmosphere, and a degree of glamour for the same dollar." This line of argument represented a decided shift from the tactics of earlier black marketing experts like Barnett and David Sullivan, who sought to raise advertising revenue from white companies but at the same time encouraged black businesses not to let these bigger, wealthier white firms drive them out of business. Nevertheless, by the 1960s, black consumers were getting much more serious attention from white advertising and marketing executives, who were scrambling to understand and attract this "new" market.[9]

Sales and marketing magazines heralded black consumerism as if it were a brand-new phenomenon. As late as 1972, one predominantly white trade magazine declared enthusiastically, "Marketing men go black for green." White corporations and advertisers looked to black "experts" for tips on how to "sell" African Americans. Caroline Jones was one of the first black women hired by the famed J. Walter Thompson advertising firm in 1964. Jones conducted marketing research and developed advertising strategies for a range of products aimed at African Americans. D. Parke Gibson, black sales consultant and author of *The $30 Billion Negro* (1969), advised white companies on how to attract African American customers. In one 1969 article in the *Marketing*

Magazine, Gibson encouraged companies to develop new products and sales techniques for the black market but warned that forethought and research were necessary to avoid inappropriate and offensive sales appeals. Early 1960s advertising depicted images of a racially desegregated society in which the discerning tastes and values of black consumers were highlighted. The rise of Black Power in the United States complicated this relatively simple and innocuous marketing approach. As Weems points out, and as we will examine in more depth in chapter 6, black nationalism was confusing to white advertising executives, who had assumed that African Americans sought racial assimilation and would be satisfied with advertising campaigns that used black models without making explicit references to racial issues.[10]

Overall, whether in the case of beauty product advertising in particular or commercial advertising in general, the presence of white-owned companies grew steadily in the 1950s and 1960s. From the perspective of black periodical editors, this was good news. Indeed, by the mid-1960s, to look at the prevalence of national-brand-name advertising in magazines like *Ebony,* one might think that the goal of black consumer citizenship, at least in terms of advertisers' recognition of the African American market, was on its way to being realized. At the same time, this success highlighted crucial problems when it came to beauty culture. African American beauty companies at the time often claimed that they were so well known they did not need to advertise very frequently (if at all) in publications like *Ebony.* But it was also true, as it had been in earlier decades, that few black companies had the means to advertise on a large scale. This would became even more glaringly apparent in the 1960s and 1970s, as much larger white companies entered the African American beauty market on an increasingly larger scale.

Advertising Black Beauty Products in African American Magazines

The emergence of successful mass-market magazines for an African American readership provided cosmetics companies with a broader-based and more versatile medium for marketing their products to black women. Black newspapers had always enjoyed circulations that extended far beyond the cities of publication, but magazines like *Ebony* were explicitly national in scope. Furthermore, magazines offered higher production values than newspapers, including glossy pages and the option of color photographs, which improved the visual impact of print advertising. At the same time, in the years between World War II and the early 1960s, the number of companies that produced beauty products for black women and advertised in black magazines increased dramatically. Newcomers to the African American beauty culture industry were largely, but not exclusively, white-owned. The slew of new white-owned companies included brand names like Silky Strate, Perma-Strate, Lustrasilk, Royal Crown, Snow White, and many others. Unlike white advertisers of the 1920s and 1930s, these companies did not attempt to pass themselves off as black-owned. They claimed no connections to the African American community, focusing instead on product promotion. These advertisements were, if anything, less ambiguous about the issue of beauty standards than the advertisements of previous decades had been. They openly promoted long, straight, flowing hair or fashionably curled styles and favored light-skinned models. Black-owned companies also advertised in the new African American magazines in the 1950s, but as in the 1920s and 1930s, they did so less frequently than did white-owned companies. The Madam C. J. Walker Manufacturing Company was one African American company that maintained consistent and large-scale magazine advertising throughout the 1950s and early 1960s. Nevertheless, the Walker advertising that appeared in this period, like that of white advertisers, focused more on selling beauty products and less on service and racial pride than it had in earlier decades. More and more, black-owned companies, like Walker, Apex, and the newly founded Johnson Products Company, played down racial consciousness in their advertising throughout the 1950s and most of the 1960s, even as the civil rights movement was emerging. This was not so much the case in other branches of the beauty industry. Writers in black magazines put recognition of African American women's beauty on the table as part of the integrationist agenda; black beauty culturists fought for equal treatment in their industry and actively supported desegregation and voting rights campaigns. It was not until well into the 1960s that beauty product advertising registered consciousness of the contemporary racial and political climate.

In 1945, David Sullivan sent the Madam C. J. Walker Company a package of information that echoed Claude Barnett's letter of sixteen years earlier. Under the headline "The New Negro Market Unexplored

Untouched by Madam C. J. Walker Co. What Shall We Do?" Sullivan pointed out that, although the company "was first" and continued to be "tops in quality," white businesses were getting a larger share of the growing black cosmetics market because of "consistent advertising, better packaging," and "popular prices." Sullivan pointed out that younger black consumers were, according to his survey results, unfamiliar with Madam C. J. Walker Company products, and only a concerted effort that included magazine and newspaper advertising, billboards, free samples, and demonstrations could remedy the situation. The old method of using beauty operator agents to sell products was out of date, Sullivan added. Companies like Lucky Heart of Memphis and, of course, Avon continued to depend on agent sales, but in a trend that began in the 1920s and 1930s, the beauty industry was increasingly focused on using media advertising to promote sales in retail stores. The Madam C. J. Walker Company was certainly aware of this shift. Company sales records from the 1950s show that at least half of its yearly sales went to the Indianapolis-based drugstore wholesaler Kiefer-Stewart, while the rest went to other wholesalers, stores, and agents. Because he was trying to sell his services, Sullivan almost certainly exaggerated the degree to which the Madam C. J. Walker Company was out of touch with black consumers. However, as we have seen, the vast majority of beauty product ads found in magazines like *Ebony* were hawking goods manufactured by white-owned companies. There were old, established businesses like Plough's and Nadinola and a slew of new companies like Snow White, Valmor, Perma-Strate, Lustrasilk, Silky Strate, and Dixie Peach. There were also larger white companies, like Clairol, Helene Curtis, Avon, and Noxzema, that had once advertised only in white publications but now were beginning to market their products to black women, in black magazines, using black models. These companies (with the important exception of Avon) did not tell women to contact an agent about products but instead hoped name recognition would drive retail sales.[11]

Black-owned beauty product manufacturers were a smaller presence in the new magazines than one might assume given the increased prosperity of African Americans and the likely attractiveness of an advertising venue that could reach a national market. Their advertisements were either quite small (as in the case of Murray's Superior Products) or very infrequent (as in the case of Apex). The Madam C. J. Walker Company ran only one advertisement in every other issue of *Ebony* in the 1950s, and its advertising appeared even more infrequently in magazines with smaller circulations, like *Our World* and *Sepia*. One exception was the Johnson Products Company. Founded by *Ebony* editor John Johnson's brother in the late 1950s, this company ran large and frequent ads in that magazine, itself eager to get advertising revenue in the early years of its publication. The limited resources of African American beauty business-es in comparison with many white-owned companies partly explains the small scale of advertising by black firms. Many simply could not afford to advertise as much as some of the larger, more affluent white cosmetics companies could. Additionally, several of the more famous companies (like Walker, Apex, and Murray's Superior Products) were reluctant to pay money for publicity if word of mouth, beauty operator and agent sales, and free newspaper coverage could do the job. There is some evi-dence that these older black companies felt they were so well established in the minds of African Americans that they no longer needed to spend a lot of money advertising. Claude Barnett, who was still a prominent presence in African American media circles in the 1940s and 1950s, complained about black businesses that wanted their self-aggrandizing press releases published in African American newspapers free of charge while they declined to buy advertising space in the same publications. Barnett was willing to distribute beauty companies' promotional mate-rials as news, but he struggled to collect the recommended subscrip-tion fees for this service from black companies. To marketing executives like Sullivan, this was an old-fashioned and ineffective marketing ap-proach in a domestic economy dominated by mass-media advertising and competition for retail sales. White-owned companies, particularly those new to the black beauty product industry, had little name recog-nition at first and no real community ties to their consumer base. They depended on mass national advertising, which was convenient to run in the new nationally marketed African American magazines, to spark customer interest and name recognition.[12]

Selling Beauty to Black Women

During the 1920s and 1930s, black-owned companies like Madam C. J. Walker and Poro made race ownership a central selling point. This strategy made sense considering the respect "race" institutions enjoyed in black communities and given the influence of leaders, like Marcus Garvey, who promoted black economic independence. White companies used similar rhetoric in order to compete, hoping that larger marketing budgets and bigger ads would make up for the lack of a genuine presence in black communities. There is little evidence that black consumers really believed that Plough's or Golden Brown was black-owned. On the other hand, they were almost certainly familiar with Walker and Poro. These companies enjoyed extensive black media coverage, their beauty schools and factories were established in black neighborhoods, and their agents and operators were scattered throughout black communities. Still, the bigger white companies were successful. They advertised more, distributed their products widely in the drugstores of black neighborhoods, and ultimately outsold their black competitors. They might have justified their advertising rhetoric, convincing or not, as good publicity and a gesture toward community relations.

After World War II, white-owned manufacturers of black beauty products made no such attempts at subterfuge. Likewise, companies like Walker and Johnson did not stress that they were black-owned, although Walker ads continued to mention the longevity of the company and to boast of its leadership in the field. During the post–World War II period, African American beauty product ads focused more than ever on familiar themes of cosmetics advertising—that beauty was woman's duty and prerogative, that an attractive appearance was essential for female success, that women naturally wanted to indulge in glamour, and that the use of the right beauty products would lead to love and happiness. Gone completely was the use of preachers' and community leaders' wives as product endorsers. Hardly ever did advertising promise independence or a better life for black women who became beauty operators and agents (even though this was a period of tremendous growth and opportunity for beauty culturists). In white companies' ads especially, but in black companies' ads as well, the beauty ideal promoted continued to be one of smooth, shiny hair and light brown skin. To some extent, this ideal was taken for granted more than it had been twenty years before. This advertising neither encouraged black women to do their hair "any way they wished" nor made crude and derogatory references to "ugly kinky hair." Black beauty culture in the 1940s, 1950s, and early 1960s assumed that all black women wanted shiny, wavy hair and would not hesitate to straighten and style their hair to achieve this look. Thus references to race were more muted in the ads of this era than they had been (and than they would be later in the 1960s and 1970s). In the early years of the civil rights movement, black beauty culture advertising seemed to present a message of complacency about race and beauty standards.

In his bid for the Madam C. J. Walker Company account, David Sullivan used familiar appeals to racial pride and economic independence to convince the venerable cosmetics company that it needed to spend more on advertising. He warned that white businesses were getting "more and more of a market formerly dominated by Negro concerns . . . those intrepid pioneers who started what is considered today—Big Business, Profitable Business." The advertising of these new white players in the black beauty culture industry did dominate the pages of black magazines, particularly *Ebony*, whose large circulation attracted the most advertising revenue of all the new African American magazines. The ads themselves were cheerful and upbeat, promoting a fun, glamorous, romantic image of beautiful black womanhood. Snow White, maker of hair dressings, pressing oils, and other cosmetic products, invited women in a 1947 advertisement to "delight your man tonight with your . . . Satin-Smooth Lustrous Hair." The advertisement featured a photo of "Glamorous Una Mae Carlisle, famous entertainer," wearing her highly glossed hair in a typical 1940s upswept style. Snow White, a white-owned company, featured the advice of African American beauty consultant Sandra Powell in each advertisement and offered women Powell's "Guide to Correct Make-Up" free by mail and at cosmetics counters. Royal Crown ran an advertising campaign in the 1950s that billed its product as "America's largest selling hair dressing" and claimed it would put the "Love Look" in women's hair. Royal Crown ads focused on youth, using real-life high school students (complete with white ankle socks and white buck shoes) as models and featuring pictures of young women sporting the latest 1950s hairdos, from poodle curls to curly bobs and straight, brushed-back styles. Royal Crown billed its hair dressing as light, modern, and fashionable, unlike the heavy, greasy pressing oils of the past. Dixie Peach ran advertisements for its hair dressing in the 1950s and 1960s that highlighted the necessity of beauty for African American women. Glamorous models appeared with captions like "My Hair Just *Has* to Look Perfect All the Time" and "A model's hair must be extra lovely!" Not all black women were models,

Royal Crown advertisement, 1956: "Beauty begins with Smooth, Glossy Hair!" (*Ebony*)

of course, but, these advertisements suggested, they should all strive to look like models.[13]

African American companies' advertisements differed little from those of white companies in these years. The images of ideal beauty they presented also favored straightened hair, light skin, and middle-

Madam C. J. Walker advertisement, 1950s: "Now I'm Going Steady . . . with Glossine!" (Madam C. J. Walker Collection, Indiana Historical Society)

class lifestyles. Posner, a well-established black company, ran an advertisement for a hair relaxer in 1960 that featured a black model typical of the era: short Jackie Kennedy–style haircut, a medium-brown complexion, and a string of pearls around her neck. Supreme Beauty Products Company marketed its Raveen Hair and Scalp Conditioner with the endorsement of Helen Williams, "famous model and cover girl," and told women to "look for Raveen at your favorite drug store or cosmetic counter." The Madam C. J. Walker Company ran a series of advertisements in the 1950s for its standby pressing product, Glossine, using pictures of glamorous women. Walker advertising typically employed models with stylish but short and conservative hairstyles, wearing refined makeup and expensive-looking jewelry. Johnson Products Company's Ultra Sheen models had a similarly glamorous, yet refined, look. One Apex advertisement featured a woman driving a convertible, and another suggested that women who knew the "secret" of beautiful hair (using Apex products) would attract men wanting to shower them with expensive gifts like orchids and diamonds.[14]

With their photos of models in evening gowns, pearls, and tennis outfits, the advertisements of all of these companies portrayed a fashionable, affluent, middle-class ideal of beautiful black womanhood. These were not women who worked (except as models or entertainers). Their goals, often explicitly stated, were to be fashionable, to enjoy leisure activities, and to look beautiful for their men. These were images few black consumers, even those among the disproportionately middle-class readership of the new black lifestyle magazines, could identify with, since so many black women, regardless of class, had to work outside the home and hardly led lives of suburban leisure. Nevertheless, such images held meanings that might have resonated with a broad range of African American women. Black women, as we have seen, were rarely portrayed in the white-controlled media as glamorous or beautiful, and the particular focus in these advertisements on gorgeous black models was refreshing. Furthermore, as historians Shane White and Graham White, Robin Kelley, and Tera Hunter have observed, working-class black men and women frequently wore high-end clothing in their leisure time as a potent expression of independence and personal dignity. Although these scholars sometimes see class distinctions in particular styles of clothing favored, they also recognize that working-class blacks drew, at least in part, from the fashions of middle- and upper-class blacks and whites for inspiration. Additionally, hair product advertisements' portrayals of black women dancing and playing sports suggested (truthfully or not) that these treatments prevented processed hair from going back to its natural texture even if a woman perspired. This was an issue of constant concern to black women, many of whom had neither the time nor the money to get their hair done more than once a week. Working-class and middle-class black women straightened their hair using similar products in this era, and women from both classes might have responded favorably to advertising promising beautiful, worry-free hair that would keep its "process" through a hard day's work, exercise, or a night on the town. Beauty culture ads certainly exemplified the middle-class image that black consumer marketing experts and magazine publishers wished to portray, but middle-class black women were not the only audience affected by such appeals.[15]

Old and New Products and Their Advertising Campaigns

Many of the tools and treatments for black women's hair common from the 1920s through the 1940s enjoyed continuing popularity and were actively marketed in the 1950s and 1960s. The use of a hot comb with pressing oils, creams, and pomades was still the most common method of hair straightening. Still, new treatments began to emerge that were promoted in advertisements and available in beauty salons during these years. Beauty culturists and producers of beauty products alike promoted new methods for straightening hair and for curling hair that had been straightened. Advocates of these innovations promised softer, more versatile hair. The new products would allow for easier straightening and curling of short hair (accommodating the popularity of the shorter styles of the 1950s) and would require hair to be straightened less frequently. African American beauty culturists adapted the methods of perming, setting, and styling hair that were commonly used in white salons for use on their black patrons. Manufacturers of products for black women responded to this trend, marketing hair-setting lotions, curling fluids, and lighter hair dressings to accommodate the demand for softer, lighter hairstyles. Chemical hair relaxers were just one of the more prominent "new" products advertised to black women in the years after World War II. Hair relaxers, both commercially made and homemade, had been around at least since the turn of the century, but they had always been more popular with men than women. The "conked" styles of 1940s and 1950s male hipsters are well known, but trend-conscious urban men may have used chemical preparations earlier in the twentieth century as well. Women, however, relied almost exclusively on the pressing method to straighten their hair. Beauty manuals and textbooks published before the late 1960s did not provide any instruction to beauty culturists on how to chemically straighten black women's hair. Until the 1950s and 1960s, the best-known makers of beauty products did not produce hair relaxers. Early chemical straighteners were considered too harsh and damaging to hair, particularly the longer hair of women; they often caused hair to break or turn red. At the same time, hot combs were not practical or effective tools for straightening shorter hair on black men. Around the time the conk was at the height of its popularity for men, advertising for chemical straighteners directed toward both genders, and toward women in particular, began to appear in magazines.[16]

Several new chemical hair straightening products hit the market in the late 1940s and early 1950s: Silky Strate, Perma-Strate, Hair Strate, and Sulpher-8, among others. Advertisements assured black women that these chemical relaxers were safe and effective. Perma-Strate used celebrity endorsers like Sarah Vaughan, Hadda Brooks, and Dinah Washington to convince women that using a relaxer was an appropriate way for them to straighten their hair. A 1955 Silky Strate ad pictured a woman confidently standing with uncovered hair in the rain and prom-

Silky Strate advertisement, 1955: "No Rainy Day Blues" (*Jet*)

ised "New Hair Beauty That Lasts for Months!" "One simple application of Perma-Strate Cream Hair Straightener keeps your hair beautifully straight up to 6 months," declared another company's advertisement. "No Burn! No Redness! No Scalp irritation!" ran another Perma-Strate ad. "Hair becomes softly, smoothly straight . . . just as you've always wanted it to be . . . without the use of heavy, greasy dressings . . . without any 'pasted down' or waxy look. . . . No wonder Perma-Strate is preferred and recommended by so many famous stars of stage, screen, radio and television." In spite of such appeals, it seems that black women did not throng to have their hair straightened the "modern" way. Some were undoubtedly concerned that the products were not as safe as they were purported to be. The old pressing method was still considered the popular, respectable choice. As will be discussed later, chemical relaxers did not gain wide acceptance for black women until the late 1960s. For African American women who wanted to avoid altogether the question of how to straighten, wigs offered a viable option. Advertising does not suggest that wigs were common among black women before the 1940s, but in the decades after World War II, African American magazines featured page upon page of wigs, natural and synthetic, long and short, black, brown, blond, and red. Wigs could be had in any of the latest hairstyles and required no weekly trip to the beauty salon.[17]

On the cosmetics front, entire lines of makeup designed for African American skin tones were available to black women by the late 1940s. Beauty culturists like Marguerita Ward and Rose Morgan marketed their own lines of makeup produced exclusively for black women, while companies like Madam C. J. Walker, which had manufactured such products for decades, continued to promote cosmetics tinted to complement African American skin tones. African American magazines frequently offered makeup advice to black women. *Our World*, for example, printed several cosmetics pieces in the 1940s. "I don't have to tell you what a job it is to match face powder to Negro complexion tones," nightclub singer Norma Shepard said to *Our World* beauty columnists in 1946. Light shades look gray, darker shades look too orange, and though "the grapevine reports that suitable shades are about to be packaged and placed on the market," until then, black women were obliged to blend three shades at home to achieve the right look. "Your complexion is your treasure," declared *Our World* in 1949. "And it's the key to your make-up. Choose cosmetic colors appealing to your natural skin tones. They will enrich your beauty." The article continued with makeup suggestions for complexions from "mahogany brown" to "bronze" and "olive tan."[18]

Intensified efforts to produce and promote makeup that suited darker complexions did not alter the media-promoted beauty ideal

Nadinola advertisement, 1953: "Don't Depend on Daisies!" (*Ebony*)

of light- to medium-brown skin for African American women. Advertisements for skin bleaching creams continued to run alongside those touting brown shades of facial powders and deep-toned lipsticks. New companies and lines like Bleach and Glow and Artra joined old ones like Nadinola and Plough's Black and White. As in the 1920s and 1930s, bleaching cream advertisements mixed blatant claims for the skin-lightening properties of the product with assertions that the cream was really for overall improvement of skin tone and texture. Artra ads promised "lighter, lovelier skin beauty for you" but also "luxurious softness . . . without oiliness." A 1957 advertisement for Golden Peacock Bleach Creme pictured the familiar dark-skinned "before" and light-skinned "after" pictures of a model with a headline stressing that the cream "turns skin shades lighter." The accompanying text, however, listed reductions in "oily skin," "blackhead bumps," and "dark splotches" among the benefits of using the Golden Peacock cream. A 1962 advertisement for Dr. Fred Palmer Skin Whitener promised "lighter, brighter skin" in only seven days "plus a clearer complexion too!" Bleach and Glow advertisements told black women that its cream "lightens, brightens your skin tone to one creamy *even* tone" and causes "blemishes, blackheads and dull, drab skin" to vanish. Bleaching creams were not offered only by white-owned companies. In the early 1960s, Posner promoted its new Skintona cream "for lighter, brighter, exciting skin tone!" Nadinola, long a big name among skin bleach manufacturers, continued to be a frequent and highly visible advertiser in magazines in the 1950s and 1960s. "What's more fun than being a girl?" asked one advertisement—especially if she has "skin that's clear, bright, Nadinola-light." Another advertisement claimed that "men notice and admire girls with clear, bright, Nadinola-light complexions." One advertisement asserted, "I discovered Nadinola—then he discovered me." Others declared that Nadinola skin bleach provided "the lighter, brighter complexion that welcomes Close-ups" and that "lighter skin leads the way to brighter evenings!" All these advertisements promised an end to pimples, blackheads, and other blemishes, as well as a lighter complexion.[19]

Overwhelmingly, skin bleach advertisements connected light skin with femininity, beauty, and romantic success. That these products were sold to eliminate various skin blemishes as well as lighten skin does not indicate an attempt to justify the sale of the bleaching creams or an admission that there was anything wrong with trying to change one's skin color. On the contrary, using skin lighteners along with cleansers and moisturizers and taking measures to prevent and heal breakouts were portrayed unquestioningly as equally important parts of a black woman's daily skin regimen. This trend was not new, but whereas some bleaching cream ads produced by white companies in the 1920s and 1930s had portrayed dark skin as ugly and undesirable, in the 1950s both white and black companies presented more muted and complex arguments for using these products.

The "Natural" Look

Advertisements for African American hair products during the 1950s often promised natural-looking hair to black women. This was a new sort of appeal that reflected changing methods and products for straightening African American women's hair. By "natural," advertisers did not mean the unprocessed Afro that would gain favor with young black men and women in the 1960s and 1970s. "Natural" in this earlier context meant hair that remained soft, smooth, and free flowing after it had been straightened. Advertisers, like leading beauty culturists at the time, assured women that they no longer needed to put up with stiff, hard-pressed hair covered in sticky pomades. New products and methods of straightening and styling black women's hair offered alternatives to the use of the hot comb. Advertisers sought to convince black women that these new products were effective and desirable alternatives to the familiar press-and-curl service they had used for years. The "natural" look, of course, could be achieved only through the use of considerable artifice, as well as time and money. Promotion of so-called natural beauty is certainly a familiar aspect of white women's beauty culture. Nevertheless, in this case, the hair texture being promoted to black women was not, for most, even close to being natural. This line of promotion not only maintained that straight, smooth hair was desirable, as earlier advertising had done, but it also assumed that flowing, glossy locks were a beauty norm that women needed to live up to. Although there were now more choices in how to straighten one's hair, the necessity of straightening and the ideal look to achieve seemed more rigid than ever.

In 1953, Willard B. Ransom, Freeman B. Ransom's son and the assistant manager of the Madam C. J. Walker Company, wrote a letter to

Madam C. J. Walker advertisement, 1953: "*Your Own Natural Beauty*" (Madam C. J. Walker Collection, Indiana Historical Society)

the company's advertising firm, enclosing an advertisement for Lustrasilk home permanent kits. He commented that the Lustrasilk ads were "excellently done" and complained that "they're all trying to steal the Natural Beauty theme." In fact, Walker had no exclusive or original claim to the use of natural beauty as an advertising hook; "natural" was an unusually common adjective in black beauty culture advertising in the post-

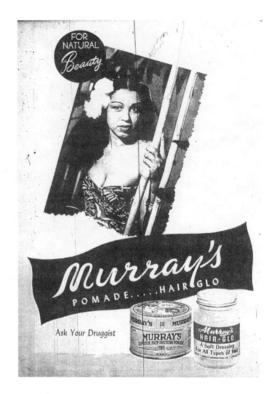

Murray's Superior
Products advertisement,
1946: "For Natural
Beauty" (*Ebony*)

war period. Walker ran a campaign for several years in the early 1950s touting its hair and cosmetics products with the motto "Only Madam Walker brings out your own natural beauty." Advertisements promoting the natural look promised that Walker hair-straightening products and methods were neither heavy and greasy, as old pressing oils had been, nor damaging, as new chemical relaxers were. Lustra- silk, the company Ransom mentioned in his letter, marketed a home permanent similar to those that had been available to white women for decades. A setting cream was put on damp hair, but instead of being dried on curlers, the hair was pressed with a (not-too-hot) pressing comb or iron. "Super Safe," a typical advertisement declared, "Lustrasilk brings out *natural* hair beauty . . . protects as it straightens!" "No discoloration— no oils—no damage," promised another ad. "Lustrasilk works real 'beauty magic' on super-curly or hard-to-manage hair, leaving it softer, easier to style and manage . . . gleaming with brilliant *natural* highlights." The Madam C. J. Walker Company had come out with its own permanent, Satin Tress, but it was designed for professional use only.[20]

Meanwhile, hair dressing manufacturers assured black women that their products were new and lighter and made the old hair-pressing methods more effective than ever. A Murray's Superior Products advertisement from 1946 promoted the company's hair pomade "for natural beauty" with a photograph of a long-haired African American model. Apex advertisements featured models brushing long, luxurious curls under captions like "Naturally! . . . Good news for women everywhere with super curly hair." In 1957, the company renamed its hair dressing Naturalizer, promising that hair required only light pressing. With Apex Naturalizer, "Wind . . . rain . . . moisture . . . perspiration . . . your hair will not go back! Now you can have surprisingly *softer*, more convincingly *natural* waves . . . longer lasting too . . . encouraging *natural* hair growth!" Johnson Products Company touted its Ultra Sheen Creme-Press, putting quotation marks around the word "natural" in one 1964 advertisement, while promising that the pressing cream "gives hair natural looking, healthy sheen . . . not oily 'pomade shine.'" These advertisements clearly recognized that the products were designed to alter black women's hair, that "natural" was not truly natural. The advertising copy used quotation marks and phrases like "convincingly natural" and "natural-looking" to suggest that the creation of natural hair required the artifice of beauty culture.[21]

Magazine articles of the time echoed this trend toward softer styles. "Pressed or unpressed your hair can be lovely if you know how to treat it and how to wear it," proclaimed beauty writer Thyra Edwards in 1946. Edwards advocated brush-dried hair, light oils, and careful pressing with a not-too-hot comb. Although she gave due recognition to "chic women from the Caribbean" who wore their hair "unpressed in all its natural crinkliness," she told American women to value their "coarse, kinky hair" only because it lent itself better, once it had been straightened, to the various waved and curled styles popular at the time. African American women were consistently told that soft, wavy, smooth, natural-looking hair was modern, fashionably urban, and highly desirable. Of course, the ideal of naturalness had long been a common motif in the promotion of beauty products to women regardless of race. Kathy Peiss points out that even as cosmetics gained wider acceptance in the twentieth century, fashions vacillated between the natural look and a more artificial, theatrical, and glamorous style. The natural look pro-moted by the beauty industry dictated that makeup and hair products be used artfully to make the woman look as if she had applied nothing at all. In this way, Peiss shows, the natural look was as artificial as any. Nowhere was this more powerfully demonstrated than in the natural look promoted to black women in the 1950s. Selling soft, wavy, flowing hair as the natural ideal for African American women denied the artifice of hair straightening.[22]

In the postwar era, the African American beauty culture industry grew tremendously in tandem with rising prosperity and an increased focus on black consumerism. The ideal of consumer citizenship meshed well with the goals and rhetoric of the era's civil rights movement. Although tensions persisted between the desire for white advertisers to recognize African American consumers and the desire of black business owners to protect their interests, for the moment, the integrationist vision of consumer citizenship won out. This was partly the result of the in-creasingly national scale of product manufacturing, distribution, and marketing, a trend that hurt smaller, black-owned firms that could not afford extensive advertising campaigns. The success of post–World War II marketing campaigns designed to promote black consumers to white advertisers may therefore have initiated the decline of African American beauty product manufacturers, many of which would have serious fi-nancial difficulties by the early 1970s.

Chapter 4

"Beauty Services Offered from Head to Toe"

Promoting Beauty to African American Women in the 1940s and 1950s

In 1946, the new Rose-Meta House of Beauty opened in Harlem. Co-owners Rose Morgan and Olivia Clarke, who had run a smaller shop together for several years, bought the property for $20,000 and spent $28,000 on lavish renovations. At its height, this beauty salon would employ sixty operators and style the hair of three thousand women a week. Less than a decade earlier, in Washington, D.C., three sisters founded the Cardozo shop, a smaller salon that nevertheless saw hundreds of customers a week in 1947. By the early 1950s, several beauty emporiums were located in big northern cities, including New York, Chicago, Washington, D.C., Detroit, and Philadelphia. Although these establishments did not replace the one-room shops and home-based operations that had flourished in black neighborhoods for decades, their emergence did indicate a shift and an expansion in African American beauty culture. The rise of the full-service luxury beauty salon in many respects represented the pinnacle of African American beauty culture in the years following World War II. Even as African American beauty product manufacturers faced increasing competition from white-owned companies, black beauticians themselves enjoyed new prosperity and

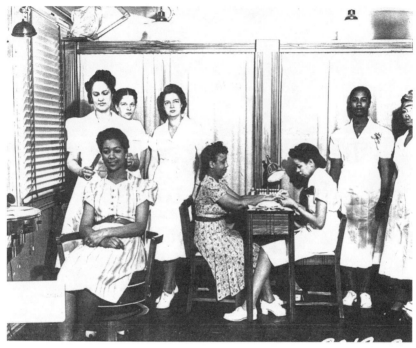

Cardozo shop, Washington, D.C., 1940s (Women's Bureau, U.S. Department of Labor, National Archives)

demands for their services. Continuing segregation, whether voluntary or imposed, in beauty salons, training facilities, and even in some states' certification requirements ensured that African American women would still run and work in African American beauty shops. These shops offered black women a full range of treatments and services that could transform them into glamorous beauties. Salons like Rose-Meta and Cardozo brought black beauty culture to new heights of professionalism and commercialization. At the same time, these luxury salons suggested deepening class distinctions among the newer and bigger beauty shops, smaller businesses, and beauty workers.[1]

The rise of these megasalons was not an isolated development; it was accompanied both by a significant rise in the number of companies producing beauty products for African Americans and by a surge in African American media interest in the subject of beauty. Beauty product advertisements, articles and advice columns about beauty, and coverage of black beauty pageants, models, and celebrities filled the pages of the newly launched national black magazines. Many articles presented African American female beauty as an "issue." Writers complained that the mainstream white media ignored the beauty of black women, and they sought to define and promote African American beauty in various articles and photo spreads. The beauty ideals depicted in advertisements and magazine articles continued to favor lighter complexions and hairstyles similar to those that were fashionable among white women. Critiques of this standard were rarer during this period than they had been in earlier decades or would be by the mid-1960s. Beauticians continued to portray themselves and their business as beneficial to African American women, and they no longer took pains, as they had earlier in the twentieth century, to justify their services or to counter charges that they encouraged a white beauty ideal. Increased demand for beauty services among black women suggested that such charges had not slowed the growth of the African American beauty industry.

The Beauty Emporium

The proprietors of the large African American beauty salons that opened in the 1940s and 1950s took pride in offering black women head-to-toe luxury beauty services in modern, attractive, and professional settings. Coverage of these shops in the black media gushed over their opulent settings and the fashionable, up-to-the-minute hair and cosmetic treatments they made available to black women. *Pulse* magazine lauded Rose Morgan and Olivia Clarke's original House of Beauty in 1943 as the only establishment where "Negro women are welcomed and can get all of the beauty services offered, from head to toe." Not only could women have their hair "shampooed, styled, bleached, tinted, and trimmed," but they could also get "scalp treatments, manicures, pedicures, body massage, bubble bath, electric vibration, and reducing baths." By 1946, *Ebony* recognized the newly relocated House of Beauty as the "biggest Negro Beauty parlor in the world . . . attracting customers from coast to coast," including "outstanding notables" like Eslanda Robeson and dancer Katherine Dunham. In 1947, a reporter for the *Baltimore Afro-American* named the Cardozo sisters' shop one of the most modern beauty salons in Washington, D.C. It offered manicures, the latest hairstyles, and attractive surroundings to patrons. That same year the *Afro-American* ran a full-page spread under the headline "Thriving Beauty Shops Prove Women Pay for Glamour." In Newark, New Jersey, the article reported, a woman who started out doing hair in her home at twenty-five cents a head now owned two establishments grossing $20,000 a year. A competing shop, the Orchid, made $25,000 annually and boasted purple tinted glass, booth dividers, and walls "colored in conformity with the [store's] name." In Philadelphia, a prominent salon that was painted "Nile green and buff, as a background for black and chrome fixtures," provided patrons with scalp treatments, facials, manicures, and pedicures along with hairdressing services. By 1950, House of Beauty franchises had spread to Norfolk, Virginia; Chicago; Detroit; Denver; Los Angeles; Washington, D.C.; Philadelphia; Kingston, Jamaica; and San Juan, Puerto Rico. In 1955, Morgan's newest House of Beauty opened in New York, "loaded with the latest gadgets and machines for hair and body" and featuring a children's department, a clothing designer, and a charm school. Detroit's House of Beauty boasted a Motor City–style assembly-line service that efficiently whisked patrons from the shampoo-and-curl room to stylist, beauty analyst, facialist, pedicurist, manicurist, and fashion consultant. The husband of salon owner Carmen Murphy told *Ebony* in 1951, "Leave my wife alone, and the House of Beauty would be as large as the Ford plant at River Rouge."[2]

The African American beauty emporium emerged during what Julie Willett refers to as the "golden years" of the independently owned beauty shop. Although women had continued to get their hair done during the Depression, Willett notes, during World War II women's trips to the beauty parlor became one part of home-front patriotism, helping women to maintain "feminine beauty even in the toughest of times." After the war, and into the 1950s, regular trips to the beauty shop "had become part of a woman's routine"; more than half of American women reported getting their hair done in salons in 1953. By 1958, there were 110,000 salons in the United States; by 1961, that number had risen to 150,000. The increased demand for beauty services contributed, Willett observes, to a shortage in beauticians and a subsequent rise in beauty culturists' wages. African American women were a part of all these trends. During the 1950s and 1960s, black beauty shops grew in size and number, becoming central social, cultural, and economic institutions in African American neighborhoods. The Cardozo sisters ran their business in a succession of apartments in the 1930s but used New Deal financing programs for small businesses to build a salon in 1937. Rose Morgan rented a booth from another salon owner for years, until she was able to open her own shop after the war. Postwar prosperity, along with increasing urbanization of African Americans after World War II, helped to create the conditions that allowed many African American women to expand their beauty culture businesses. Commentators credited increased demand for beauty services, along with more stringent state regulations, for making beauty culture a lucrative occupation for women. In 1947, the *Baltimore Afro-American* cited weekly salaries of $25 to $75 for District of Columbia beauticians and $40 to $50 a week for those in New Jersey.[3]

The luxury and comprehensiveness of the new African American salons were not their only attractions. The salon owners and the writers who reported on them always stressed that these shops offered services designed for the specific needs of black women. *Pulse* noted in 1943, for example, that the Rose-Meta salon not only brought "scientific, modern beauty services to the Negro woman" but also offered guidance to African American women in finding cosmetics and hair treatments appropriate to their hair textures and skin tones. The House of Beauty in Detroit offered its own line of cosmetics "designed especially for women of color." Carmen Murphy claimed she had "taken the guesswork out of beauty care for colored women" by making cosmetics "which suit all types and shades of skin." Elizabeth Cardozo Barker, co-owner of the Cardozo salon in Washington, D.C., attributed the success of her salon to the expertise her hairdressers had in caring for all types and textures of African American women's hair. Her sister, Catherine Cardozo Lewis, believed that by providing women with the most up-to-date methods and products, particularly those that were not available in other black salons, they were "contributing to the self-respect of Negro Women at that time." Writing about the Rose-Meta House of Beauty in the *New York Age*, Betty Granger made a similar point. "As Ziegfeld typified the American Beauty of his day," she wrote in 1949, "so will Miss Morgan and Mrs. Clarke glorify the Negro woman."[4]

Of course, these spacious, glamorous salons were located in cities and were not easily accessible by women from small towns and rural areas. Moreover, a trip to a House of Beauty was considerably more expensive than getting a wash-press-and-curl treatment at a smaller neighborhood beauty parlor or a home-based business. Basic hair treatments could run as high as four or five dollars, and more elaborate services, such as permanents, hair coloring, manicures, and pedicures, cost even more. Middle-class women could more easily afford regular trips to the new salons than could working-class women, but the former were not the only patrons. *Pulse* reported in 1943 that the Rose-Meta salon had "the distinction of serving Negro women from all walks of life, from all parts of the country." By 1955 the salon employed eighty hairdressers and could handle 125 customers at a time. Carmen Murphy's House of Beauty in Detroit claimed to have filled 75,000 appointments between 1948 and 1951. The Cardozo sisters' shop averaged 60 customers a day in 1947. Catherine Cardozo Lewis recognized that the shop had a reputation for "cater[ing] only to the elite" but maintained that that was misleading. All were welcome, she said, though she admitted that the shop's appointment system and long list of regulars sometimes gave the appearance of exclusiveness. Cities like New York, Chicago, and Washington, D.C., boasted scores, sometimes hundreds, of African American beauty parlors in the 1940s and 1950s, increasing numbers of which offered the kinds of luxury services Rose Morgan had innovated. By all accounts, demand for beauty services, and venues for getting them, exploded in these years, and one can safely assume that not all of these patrons were elite or middle-class black women.[5]

The proliferation of luxury beauty salons in black neighborhoods was part of the overall growth of the African American beauty industry that sprang from larger social and economic changes affecting African Americans during and after World War II. Black troops served in the war effort, unprecedented numbers of African American workers got industrial jobs and joined unions, and black politicians and activists intensified their campaigns for civil rights. The "double V" campaign, led by African American publishing, political, and labor leaders, was founded on the premise that black people needed to fight for freedom at home as well as overseas. African American labor leader A. Philip Randolph, along with the NAACP and the National Urban League, pushed the U.S. government to desegregate the war production industries—a cause that culminated in a threatened march on Washington in 1941. Throughout the war, African Americans slowly and painstakingly won jobs in war industries and made inroads toward inclusion in industrial unions. This, along with black participation in the war effort abroad, heightened the visibility of African Americans in public life and strengthened their sense of entitlement as American citizens. Additionally, World War II and the industrial boom that accompanied it brought a second wave of black migrants to cities in the Northeast and Midwest and drew unprecedented numbers of African Americans to the urban centers of the West Coast. By 1945, 60 percent of African Americans lived in cities, and black incomes overall were on the rise. Beauticians and cosmetics companies rushed to take advantage of this new opportunity.[6]

One of the reasons so many large beauty salons could be successful during and after World War II was that income levels for African Americans in general were somewhat higher than they had been in the 1920s and 1930s. These higher income levels, combined with the growth of densely populated urban black communities, created a huge and concentrated market for goods and services aimed at African Americans. Increasing numbers of African American women, working class as well as middle class, lived in cities and wanted to get their hair done. Many could afford to go to more expensive shops at least once in a while. Certainly smaller shops were thriving in this era too, further indicating continuing demand for many kinds of beauty services. Although the market for full-service, luxury beauty treatments probably did come disproportionately from the ever-expanding black middle class, these prominent shops served a range of women living in black urban neighborhoods: longtime residents and new arrivals, laundresses and cooks, teachers and nurses, nightclub singers, and politicians' wives. Store owners like the Cardozo sisters and Rose Morgan noted that they did the hair of black women from all classes and that everyone in their shops, clients and staff, was treated with respect regardless of background. Morgan remembers that she strove to maintain an atmosphere of dignity in her shop and that all women, operators and customers alike, were addressed as "Miss" or "Mrs." For working-class black women, so frequently employed as domestics in the service of others, the indulgence of a trip to the beauty parlor where they were pampered and given respect must have been appealing.[7]

The culture of the new, big salons was, their proprietors claimed, more "refined" than that of the home salons and small shops common in African American neighborhoods. Morgan, for example, made sure that her Houses of Beauty were not houses of gossip by maintaining a strict policy of silence for her operators. The only subject of conversation between hairdresser and client was to be beauty. The Cardozo sisters upheld a similar policy. In both cases, and in the cases of other large beauty salons, the assembly-line strategy precluded the use of black beauty shops as communal centers, where African American women could meet, exchange news, relax, and socialize. Some African American women may have missed this, and one wonders how successful Morgan and the Cardozos were in maintaining their strict guidelines. In her 1939 interviews conducted in Harlem beauty shops, Vivian Morris revealed that the shops she visited, from what she called "elite" beauty parlors to the neighborhood salons frequented by the "average Harlemite," were lively places of gossip and social interaction. In her study of beauty shops, Julie Willett cites Alice Murray, an African American woman and thirty-six-year owner of a Washington, D.C., salon, expressing what was probably a typical view on the subject. "Beauticians have to be more than hairdressers," she observed; they also have to be "doctors, advisors, good listeners, relaxation therapists and more." When women are troubled, she went on, articulating a pervasive gender stereotype, "they will either go shopping or to their hair parlor seeking relief."[8]

Still, some patrons might have appreciated the efficiency and relative quiet of the new salons. Barker observed that the "majority of our customers were women who worked and had no time to come to the shop for a social hour." Barker recalled working as an apprentice in a shop with no appointment policy and a liberal atmosphere. When she volunteered to get an appointment book, the salon owner said, "Oh, yes indeed, dearie, you go right ahead and get me this book," but in six weeks Barker was the only one who used it. The salon was set up with a comfortable "living room" type waiting area where customers were "quite satisfied" to "sit in there for hours, sometimes. They'd play cards; sometimes they'd gossip. . . . I hadn't worked with her very long before I realized that I wasn't going to learn. . . . I didn't want to be that kind of hairdresser." So the Cardozos did things differently. Barker noted that, with their appointment system and no-gossip policy implemented, "we did get real teamwork then, and customers used to really appreciate it. Because they'd come in tired and worn out and they would want to relax, come in and get their hair treated, and not be hearing about anybody's problems or not be hearing any gossip, they'd just want a relaxed, quiet atmosphere." But Barker admitted that not everyone liked the policy. "Some people say we were 'hinkty' [snobbish]! They didn't like to go to a beauty shop with all that quiet: 'Think you're going to church.'"[9]

Whether beauty operators came from the black middle class, aspired to it, or just hoped to earn a decent living, the beauty culture industry encouraged them to present themselves as refined professionals and to make their shops appear modern and luxurious. Lessons in proper appearance and deportment began at beauty school. Students of the Poro schools received lessons in how to walk, talk, and eat "properly" along with instruction in hair pressing and styling. Implicit in this curriculum was the assumption that most of the women training in beauty culture did not enter the program adequately versed in middle-class standards of appearance and deportment. The Cardozo sisters welcomed former domestics into their apprenticeship system, suggesting that their shop could be a transformative experience for some. Barker noted that many of her beauticians had started out as "ordinary looking black women who looked like domestics," but "all somebody needed to do was scratch the surface" to see their true abilities. Barker explained that she and her sisters decided that all their workers, be they beauticians, clerks, or cleaners, should be treated with equal respect and gentility as long as they were "good" and did "good work." This was, Barker went on to say, "to encourage them to be professional, to be businesslike ladies." In this way, these salons extended an atmosphere of respect and civility to all employees regardless of their backgrounds. At the same time, such shop owners attempted to exert considerable control over their operators' work habits and behavior.[10]

The most prominent black beauty culturists sought, with limited success, to define what beauty shops looked like and to control how they were run. For the most part, they welcomed the midcentury trend toward increased state regulation and more rigorous certification requirements for beauticians. Those connected with beauty colleges were certainly helped by this trend: State regulation meant increased enrollment and more time in school to complete the minimum one thousand hours of training required in many states. Some hoped that tough certification exams would weed out the ignorant and unmotivated and help raise the professional status of beauty culture. Many prominent beauticians fought segregation and bigotry to win positions on state cosmetology boards. For the most affluent, influential, and best-educated African American beauticians, regulation was a positive development. At the same time, the increased time and tuition costs, along with state licensing fees for salons and beauticians themselves, must have posed a financial hardship to many aspiring black beauticians. Some young black women who could not afford to finish their schooling got stuck working as maids in white salons with little pay and no chance for advancement. Salon owners were often sympathetic to this situation—and not only those owners like Rose Morgan, who was the daughter of sharecroppers, but also those who had quite privileged backgrounds, like the Cardozo sisters, who came from a prominent Washington family. Barker remembered fighting hard to get the District of Columbia's cosmetology board to recognize apprenticeships in licensed shops as equivalent to the required hours of training in a beauty college. "Well unfortunately, in our race, in so many instances, we start off just a little underprivileged compared to those white students," commented Barker. The Cardozo sisters "were determined to see to it that [young black women] were going to get their education, they were going to get to be beauticians if they wanted to."[11]

African American Beauticians and Their Customers

By all accounts, demand for beauty services among African American women was up in the 1940s and 1950s. Beauty salons now offered a much wider range of procedures than they had in the 1920s and 1930s, when the basic wash-press-and-curl was ubiquitous. Now even those women who went to salons primarily to get their hair done had a range of new straightening methods to choose from, from the natural-look techniques pioneered by beauticians like Morgan and Barker to the new, gentler chemical hair relaxers that manufacturers were beginning to produce. Whatever hair care method they chose, most African American women, regardless of class or region, did not question hair straightening itself.

Like the beauty-product manufacturers cited in the last chapter, many beauty culturists in the 1940s and 1950s promised new, more natural-looking hair to African American women. Before World War II, Walker, Poro, Apex, and other African American beauty institutions in the 1920s and 1930s, in spite of their rhetoric of corporate rivalry, taught beauticians basically the same hairstyling methods. After the hair was washed and conditioned, a styling oil (which could be liquid or semisolid) was applied to the hair to protect it while a heated metal comb was drawn though the hair, one small lock at a time, until the hair was straight. Curling irons could then be used to make tight curls or loose Marcel waves. The result was a shiny, gleaming, but often hard, even lacquered, look. The method certainly suited the short, sleek, close-to-the-head styles popular for black and white women alike in the 1920s and 1930s, but it did not work as well for looser styles, nor did it suit those African American women with less tightly curled hair. As Barker observed, even those women with tightly curled hair often underwent unnecessary and damaging styling processes. "Some black shops then," she recalled, "after they shampooed your hair, they would take this wet hair, stand it all over your head and stick you under the dryer. So that when you came out of that your hair *had* to be pressed hard to undo what they had done."[12]

Barker claimed that she and her sisters innovated what would become the natural-look alternative to the hard press. The method used a softening shampoo and then a light oil applied sparingly to the scalp. "We did not see any reason why black folks' hair had to be gummed down and laid down with grease," she said. Then the hair would be brushed to distribute the oil and get the tangles out, brushed dry using a blow dryer, and pressed or curled ("croquignoled") into the desired style. "Well, people used to be amazed at the way their hair looked when it was handled this way," Barker recalled. "So very much less pressing was necessary. And in some cases almost none." Morgan described a similar method that was used in her Harlem salon. In fact, according to Barker, her sister Meta Cardozo Hurley, Morgan's original partner in the Rose-Meta salon, taught Morgan the technique, which, Barker noted, "went over very big in New York. Naturally it would, because all they had at this time was what they called 'hard press.'" Morgan herself attested to the popularity of the natural-look method, observing that "people would say: if you want 'blow' hair [hair that will move in a breeze], go to Rose-Meta." At Carmen Murphy's House of Beauty in Detroit, *Ebony* reported in 1951, "beauticians were taught to give the natural hair type of treatment. . . . [They] did away with heavy oils, learned to use controlled heat," and the "natural look became the rage of Detroit." Meanwhile, new setting lotions (such as Madam C. J. Walker Company's Vapoil) for putting curls into straightened hair using curlers instead of heated irons, and new, gentler chemical straighteners (such as Walker's Satin Tress and Lustrasilk home permanents), promised looser, more natural straightened and curly looks. The new methods

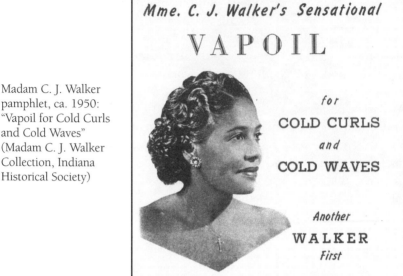

Madam C. J. Walker
pamphlet, ca. 1950:
"Vapoil for Cold Curls
and Cold Waves"
(Madam C. J. Walker
Collection, Indiana
Historical Society)

Mme. C. J. Walker's Sensational

VAPOIL

for

COLD CURLS

and

COLD WAVES

Another

WALKER

First

facilitated the puffed updos of the 1940s; the short, tousled styles, such as the poodle cut, popular in the 1950s; and many of the swingy shoulder-length looks that women favored in the early 1960s.[13]

Beauticians and product manufacturers claimed that the natural look was available to African American women with any type of hair. Margaret Cardozo Holmes, for example, countered the notion that her and her sisters' method was appropriate only for black women who naturally had more loosely curled hair. "It has been said that we can only do good hair," she told the *Baltimore Afro-American* in 1947. "That is a fallacy—we can handle any kind of hair and bring out the best in it." All the purveyors of the natural look profiled in the black press seemed to be doing a booming business in the postwar years. The popularity of certain products also attested to the desirability of an alternative to the hard-press look. In 1953, Eunice Wood, the director of a modeling and charm school for African American women in Columbus, Ohio, offered her endorsement of Vapoil setting fluid to the Madam C. J. Walker Company. "A more natural looking hairstyle is accomplished by pin curling," she wrote to Willard B. Ransom. "Vapoil by Mme. Walker Company was the preparation so easy to apply at home and still get 'professional' looking results." Wood acknowledged that "every smart woman has a competent beauty operator," but "between-appointment

Walker Satin Tress demonstration, Kansas City, 1950s (Madam C. J. Walker Collection, Indiana Historical Society)

care at home is a must," and Vapoil helped her students maintain their "softly turned crew cut," "hoydenish poodle," and "sleek cap" hairstyles. Ransom later used Wood as a spokeswoman in print advertising campaigns. The Walker Company newsletter also reported success for its Satin Tress hair relaxer and reprinted many letters from beauticians' satisfied customers. In the March 1949 issue, a Kansas City beautician wrote that the product was "the best on the market today," and an operator from New York gushed, "Last week we did a girl's hair who had difficulty keeping it straight over a week; yesterday she was caught in the rain, yet her hair looked lovely." By 1955 beauticians were writing in to the *Walker Newsletter* calling Satin Tress "wonderful" and "a Honey."[14]

In spite of such reports, old-fashioned wash-and-press methods continued to dominate African American beauty culture, in part because the new chemical relaxers could be unreliable and dangerous in untrained hands. In 1949 Robert Brokenburr, a Madam C. J. Walker

Company lawyer, wrote Marjorie Stewart Joyner to tell her that the company had "slowed down on pushing Satin Tress for the reason that we have gotten so many complaints. . . . People have complained that their hair has just come out in great quantities after undergoing more than two treatments." Although Brokenburr seemed convinced that "the fault is with the beautician," the threat of "at least two lawsuits" was enough to convince him that the company needed to hold off on promoting the product while Joyner set to work educating Walker beauticians on how to use it safely. By the mid-1960s, however, chemical relaxers for women were increasingly common. In 1966, for example, a black beauticians' trade magazine reported on a beauty salon in a Detroit department store (managed by an African American woman but serving whites and blacks alike) that did not press hair at all. The shop offered permanent straightening and styling and setting services for women with already-pressed hair. Still, chemical relaxers had by no means superseded pressing. African American beauty schools continued to teach pressing techniques, and the straightening comb was still the most ubiquitous tool in black beauticians' supply kits throughout this period. In spite of the efforts of natural-look proponents, the hard-press look of the hot comb was very likely still the most popular straightening method for African American women, and it is certainly the method most commonly cited in references to black women's hair care during the period. The trend toward light hair oils was not necessarily universal either. In a 1949 *Chicago Defender* poll of working-class African American women, most respondents said they preferred a hair dressing of a "light texture," but 16 percent said they used Vasoline as a hair dressing—hardly light in texture, but very affordable. Further, 21 percent said they didn't know what product they used (perhaps because they got their hair done at salons). It is quite likely, too, that the more elaborate curled styles that urban salons specialized in were slow to gain favor in smaller towns and rural areas. Andrea Benton Rushing, who grew up with a hairdresser mother in New York and spent vacations with beautician relatives in South Carolina, remembers that none of the southern women "would have done the fancy styles New York customers wanted because no self-respecting, church going family woman . . . would wear those bold styles." These women could not understand "what kind of person would want to get herself gussied up like the women in *Ebony* and *Jet*."[15]

Whatever method they might have used and whatever style they wanted, almost all black women in America straightened their hair from the late 1940s to the early 1960s. Earlier in the twentieth century, many advertisers and beauticians had spent time promoting the idea of straightening itself, whereas in the postwar years none did; they focused instead on touting one method or another. In the early decades of the century, black women who straightened their hair and beauticians who offered hair straightening had to contend with criticism not just from black clergy members but also from separatist publications like Marcus Garvey's *Negro World*. By the 1950s and 1960s, it was hard to imagine an African American preacher anywhere in the United States who would rail against beauty parlors to pews filled with gleaming, wavy-headed black women. Similarly, the most prominent black nationalist organization of this period, the Nation of Islam, did not maintain a universal policy on the issue. Although some articles in the group's newspaper, *Muhammad Speaks*, criticized women for using cosmetics or concerning themselves with fashionable clothing, the publication also invited readers to send in pictures of African American women for its "Natural Beauty" feature, which ran in 1962 and 1963. Whether or not they covered their heads, all the women whose hair was visible in the photographs appeared to have straightened hair.[16]

Photographs from the 1930s depict rural southern black women wearing braided and wrapped hairstyles that dated back at least to the nineteenth century, but memoirs of southern African Americans who grew up in the 1950s and 1960s do not mention women wearing their hair this way. They frequently mention the ritual of hot-comb hair straightening, especially in the home-based business that persisted in these decades. Although these writers are well aware of (and often participated in) later critiques of the straightened-hair aesthetic, many remember that, at the time, such hairstyling practices did not seem to represent the damaging influence of a white beauty standard. Rather, many African American writers look to hair straightening, sometimes quite nostalgically, as an essential part of black women's communal and social lives, as well as an important step in an African American girl's coming of age. In her memoir of growing up in Bessemer, Alabama, English professor Deborah McDowell remembers that, "for the local Pipe Shop scuttlebutt, the women and girls of the neighborhood flocked to Ophelia's to get their hair straightened and styled." Ophelia's home beauty parlor was so popular that she sometimes rushed through a job and accidentally singed a person's head with the hot comb. Customers "were sure to sit all day long, as other girls and women trickled into the house to wait impatiently for Shirley Temples or bangs and kissy curls held down by shiny black crisscrossed hairpins." In his memoir of growing up in 1950s Piedmont, West Virginia, Henry Louis Gates fondly recalls watching his mother doing the hair of women in the family's kitchen. "There was an intimate warmth in the women's tones as they talked with my mama while she did their hair," he writes. "How that scorched kink could be transformed through grease and fire into a magnificent head of wavy hair was a miracle to me. Still is." And bell hooks remembers Saturday mornings at home when she and her five sisters "would gather in the kitchen to get our hair fixed—that is, straightened" by their mother. "In those days," she observes, "this process of straightening black women's hair with a hot comb was not connected in my mind with the effort to look white, to live out standards of beauty set by white supremacy. It was connected solely with rites of initiation into womanhood." Getting one's hair straightened was "a ritual of black women's culture" and "an exclusive moment when black women . . . might meet at home or in the beauty parlor to talk with one another or listen to the talk." There seems to have been less unquestioning support for other products, such as cosmetics and skin bleaches. Reports on new beauty salons mentioned the availability of these products and services, but there is little evidence that they were anywhere near as popular as hair straightening.[17]

The Black Media and the "Issue" of African American Beauty

The postwar beauty standard of shiny, wavy, styled hair was made even more powerful by depictions of African American "beauties" of various sorts in the black media. In 1947 *Our World* called upon Ed Brandford, owner of a prominent African American modeling agency, to answer the question "What is Negro Beauty?" Brandford offered examples of Negro beauty in photographs and descriptions of popular black models and entertainers of the day. At one point he observed sardonically how "strange" it was that "no Negro girl has ever competed in the Pageant of Beauty at Atlantic City. Strange that millions of Negro girls, of varied and interesting beauty, are shut out from the parades." Blaming Hollywood for inequities in the business of beauty, Brandford concluded that beauty in America was "a monopoly which permits no Negro girl to pass." While complaining about racism in modeling agencies and the entertainment industry, the professional modeling agent unquestioningly accepted the notion that Hollywood starlets, beauty pageant winners, and fashion models defined modern American beauty.[18]

In the American entertainment industry in the late 1940s, as Brandford noted, black women were not much more likely to be celebrated as glamorous beauties then they had been before World War II. There were a few notable exceptions. When Josephine Baker returned to a singing engagement in the United States in 1951, after living in Paris for twenty-five years, black and white media alike remarked on her fashionable image. *Jet* called her "The World's Best-Dressed Woman" and gushed over her green velvet dress by Dior and her $32,000 gown by Balmain. Judging from her "11 oversized trunks and 7 small suitcases," it is no surprise that, according to Baker biographer Phyllis Rose, a "writer from *The New Yorker* who came to interview Baker at the Strand was introduced to her wardrobe instead." Baker's earlier American tour, in 1935 and 1936, was an abject failure, in part, Rose argues, because white audiences were not ready then for a black woman to take the role of elegant and sophisticated chanteuse. Baker's popularity among white and black audiences in 1951 suggests a more widespread acceptance of glamorous black women celebrities, but this was often limited to women best known as sensuous nightclub singers or portrayers of whores and "tragic mulattos" in a few popular films. Actresses in Hollywood, on Broadway, and on television still rarely got leading romantic roles. At the same time, black media observers continued to celebrate African American female entertainers, holding them up as proof that black women were as beautiful and glamorous as any women in the world. But even as African American entertainers received praise from black and white critics alike for their beauty and talent, they struggled in their careers. Champions of the new black female celebrities constantly complained about Hollywood's color prejudice in casting. African American media efforts to promote black glamour echoed and reinforced efforts by the African American beauty culture industry to sell commercial beauty to black women and, later, to integrate beauty standards in the United States.[19]

Two of the most prominent representatives of African American beauty in the 1940s and 1950s were Lena Horne and Dorothy Dandridge, both of whom appeared constantly in adoring publicity stories in the black press. At the same time, it was clear that these women achieved commercial success at least in part because they fit a particular beauty ideal, perpetuated in Hollywood, of a light complexion, "good" hair, and "sharp" features. Black publications, as they always had, mostly avoided direct discussion of this particular issue. In fact, many magazines used celebrities as examples of the "diverse" beauty of African American women, even as they continued to feature a quite narrow range of hair types, skin tones, and facial features. Many black commentators did observe that even the fairest of black women could not hope to get a wide range of leading roles, and they criticized the white-dominated entertainment industry for offering limited opportunities to actresses like Dandridge and Horne. Yet when black media observers called for integration of American glamour and stardom, they failed to seriously address controversies over female beauty standards that remained salient within African American society. Articles seemed to argue only that there were black women out there who could resemble the established ideal beauty type, rather than that the standard should be altered to reflect the diversity of African American women. At the same time, it is important to recognize that even limited inclusion of glamorous black women in the mainstream entertainment industry was something of a breakthrough. The late 1940s and 1950s did bring somewhat greater recognition of and opportunities for African American performers in white-controlled venues, especially jazz singers in nightclubs and actresses in movies. Their popularity, along with the devoted fascination with black celebrities of newly launched black magazines like *Ebony*, *Jet*, and *Our World*, ensured a proliferation of publicity about black female stars and engendered a newly intensified quest to define African American beauty by glorifying African American women performers. Many articles answered the question "What is Negro Beauty?" by offering a selection of ideal types drawn from the ranks of well-known African American actresses, singers, and dancers.[20]

In a 1952 *Our World* article titled "What Is Sex Appeal?" surreal photographs of various famous black women's legs, waists, lips, eyes, and bust lines compartmentalized beauty into particular physical traits.

Black cartoonist E. Sims Campbell responded in a similar vein when *Jet* asked him in 1952 to define "The Perfect Negro Beauty." Campbell commented, "If I were to draw a picture of the perfect Negro beauty, I would have to select at least one feature from each of nine lovely women," including Lena Horne's nose ("I like the refined, extremely sensitive curves of her nostrils") and "full-bodied" but "not overly sensuous" lips. Campbell praised Marian Anderson's "chin, throat, and shoulders," Dorothy Dandridge's "sensuous and weaving" waist, Pearl Bailey's arms and hands, Katherine Dunham's hips, and Josephine Baker's "autumnal brown complexion." Evoking a consistent theme in the black media's musings on African American beauty, *Jet* observed, "Selecting a perfect Negro beauty is an extremely difficult task . . . because of the many different kinds of beauty evident in the race." Yet, of course, selecting an image of "perfect Negro beauty" was exactly what Campbell was doing, and that was not the only contradiction he expressed. Though insisting that "hair needn't be straight to be beautiful" and noting how "foolish" straight hair would look on the "tall, arrogant women of the Watusi tribe in Africa," Campbell said, "With all the hair preparations on the market, and all the skilled stylists who can use them, women can have beautiful hair."[21]

For the most part, articles on the issue of African American beauties and the entertainment industry divided their time between praising black female entertainers and attacking white Hollywood for failing to adequately appreciate "brownskin beauty." Some celebrity profiles seemed on the surface to differ little from the promotional fare of *Life* and other popular magazines. Articles in *Our World* created false controversies, as in a 1954 piece titled "How Evil Is Eartha?" Trading on Eartha Kitt's media image as a calculating sex kitten, the journalist assured readers that Kitt was not evil but that her hard-luck childhood and adolescence had toughened her. "Now that she knows what she wants," concluded the author, "she has gone after it with all claws." In 1952, *Our World* asked, "Can Dandridge Outshine Lena Horne?" In a thinly veiled attempt to introduce a new young star by manufacturing a competition with an older one, *Our World* gushed over Dandridge's "nut brown skin" and "lush body." But there were real controversies for black women in the entertainment industry. In 1951, *Jet* introduced African American readers to young black women in Hollywood who struggled to make ends meet while trying to break into the tough movie business.

Like all aspiring actresses, the article noted, these young starlets faced few opportunities, small roles, and small paychecks, but as black women they also had fewer parts open to them. As Donald Bogle notes, the hopeful atmosphere of post–World War II civil rights activism did not markedly improve movie roles for most black women.[22]

Lena Horne and Dorothy Dandridge were easily the most successful black female stars of the era, but even they found it difficult to break out of old stereotypes. *Our World's* fourth anniversary issue, in April 1950, featured Horne as its first cover girl. The accompanying article described her professional successes, including her eight-thousand-dollar-a-week income for headlining at the Copacabana Nightclub, and provided several photographs of the glamorous star in exquisite clothing. Further on, however, the tone of the article changed. Mentioning an upcoming tour of Europe, the author observed that "other Hollywood stars, feeling throttled by movieland's restrictions, have preceded Lena to Europe." Referring more pointedly to race, the author admitted that when Horne first appeared in movies, "in all her glamour, it marked an upheaval in traditional 'Uncle Tom' casting of Negroes." Nevertheless, Horne mostly played in short musical scenes that "could easily be cut to appease the Southern market." Even movies about miscegenation tended to use white actresses to play alongside white actors in the popular "Negro problem" romance plots of the late 1940s and 1950s. Horne herself noted, "From here on, I hope films will present Negroes as a reality, not as a problem." Horne's comment recalls W. E. B. DuBois's reflections in *The Souls of Black Folks* on how it felt to be a "problem," a connection Horne may well have been aware of as a result of her series of appearances at Café Society in the early 1940s. Horne's biographer, James Haskins, notes that the intellectual, left-wing, and politically conscious patrons of that nightclub encouraged Horne to explore African American history and read the works of important black writers.[23]

Horne and Dandridge faced similar dilemmas in the 1950s. Critics, black and white, recognized their talent. Observers of both races waxed poetic over their beauty. But neither woman was able to break the color line in films by getting consistent work as a leading lady. Horne remained stuck as the sultry nightclub singer, and Dandridge settled into one "tragic mulatto" role after the other. As *Jet* observed in 1952, Hollywood had no place to put Horne or Dandridge, in part because of their light complexions. Like the chorus girls and nightclub singers of the 1920s and 1930s, both younger actresses had achieved much of their success as club singers because of their skin color, which admirers described with words like "golden," "honey," and "copper." On the *good* other hand, as *Jet* put it in 1952, "dark" women could always find roles as "maids" or "Queens of Sheba," but lighter-skinned women had a harder time finding jobs in the movies. Dandridge was asked to wear makeup to "darken up" for a role in 1952; producers told Horne early in her career that she was too light and her hair was too short and she should try to pass as Spanish. She refused. In 1953, *Jet* berated Hollywood for failing to "glamorize Negro girls," citing Lena Horne as the most prominent example of an underused black star. Commentators on African American female celebrities reflected the contradictions of the age. Following an old tradition in the black press, writers continued to glorify the beauty of black celebrities. Entertainers and journalists alike hoped that Hollywood would not only create more space for black glamour girls but also accept a more diverse beauty ideal. At the same time, African American media observers continued to perpetuate quite narrow beauty standards for women of color in the post–World War II era.[24]

African Americans Ed Brandford and Barbara Watson founded the first black modeling agency in 1946. Brandford highlighted the racial dimension of his enterprise by referring to the outfits his models wore for photo shoots and fashion shows as "freedom clothes." The relative novelty of professional black models in the early 1950s led to occasional speculation over their virtue. The author of a 1953 article in *Color* magazine, for example, warned of the "beauty" who is transformed by fast living from "a naïve young girl into a calculating call girl." Actually, black models exemplified African American beauty by this time, just as white models had twenty years before, and accusations of loose morals were rare. More common were celebratory profiles of famous black models like Dorothea Towles, Sara Lou Harris, and Sylvia Fitt. Commentary on African American models in the 1950s and early 1960s focused on the dearth of jobs open to black beauties, especially in white magazines and fashion shows. Not until the late 1960s and early 1970s were African American models even beginning to be featured in big fashion shows, mainstream print advertising, or predominantly white fashion magazines.[25]

In the 1920s and 1930s, African American cosmetic and hair product advertising featured relatively few professional models hawking products. Many companies turned, as we have seen, to famous African American stars of stage, screen, and nightclubs. The Madam C. J. Walker Company often used Walker herself in advertisements, even some years after her death in 1919. The Walker advertisements also used prominent African American society women, preachers' wives, and community leaders in ads. Often, cosmetics companies used sketches and illustrations of women in advertisements, which may or may not have been inspired by real African American women. In 1925, Claude Barnett wrote to Poro with advertising copy ideas and a sample drawing. "The artist is one I have nursed along for years," he wrote, "and finally got to the place where he draws, I think, good Negro types." Nevertheless, even in these early years, some companies' advertising occasionally used photographs of young, beautiful African American women. By the 1930s, companies like Nadinola, Palmer, Poro, Apex, and Walker regularly used photography and often featured the same model over and over in advertisements. This, along with packaging, must have helped create brand-name recognition, as well as establish a particular type of beauty the company wanted to project. Unlike famous cosmetics "spokesmodels" of today, these women were unnamed, but they played a similar role, promoting a particular image for the company. In these cases, the images conveyed fun, youth, womanhood, and a beauty ideal of light skin and straight hair.[26]

By the 1940s, and especially in the 1950s and 1960s, black cosmetics advertisers used models regularly, reflecting the role black models now played in commercial beauty culture as representatives of ideal beauty. A 1960 advertisement for Raveen Hair and Scalp Conditioner featured "famous model and cover girl" Helen Williams declaring, "Thank goodness for New RAVEEN! It makes my hair look longer, more beautiful and more glamorous!" In 1955, white-owned Lustrasilk hawked its home permanent kit with photographs of models and the observation "Leading models stress importance of hair care for good grooming! . . . For straightening and styling super-curly or hard-to-manage hair . . ." The Madam C. J. Walker Company was relatively slow to use professional models in its advertising. In 1959, June Taylor wrote a letter to the company, with publicity shots of herself and another model enclosed, inquiring about possible employment: "If we can be of any service in advertising any of your products, we would be deeply grateful." (Significantly, Taylor and her friend were both graduates of the John Powers School of Modeling in Los Angeles, one of the first all-white modeling agencies to integrate.) The Madam C. J. Walker Company had previously "used graduates from our Beauty Schools" in its advertising, but by the 1960s, professional models had taken over there as well; company files from this era overflow with publicity shots sent in from aspiring models. Silky Strate, a white-owned producer of chemical relaxers, created advertisements that used a device familiar to anyone who regularly peruses fashion magazines: juxtaposing models with "ordinary" women. In 1957, the company ran a series of ads with two close-up photographs under the headline, "Which Girl Is the Professional Model?" Beneath the pictures the advertising copy observed, "One of the two girls pictured above is a professional model. Her career demands beautiful hair. The other is a college student. Her hair is just as lovely . . . thanks to SILKY STRATE. Can you tell the difference?" The company then offered female readers a prize of one thousand dollars if their picture was chosen for use in its advertisements. By the 1950s, professional black models were a permanent fixture in most African American cosmetics advertising and were consistently held up as experts on and examples of beauty.[27]

Black observers' commentaries on modeling, like their writings on the entertainment industry, constantly invoked race, whether celebrating "varieties of racial beauty," reporting on African American models who "made it," or complaining about racial bias in the industry. In July 1948, *Ebony* reported on the "First Interracial Charm School," the International Finishing School in San Francisco. Citing "Caucasian standards of beauty" as the reason that black models failed to find work, the article profiled the San Francisco school's innovative efforts to promote varied examples of beauty by including white and black women, as well as Native American and Asian women. Founded by Lucille Sanderson, a descendant of Harriet Beecher Stowe, the school promoted interracial cooperation, participating in a National Brotherhood Week fashion show and declaring that "each race, color or nationality should have its own recognized standard of beauty." For the most part, as the *Ebony* article attests, white-run modeling agencies excluded women of color, forcing the creation of the International Finishing School, the Brandford agencies, and other firms that specialized in representing black women.

Although Brandford had achieved a certain amount of success by the mid-1950s, boasting six agencies throughout the United States in 1954, smaller black agencies struggled. Sandy Edmonson had trouble getting investors for her interracial Glamazons agency (for beautiful women five-feet-seven and taller). Edmonson was proud that her charm school and agency accepted beautiful women who had been rejected elsewhere because of racial bias, but she had to admit that there was little demand for "Negro Glamazon clothes models."[28]

Nevertheless, there were undoubtedly more modeling opportunities for African American women in the 1950s than there had been in earlier decades. In 1950, *Ebony* reported on the proliferation of modeling schools and agencies that had sprung up to meet the demand created by increased advertising directed at African Americans, along with the increased number of African American magazines. For years modeling had been a "lily-white profession," but "sudden recognition of the booming postwar colored market" had spurred the founding of many black modeling firms. Now, *Ebony* observed, "dozens of colored models are being used in advertising campaigns aimed at corralling the one billion dollars that Negroes spend annually on clothes and cosmetics alone." The magazine warned of "fly-by-night" teachers and beauty school "rackets" but assured readers that most of the schools thriving in major cities were legitimate businesses. Even so, because of the lack of jobs for black models, most African American modeling schools also served as charm schools, where housewives and high school girls could learn the "proper techniques of hair styling, make-up, personality development, and social etiquette." In fact, African American modeling schools and agencies, like their white counterparts, helped perpetuate the notion that female social and personal success lay in one's appearance, specifically in achieving the high standard of beauty set by the beauty culture industry. Following Brandford model Sylvia Fitt one working day, *Ebony* observed her rushing to assignments, leading a charm school exercise class, and window shopping. "Even when not working, models must dress well, [and] live up to glamour expectations," *Ebony* commented, and pointed out that models ate dinner at home to stay slim.[29]

Many African American magazines rushed to assure their mostly middle-class readership that the image of models as reckless party girls with loose morals was much exaggerated. In an informal poll of African

American models from New York, Chicago, and Los Angeles in 1951, *Ebony* found that they were "neither the husband snatchers nor night club barflies that tabloid sensationalism has pictured them to be." Models led serious, busy lives, according to the article, working as teachers or using modeling to help pay their way through college. "I don't have time to go to nightclubs or bars," said Fitt. "With the hours I keep," said Chicago model Vera Green, "I don't see how anyone could get the idea that a model has time to be a playgirl." Vera Francis, a Los Angeles model, commented, "I always keep a regular job, it's one sure way of staying out of trouble." Another Los Angeles model, Dorothy Brown said, "Modeling is fun, but it can also be hard work." Observed New York model Ellen Helty, an aspiring film editor, "The models I know are just like other people—clean living girls, neither sober nor fast." Courtney Olden of New York assured *Ebony* readers, "My career is far from glamorous. I love my home and my children. I love to cook and take care of my husband's needs. His career comes first, mine second. And I don't mind it at all." Expressing a desire for both a traditional and a more progressive female role in society, Juanita Green, also of New York, told *Ebony* that she took up modeling because she thought she needed "poise," but, she explained, "I'm interested in more serious things . . . a law career, a home, and family." These young women presented a clean-living, respectable image of modeling, one that meshed well with the bourgeois editorial perspective expressed in many African American magazines at the time. But the question of how race affected the modeling careers of black women was left unasked in many of these promotional articles.[30]

Other commentators were less reluctant to invoke racial politics in their discussions of modeling. In 1953, *Our World* outlined the requirements for becoming a model, including "proper training" (a six- to sixteen-week course covering "everything from walking to talking, make-up to diets") as well as intelligence, "personality," good looks, hard work, "sacrifice," good grooming, poise, grace, and an outgoing personality. Nevertheless, even with the training, the dedication, and all the right qualities, black models faced discrimination. "Top white high fashion models get $50 an hour, and earn up to $5,000 annually," noted *Our World*. "Among Negroes, only cream-colored Dorothea Towles . . . grosses over $10,000." Top black models Sara Lou Harris and Sylvia Fitt rarely made more than $4,000 annually. In 1954 *Ebony* noted the many advances made in the decade since the Brandford agency was founded, citing the growth of African American magazines and the increased willingness of designers to use black models on runways and of white-owned companies to feature black women in advertising. Nevertheless, even this relatively cheery article complained that "only a *handful*" of "200 Negro models in New York" had full-time careers. In fact, the 1951 *Ebony* article that held up models as respectable women who worked "regular jobs" too revealed that black models needed those jobs to survive. In Los Angeles in the 1950s, a group of black models, calling themselves the "Bronze Mannikins," formed to help each other secure modeling jobs. Despite charm courses, group study sessions, rehearsals, and grooming workshops, the successes of the program were limited. "For most Negro girls," *Our World* observed, "modeling, at best, is part-time work. That's why all the 'Bronze Mannikins' have steady jobs."[31]

The career of the most successful black model of the 1950s and 1960s, Dorothea Towles, illustrates the complexities of a modeling industry suffused with the politics of race. In many ways, Towles was the exception to the rule: a black woman who could actually make good money as a fashion model. She took a charm school class in Los Angeles but did not work professionally as a model until she got her big break in 1950 while on vacation in Paris. There, as a runway model, she was admired for her grace and the physical proportions demanded by haute couture designers. Towles modeled clothes for big names Christian Dior and Jacques Faith before becoming a regular model for Elsa Schiaparelli. In 1952, Towles returned to the United States, along with six trunks of French clothes, to embark on a fashion tour. Observed *Our World*, "The toast of Paris has come home to crack the big time. New York modeling, which, up to now, has been closed to Negroes. Dorothea has proved that a Negro model can 'sell' a $1,500 gown in Europe. She expects to do the same thing in America." By 1959, according to *Sepia*, Towles had become "a woman with a crusade, determined to emancipate the Negro model." Towles's desire to integrate the U.S. modeling industry points to the social and cultural stakes of racially biased racial standards in America. That Towles herself was extremely fair skinned and, eventually, had (dyed) blond hair helps to explain both her personal success and her failure to bring about greater recognition of, and opportunities for, African American models.[32]

The rhetoric of integration increasingly pervaded commentary about beauty in the African American press in the 1940s and 1950s. Before World War II, advertisers touted hair straightening as a way for women to style their hair any way they chose, but the hard-pressed look one got with hot combs and heavy dressings was nowhere near as versatile as the brushed-straight style innovated in the 1940s or the look made possible by chemical relaxers. After World War II, the beauty industry promoted these new products and services with the promise that they would create a more natural look—that is, natural-looking straight or wavy hair. The hard-press method remained popular in these years, however. Kobena Mercer has suggested that the male conk (a style popular in the 1950s) represented not an attempt by black men to look white but, rather, an exaggeration and manipulation of the idea of white men's hair—a new creation. African American women may have continued to use the hard-press method after the war to achieve a similar purpose. Even when black women followed the new methods and chose styles that were fashionable for white and black women alike, there was still room for exaggeration, for playing around with white aesthetics to create new ones. Hair dyeing, for example, was popularized by celebrities like Dorothea Towles and touted in African American magazines as a trend for black women in the 1950s and 1960s. The resulting blond look highlighted, rather than minimized, a dark complexion, and it seems to have been at least as deliberately artificial as the conk or the precise glossiness of a Marcel wave. Although blond hair was a trend worn mostly by entertainers and the unusually daring among African American women, its appearance indicates that the rise of the "natural" look did not diminish black women's ability to carve out their own visions of beauty and style within the context of a white-dominated American beauty and glamour industry.[33]

Chapter 5

"All Hair Is Good Hair"

Integrating Beauty in the 1950s and 1960s

In the twenty years following the end of World War II, the African American beauty culture industry was in most respects bigger, better organized, and more affluent than ever before. These developments were reflected not only in larger salons and the expanding cosmetics industry, but also in the growth of professional organizations, in the responses of beauty culturists to state regulation, and in the coverage of women and beauty by the black media. African American commercial beauty culture focused intensely in these years on promoting beauty, glamour, and style to black women. The commodification of beauty, which had developed extensively in black beauty culture during the 1920s and 1930s, was ubiquitous by the 1940s and 1950s. Along with this came the expectation that, in order to be beautiful, black women needed at the very least to straighten their hair. At the same time, technological innovations in beauty culture gave black women new choices in hair-straightening methods and products. By the mid-1960s, though, the promotion of many of these products had changed. Many advertisements for black women's hair and cosmetic products used the images and rhetoric of racial integration to sell their products. Some posed black and white models together, suggesting that their products, though promoted only in African American publications, were appropriate for women of all races. Throughout the civil rights era, furthermore, the success of African American women in the mainstream beauty and glamour industries became an issue in the black media. As we saw in the last chapter, dozens of magazine articles followed the careers of black models and entertainers. The fortunes of African American beauty pageant contestants also gained widespread attention. These articles characterized white recognition of African American female beauty as a political issue. In these ways, corporate advertisers and savvy journalists linked black women's hair, and black women's beauty generally, to civil rights and integration.

As they had in the 1920s and 1930s, African American beauticians denied that they were promoting a white beauty ideal, but now they too began to articulate their position in terms that reflected the emerging civil rights movement and expressed a commitment to an integrated, or at least multicultural, beauty ideal. Prominent beauty salon owners declared that there was no such thing as "bad" hair and that their salons could accommodate women of all races and hair types. In fact, African American beauty culturists increasingly drew connections between the civil rights movement and their own businesses. This is understandable, given the importance of black consumer citizenship in the early years of the civil rights era. In boycotts and sit-ins throughout southern cities, protesters explicitly claimed that democracy and racial equality rested on the equal treatment of black consumers as well as the desegregation of schools and the establishment of voting rights. Civil rights activists in the North also frequently mobilized black citizens, both to picket in sympathy with southern desegregation campaigns and to address the racial discrimination that northern blacks experienced in retail stores as consumers and employees. In a nation that, by the mid-twentieth century, often defined freedom in terms of the freedom to buy, it made sense that part of the civil rights movement was devoted to this issue. As black entrepreneurs and as community leaders, African American hairdressers both supported civil rights causes in general and fought for racial equality within their industry. Many hairdressers were at the forefront of efforts to combat segregation and discrimination in beauty schools and professional organizations.[1]

Hair and Integration

By the mid-1960s, African American manufacturers of cosmetic and hair products were running advertisements picturing both African American and white models and maintaining that their products were suitable for all women. The black beauty culture industry voiced an integrationist position that paralleled anti-segregation efforts in American social and political life, and most African American men and women working in black beauty culture saw common ground between their industry and the civil rights movement. Although many black activists would later criticize commercial beauty culture, reject hair straightening, and advocate natural hair, the connection between the beauty industry and the movement was not necessarily contradictory in the early years. Black women working in the movement in the 1950s and early 1960s usually wore their hair straightened in the fashion of the era. In fact, grooming was an important part of the movement strategy. Photographs of civil rights protesters at sit-ins, freedom rides, and other early demonstrations show African American protesters with smooth, carefully groomed, presumably straightened hair.

Nonviolent tactics, as well as the goals of integration and voting rights, were intended to, and did, give the highly publicized civil rights movement the moral high ground in the eyes of the nation and the world. Image was crucial for movement organizers, particularly those from groups like the Southern Christian Leadership Conference, led by Martin Luther King Jr., and, early on, for leaders of the Student Nonviolent Coordinating Committee. Not only were participants in sit-ins, marches, and other protests carefully trained not to respond to the taunts, threats, or physical abuse of whites, but they were also instructed to dress nicely when they attempted to integrate department store lunch counters or bus station waiting rooms. For black women at this time, good grooming always included carefully styled and usually straightened hair, and for men it meant short hair, sometimes smoothed with a light hair dressing. Both men and women were expected to wear their Sunday best at these protests. These standards were partly a product of class. Many of the participants in southern civil rights demonstrations came either from the middle class or from the ranks of "respectable," churchgoing, working-class African Americans. As historian Robin Kelley notes, describing the marchers in Birmingham's 1963 children's crusade, "the hundreds of schoolchildren . . . recruits of the direct-action campaign who marched peacefully into the hands of Eugene 'Bull' Connor's police officers, were not products of Birmingham's worst slums. Rather, the vast majority of neat, well-

dressed, and orderly children were the sons and daughters of movement supporters."[2]

The appearance of these protestors was as important as that of the
Black Panthers would be a few years later, but the looks themselves,
and their political purposes, were very different. The appearance of
civil rights activists stressed their social respectability and highlighted
their desire for fair and equitable treatment within American institutions. The strategy also complemented nonviolent tactics. Because no
one could claim that participants in a sit-in or freedom ride had acted
inappropriately or appeared unrespectable, the discrimination and the
brutal violence activists faced from white authorities were exposed as
unprovoked acts of racism. Finally, for those who participated in the
movement and faced humiliation and violence every day, maintaining
a well-groomed appearance was one way to hold on to personal pride
and dignity—something millions of sympathetic observers of civil rights
demonstrations on nightly news reports could hardly fail to notice. It
also had utility for activists in more private moments. In her memoir
Coming of Age in Mississippi, Anne Moody writes about a Woolworth's
lunch counter sit-in in Jackson during which she and her companions
were drenched in ketchup and mustard and dragged from the counter
by a jeering white mob. After the demonstration, she recalls,

> before we were taken back to campus, I wanted to get my hair
> washed. It was stiff with dried mustard, ketchup, and sugar. I
> stopped in a beauty shop across the street from the NAACP of-
> fice. I didn't have on any shoes because I had lost them when I
> was dragged across the floor at Woolworth's. My stockings were
> sticking to my legs from the mustard that had dried on them.
> The hairdresser took one look at me and said, "My land, you
> were in the sit-in, huh?"
>
> "Yes," I answered. "Do you have time to wash my hair and
> style it?"
>
> "Right away," and she meant right away. There were three other
> ladies waiting but they seemed glad to let me go ahead of them.

This moment of kindness and support among African American women
in a beauty shop is a small but significant example of the role beauty
culture played during the civil rights era.[3]

Challenging the Idea of "Good" and "Bad" Hair

Historically, and still to some extent today in African American culture, hair that would grow long and was straight or wavy was widely referred to as "good," whereas hair of the extremely curly or kinky variety common among African Americans was often described as "bad." Having good hair had been a hallmark of femininity within black communities for generations, but of course this ideal also reflected the influence of white beauty standards in American culture. The idea of good and bad hair was still powerful in African American society in the civil rights era. Michelle Wallace, an African American feminist, recalls that in the 1950s, the line between wanting to look white and wanting to be beautiful was a blurry one. As the children of middle-class parents in 1950s Harlem, Wallace and her sister would tie scarves around their "scrawny braids," pretending it was hair like that of the actresses they saw in the movies. Wallace observes, "There was a time when I would have called that wanting to be white." But, she continues, "the real point of the game was being feminine, being feminine *meant* being white to us." It is certainly true that images of female beauty from Hollywood and elsewhere in American mass media were almost exclusively white, and these images must have had an impact on black women. Black beauty culturists, the black media, and businesses that sold beauty products to African American women had long striven to promote the beauty of black women, but in earlier decades the rhetoric had centered on the celebration of black womanhood, with little reference to the lingering influence of white beauty ideals. In the 1950s and early 1960s, assertions that African American women's beauty ought to be recognized by black and white America alike echoed the cries for racial equality coming out of the civil rights movement.[4]

One of the earliest indications of this change was a shift in how black beauticians themselves represented their businesses. In 1935, future beautician, cosmetology teacher, and social worker Gladys Porter took an advanced course in beauty culture at her segregated high school in San Antonio, Texas. Part of the course required that she learn permanent waving and setting, a process used almost exclusively on white women at the time. While attending the necessary classes at a white school and beauty parlor (her school did not have the equipment she needed to practice on), Porter became friends with a white student, and the two agreed to help each other learn to do the other's hair. Both girls "questioned the necessity of our having to learn to 'fix' the other race's hair." Who could blame them? If legislated segregation did not necessarily prohibit interracial hairdressing, convention certainly did. Black and white beauty culture had always been completely separate enterprises in the North as well as the South. The training programs, product lines, methods, and beauty shops remained sharply divided along racial lines. That a few state regulatory boards required both methods for certification and that many beauty courses, black and white, included units on how to do the "other race's hair" did not alter the segregated nature of commercial beauty culture.[5]

This division was not only a matter of white people's rejecting African Americans as beauticians or as clients. For her part, Porter observed in 1935 that she "had no desire to ever do white people's hair in the beauty shop that I hoped to open someday." Beauty culture was, in the early twentieth century, a cornerstone of African American entrepreneurship. As we have seen, Jim Crow America created openings in the personal service industry for African Americans to serve their own people, and the success stories of the beauty culture business, like Madam C. J. Walker and Annie Turnbo Malone, became legends in black communities. By the 1920s and 1930s, the independence of the black beauty culture industry was seen as something to be celebrated and protected. African American beauty business leaders criticized white cosmetics companies that they saw as forcefully entering the black beauty product industry and threatening to push smaller, less affluent black firms out of business. In the 1920s and 1930s, then, integration was far from desirable from the perspective of black beauticians and product manufacturers. In fact, both the production and the service ends of the beauty business valued racial separation as beneficial to the health of the industry.[6]

By the end of World War II, African American beauticians began to move away from the separatist rhetoric of the past and to embrace a more integrationist perspective. As we have seen, a few were opening large beauty emporiums in urban neighborhoods that offered the latest styles from Europe, and some claimed to cater to both a black and a white clientele—or at least expressed their belief in the value of knowing how to care for white women's as well as black women's hair. Rose Morgan's House of Beauty served black women almost exclusively, but the grand opening of her expanded salon in 1955 attracted an interracial crowd of celebrities, politicians, and other prominent New Yorkers. Morgan also developed a line of cosmetics that, she noted, included shades appropriate for white women. Elizabeth Cardozo Barker, co-owner of the Cardozo salon with her sisters in Washington, D.C., maintained that she always wanted to be an "integrated hairdresser," able to do "all types of hair." She and her sisters attended white hairdressers' trade shows to learn new techniques and keep up with the latest styles. Both Morgan and Barker, along with others in the African American beauty business, expressly debunked the idea that black hair was bad and needed to be fixed, insisting instead that all women, black and white, needed professional care for their hair to look good. "All her life," *Ebony* observed in 1946, Morgan "has been conducting a one-woman campaign against the notion widely held among Negroes that Negroid hair is inferior." Morgan offered a tolerant, multicultural view on the matter: "Hair textures vary from race to race and type to type, and it is very wrong to classify one kind as 'better' than another." Morgan then took an opportunity to plug her business, noting, "It's all in the way that you care for the hair. All hair is bad if it isn't well-styled and groomed." Barker's sister Margaret Cardozo Holmes made a similar point to a *Baltimore Afro-American* reporter, who wrote in 1947, "The secret of [the Cardozos'] success is that [the sisters] realize colored people have far better hair than they ever thought they had." As Holmes explained, it was just that most black women's hair had been poorly cared for by previous beauticians, and "we endeavor to give it the proper treatment." Although African American hairdressers continued to stress that they were uniquely equipped to care for black hair, after World War II, some also suggested that many of their styles and methods differed little from those of their white counterparts.[7]

Most beauty salons in the 1950s and 1960s were not truly integrated, but a few stylists and shops came closer to interracial beauty services than any American beauty shops had before. In 1955, *Our World* reported that a famous stylist who went by the name "Mr. Golden Brown" and had once been employed by Morgan had opened his own salon in Harlem. Brown apparently had served both a white and a black clientele in his time and told *Our World*, "I intend to bring the best of Paris, Hollywood and Italian beauty techniques to my Beauty World." Brown hoped his Harlem shop would become "one of the centers for stunning, original hair style creations." Similarly, Barker, who had always "wanted to be an integrated hairdresser," claimed that the Cardozo shop drew customers of all races. Because, as she put it, all the Cardozo sisters "had different grades of hair, . . . we just made up our minds we were going to take care of all grades of hair." According to Barker, "personal interest caused us to become hairdressers for all races, and I mean all races. African, Oriental, Japanese, Chinese, Indian . . . and Caucasian." Barker credited the shop's expertise in the best methods for all textures of hair for drawing an integrated clientele, but in practice, given continuing de facto segregation in beauty parlors, the Cardozos and other beauticians like them more frequently applied their diverse skills to caring for various textures of African American women's hair. As Barker explained, African American companies' beauty schools and hair care systems were "built around their products and one type of hair" (by which Barker meant very kinky hair). Black women with straight or medium-textured hair often had nowhere to go to get their hair done, especially if they could not or chose not to pass into white salons. As one black woman with straight hair told Barker, "I'm a 'race' person, I'd like to go to them [black salons]. . . . In fact I have gone and they looked at my hair and told me, well, we're sorry, we don't know what to do with your hair."[8]

The Cardozo sisters' quest to run an integrated beauty shop brought them face-to-face with the realities of segregation. It was easy enough for them to learn the methods for straightening kinky hair, since they could train with black beauticians. Barker claimed that she was adept at making very kinky hair straight because it was what she had learned first. But she also noted that it was "important for us to get that look" because one of her sisters, Meta, was a chorus girl in the supposedly all-white Ziegfeld Follies. Light-skinned enough to pass, Meta (who was partnered for a time with Morgan and lent her name to Morgan's first salon, Rose-Meta) nevertheless had kinky hair. It was, Barker observed, "necessary for her to know exactly what to do or what to have done with her hair." Meta, in turn, learned the "white" methods of wet work (using semipermanent setting solutions instead of a heated curling iron to put curls into hair) while in Paris and taught the method to her sister. The popularity of wet-finger-waving among her patrons very likely opened Barker's eyes to the potential benefits of learning skills of "white" hairdressing, but segregation made it difficult to do so openly. All of the Cardozo sisters were fair skinned, noted Barker, "light enough to have 'passed' when blacks were hardly welcome anywhere." Although they "were not anxious to be white nor to socialize with whites," they wanted to learn hairdressing and business techniques from white beauticians. Since the sisters had medium to kinky hair, it was necessary that they learn the best straightening techniques so they could get into white salons and trade shows. Once there, they were able to learn from the "top white hairdressers. This was one of the advantages of passing," or "scouting," as Barker called it. At trade shows, the only people who knew the Cardozos were African Americans were their suppliers, who, Barker remembered, kept quiet because they were such good customers. Barker highlighted the irony of passing as white to establish an integrated beauty shop but did not apologize for doing it. "Neither I nor any of my sisters ever claimed to be white," she recalled, steadfastly asserting their right to be in such places. "[We] were fully prepared to state that we were colored if the subject came up. We simply passed into all places as Americans."[9]

Marjorie Stewart Joyner also prided herself on being able to do all types of hair. Joyner received her first beauty training, in 1916, at Molar, a white school in Chicago. Joyner did not pass as white at Molar and, according to Julia Kirk Blackwelder, encountered racism from her white teachers while taking the course. Joyner's first salon catered mostly to whites—she is even credited with patenting the first permanent wave machine—but this was an unusual occurrence. Within a few years, she was trying to break into the African American beauty business, but she found that she did not have the necessary skills. She recalled, "I worked on as many colored as I could" but could serve only black women who "had what I call 'good' hair . . . almost like white people's hair." It was only at the urging of her mother-in-law that Joyner took a course from Madam C. J. Walker, thus beginning her decades-long relationship with the company. Once armed with training from white and black beauticians, Joyner felt, her career really began. African Americans, she observed, are "all born with a different type of hair. . . . But if you make a study of it, you know shortly what to do with it because of your training for white people's hair," as well for various textures of African American hair. Working with so many different hair types "gave me a creative mind, not knowing what type of hair was going to be on the head of the person that sat in your beauty chair."[10]

By the 1960s, integrated beauty shops and beauticians were a little more common. In 1963, Federal Department Store hired a black woman to manage the interracial staff of a Detroit store's beauty shop in a racially mixed neighborhood. The salon, which had once served an all-white clientele, integrated its shop in response to the changing demographics of the area: in 1966, 60 percent white and 40 percent black, a ratio "expected to reverse itself before too long." In later years, the transition of this once white, middle-class neighborhood at the corner of Oakman Boulevard and Grand River would be attributed in part to "white flight," but at the time, the department store chain's home office's decision to seek out an African American manager to serve black and white patrons must have seemed like a breakthrough. The African American hairdressers' journal *Beauty Trade* heralded it as a progressive development for the hairdressing industry, reporting that the salon now "took on products they had never thought of before," such as "chemical relaxers" and "oils which have since been introduced to other stores." Alongside a photograph of what appears to be a white beautician working on a black woman and a black beautician working on a white woman, the article credited the change for increased floor traffic throughout the store. In February 1965, the Haitian American hairdresser known popularly as Mr. Frenchie staged a coiffure show at the Carlyle Hotel in downtown New York. Frenchie, well known as an innovator among African American beauty professionals, used models "of every race and hue" in the show, including "Chinese, Japanese, Negro, Indian, [and] Caucasian." It must be pointed out, however, that these were just a few instances of beauty integration. Frenchie gained notoriety mostly in the African American media, and there are no corresponding examples of well-known white stylists working on black women's hair. Furthermore, as Kathy Peiss points out, increased opportunity for black hairdressers in downtown salons was by the 1960s an ambivalent development, as they threatened to draw business away from smaller, neighborhood shops owned by African Americans.[11]

In general, black salon owners and stylists demonstrated both a knowledge of traditional hair straightening and styling methods and a willingness to use "white" methods and styles when they were applicable to black women's hair. In terms of techniques and products, methods of permanents and hair setting were adapted for use in African American shops. In term of style, the influence of "white" trends seemed more prevalent than ever in the 1950s and 1960s. African American magazines featured such familiar styles as poodle cuts, flips, and beehives.

Beauty Trade kept close tabs on European trends and offered detailed instructions on achieving each new look. By this time, the black hairdressers who could afford it were making trips to Paris, both to learn the current hair fashions and to teach what they knew about styling black women's hair. In 1950, Rose Morgan traveled to Paris, where she worked in a ritzy Champs-Elysées salon showing Parisian stylists how to press and curl the hair of African women from the French colonies. "I am seeing and taking in everything which Paris has to offer," Morgan told an Associated Negro Press reporter. "This is one time, though, that an American had brought something new to Paris, too." In 1953 and 1954, Marjorie Stewart Joyner, in her role as a prominent teacher of beauty culture and representative for the Madam C. J. Walker Company, led delegations of African American hairdressers to Paris to "swap secrets with French experts." In addition to her work for Walker, Joyner was also the founder and president of the United Beauty School Owners and Teachers Association and the supervisor of Alpha Chi Pi Omega, the related sorority and fraternity for beauty students. In the 1950s, black beauticians were still barred from white beauticians' trade organizations, and few African Americans could get into white beauty schools. When Joyner tried to enter a hairstyling contest at a white trade show, she was told that, to compete, "you'd have to be an American and then you'd have to be white." Like the Cardozo sisters, Joyner knew the value of learning a variety of hair care techniques. She explained that trips to Paris, and the trade shows that the United Beauty School Owners and Teachers Association sponsored in the United States, served to expose African American beauticians to the latest styles. At the highest level of hair fashion, black beauticians saw themselves as part of an industry that would be at its best if interracial communication and influence were encouraged. This not only affected prominent, affluent salon owners; it also shaped the textbooks and curriculums used by black beauty schools and influenced African American hair product lines. In this way, the Paris trips of a few black hairdressers quite likely affected the work of many black stylists.[12]

During the civil rights era, the black beauty culture industry was influenced by both the ideology and the practical goals of integration. Black beauty shop owners, while continuing to stress the special services they offered to black women, also cited the influence of white stylists in new methods and hairstyles they developed. The growth of state regulations of beauty culture further encouraged professional communication between the races and prompted black hairdressers to fight for and win positions on state cosmetology boards. As Tiffany Gill shows, African American hairdressers were a politically astute and active group. Their agenda began with promoting racial equality within their industry but also included broader public concerns. Beginning in the 1930s and 1940s, state licensing boards were set up to regulate the employment and training of hairdressers across racial lines. From the start, black women fought hard to have a voice in the process of determining labor and educational standards for beauticians. The National Beauty Culturists' League, the main trade organization for African American beauty culturists, was at the forefront of these efforts to make sure state boards were not segregated and that African Americans got positions as inspectors and examiners. Rose Morgan, who was appointed to the New York board in 1947, took great pride in her achievement of the position and her work promoting better wages and working conditions for beauticians. In 1955 the first African American was appointed to Florida's board of beauty culture. This breaking of the color barrier in a southern state made the news headlines in *Jet*. In 1966, *Ebony* reported that "major states" like California, New York, and Illinois required black and white beauticians to have the "same fundamental skills." The article also cited a National Beauty Culturists' League claim that 25 percent of black beauticians had some white customers.[13]

Elizabeth Cardozo Barker observed that, of the various organizations she was involved with in her lifetime, her "most rewarding experience" was her position on the District of Columbia's board of cosmetology. "We were able to do very good work there in uplifting the standards of beauty schools . . . and routing out segregation," noted Barker. By the 1960s, the board not only forced local beauty schools and salons to integrate but also required white hairdressers to learn how to do black women's hair, and vice versa. This change was reflected in cosmetology textbooks, which, starting in the 1950s, included units on how to care for both white women's and black women's hair, even if the books were written primarily for white or black students. Barker portrayed her work on the board as a crowning achievement in her career in beauty culture, but black hairdressers did not stop at fighting for racial equality within their own industry. As Gill explains, black hairdressers in the South were at the forefront of the civil rights movement, playing a particularly vital role in voter registration drives, encouraging patrons to register, and sometimes offering their salons as voter registration centers. Ironically, it was segregation that put these black beauty parlor owners in a position to do this. As independent entrepreneurs with an exclusively black clientele, these women were more independent of white economic control than other black people were and therefore did not have to fear for their jobs if they were politically active. Marjorie Stewart Joyner spearheaded the people to Congress movement in 1958, designed to encourage voter registration and political engagement. Adopting the slogan "Who you vote for and how you vote is your business—that you vote is our business," the beauticians' movement cited civil rights and national welfare as major concerns and sponsored voting drives and workshops at local chapters as well as at the national convention in Washington, D.C.[14]

Integrationist Beauty Advertising

The integrationist rhetoric of black hairdressers in the contexts of their workplaces, their professional associations, and the services they provided paralleled their direct involvement in civil rights causes. It was also echoed in advertisements for black beauty products that appeared in black magazines starting in the mid-1960s. Most common was the use of African American and white models together in advertisements for products produced exclusively for black women. This new strategy may have been a response to a 1963 marketing survey by the Center for Research in Marketing, which found that African Americans preferred "integrated" advertising. An advertising flyer for Madam C. J. Walker from the 1960s pictured two models, one white (and blond), one black, both sporting long, flowing hair. The caption read, "Women who care about their beauty look to Madam C. J. Walker for products they can trust." Apex, also an African American company, ran an advertisement for a hair conditioner in black magazines in 1967. It featured a black model and a white model, both in mod-style minidresses and both with long, straight hair. An advertisement for Raveen hair conditioner (produced by Supreme Beauty Products Company, another black-owned business) used three models: one African American, one Asian, and one white. The text asked, "Which Woman Needs Raveen?" and answered, "They All Do!" White-owned firms also ran advertisements of this type,

Apex advertisement, 1967:
"A Mini-Dab Makes Your Hair
a Swinging Beauty" (*Ebony*)

albeit less frequently. Nadinola ran an advertisement for its skin treatments (for dry and oily skin) that featured a side-by-side close-up of two models, one black and one white. The producer of Artra Skin Tone Cream used pictures of European, Asian, and African American women in its advertising, along with the caption "New Beauty for Women All Over the World."[15]

Which Woman Needs Raveen?

They All Do!

e best...
· RAVEEN.

Beautiful hair is healthy hair, lively hair, soft and lustrous hair. And beautiful hair needs conditioning...nourishment...and the best of care. Hair that makes you lovelier, noticeable...deserves the best conditioner you can buy. And that's Raveen...and that's the truth!

Raveen Hair Conditioner is rich in conditioners with built-in moisturizers. Raveen improves appearance of hair and scalp, gives more manageability, extra body, yet is so light in texture you can and should use it every single day!

SUPREME BEAUTY PRODUCTS COMPANY · · Chicago, Illinois 60605

Supreme Beauty Products advertisement, 1972: "Which Woman Needs Raveen?" (*Ebony*)

Artra advertisement, 1964: "New Beauty for Women All Over the World" (*Ebony*)

Perhaps the most overtly political of the integrationist genre of advertising was a 1963 Apex advertisement. A photograph of an African American woman and a white woman enjoying a cup of tea together was tagged by the simple caption "Progress." The copy ran, "A picture, they say, is worth a thousand words. Yet, it took uncounted words and deeds and years to make this picture possible." Touting the advertisement as a symbol of interracial friendship and the moral rightness of the

Progress

A picture, they say, is worth a thousand words. Yet, it took uncounted words and deeds and years to make this picture possible. We at Apex are proud to publish it, and we'd like you to see it as we do: two attractive American girls enjoying a quiet moment of friendship. An indication of progress, and, we hope, a prediction of future progress. More progress is essential, and quickly, be- cause Americans cannot truly be Americans until we learn to live comfortably with ourselves. This was to be an advertisement for Apex Natural-Perm. We set out to make the point that both girls use Natural-Perm. But the inner meaning of the picture itself guided us along a different, and better, path. After all, anyone can sell a good product. At Apex, we stand for much more.

APEX BEAUTY PRODUCTS, 1800 Worcester St., Baltimore 30, Maryland

Apex advertisement, 1963: "Progress" (*Ebony*)

civil rights movement, the copy continued, "Americans cannot truly be Americans until we learn to live comfortably with ourselves. This was to be an advertisement for Apex Natural-Perm. We set out to make the point that both girls use Natural-Perm. But the inner meaning of the picture itself guided us along a different, and better, path."[16] The irony in all these advertisements is that the beauty products they promoted were produced exclusively for black women in the context of a highly segregated beauty culture industry. These advertisements never appeared in fashion magazines like *Glamour* and *Mademoiselle*, and it does not seem very likely that they were they ever truly meant for a white audience. The advertisements symbolically desegregated the beauty industry by showing beautiful black models next to white ones and emphasizing that the products themselves were potentially useful for various racial types. Beauty product advertising in white magazines was not yet using black models. The black-owned companies that placed integrationist advertisements in black magazines were presenting an alternative vision of a multiracial beauty culture industry.

This distinction paralleled the actions of beauty culturists themselves. Despite the National Beauty Culturists' League's claim that 25 percent of African American beauticians had white clients, beauty culture was still largely separated along racial lines in the 1960s. Nevertheless, it was both symbolically and materially important for African American hairdressers to promote at least the idea of integration. In the case of inspection and certification boards, integration was simply a matter of equity and power. State boards had the power to regulate the training of beauticians and the running of beauty salons, and it made sense that black beauty culturists would want and need an equal voice in that process. For the sake of equity and equal opportunity, it was essential that African Americans be qualified to work on white women's hair and in predominantly white shops, and it was equally important that the skills of caring for black women's hair be included in state certification standards. Furthermore, African American hairdressers took pride in the breadth of their skill, their ability to care for any texture of hair, and their proficiency in creating all the latest styles. Trips to Paris and attendance at white beauty trade shows meant access to new methods and styles that might be applicable to their predominantly black clientele. Such activities also gave black beauticians the chance to demonstrate their abilities to an interracial audience and countered the notion that all they could do was press black women's hair straight. African American beauticians may not have expected the full integration of black and white beauty culture, but they did hope to achieve equal quality of education, equal treatment by regulators, equal access to new techniques, recognition of their skills, and the chance to contribute to the making of beauty and fashion. The African American beauty culture industry thus combined politics and business in a fascinating way, commodifying the political and, at the same time, politicizing commodities through advertising rhetoric and the actions of beauty culturists.

Integrating the Glamour Girl Image

African American media in the postwar years sought recognition for African American women in the business of beauty. As we have seen, black magazines like *Ebony*, *Jet*, and *Our World* covered prominent beauticians and their salons and also included multiple articles following the efforts of African American women to make it as models, actresses, and beauty contestants. Often, the career challenges these women faced were articulated as a civil rights issue, and many commentators called for integration of the various glamour girl industries. A 1951 *Jet* article that featured photographs of African American actresses noted that racism made the already-tough prospect of breaking into the movies doubly hard for black women. The cheerful tone of the piece when introducing young would-be starlets was dampened by the disheartening statement that, "as it is, Negro beauties must scramble for what they can get: maid parts, jungle roles, and chorus girl bit parts, and live for the day when they can be free of the color hex." In an editorial report titled "Why Hollywood Won't Glamorize Negro Girls," *Jet* writers Jim Goodrich and A. S. Young complained that even well-known black actresses like Lena Horne and Dorothy Dandridge were relegated to "mammy" roles and denied romantic leads. "Hollywood just does not associate glamour with Negroes," Goodrich and Young noted. "Hollywood, being color-conscious, lumps all Negroes together in a certain hue, adds stereotyped physical features and arrives at its unglamorous, composite Negro." The authors did not stop at mere complaints, though: perhaps influenced by civil rights boycotting strategies already in use by 1951, they suggested that African Americans use their spending power at the box office to pressure movie studios into creating more diverse parts for black actresses.[17]

As we saw in the last chapter, magazine articles also followed the fortunes of black models like Dorothea Towles and other women emerging from recently founded black modeling schools and agencies. The articles frequently pointed out how difficult it was for black models to secure employment; they had to scramble for the few modeling jobs provided by the small but expanding black media. Black women did not grace the pages of white fashion magazines in these years, nor were they much used in fashion shows or mainstream advertising. Some magazine articles treated black women's beauty in general as controversial, featuring absurd titles like "Are Black Women Beautiful?" and "Are Negro Girls Getting Prettier?" In 1954, *Hue* asked, "Are Whites Accepting Brown Beauties?" According to the author, they were. Whereas once the only acceptable African American beauties had been, like Horne, fair skinned and sharp featured, *Hue* noted the recent popularity of "Negro entertainment queens whose features are strictly Negroid." Further proof of this trend, according to *Hue*, was an increase in interracial romance among Hollywood stars and on college campuses.[18]

Nearly ten years later, writers were making similar observations about white recognition of black beauty. A. S. Young noted in *Sepia* in 1963, "No longer is Lena Horne or Dorothy Dandridge viewed as the exception to the rule" of white-dominated beauty. There is promise, Young predicted, that "Negro beauty will soon command as much respect as any other form or kind of feminine beauty." Young also suggested that black women's beauty was no longer exploitative but now was based in the progress of the civil rights movement and in respect for black womanhood. "The modern Negro beauty," he wrote, "is a beneficiary of changing times. Her recognition is proof of a growing democracy, a growing liberalism among the majority people. To see a Negro beauty in the center spread of a Caucasian-published, predominantly Caucasian-read national magazine is witness to history in the making." Here again, the black press, still dominated by men, portrayed the commodification of a black woman's body in a white magazine as a sign of civil rights progress. To Young, the first African American centerfold in *Playboy* amounted to a major victory for racial justice.[19]

Articles about black movie stars and singers, photo spreads of "beautiful Negro women" from various American cities, and stories about black models and beauty contest winners were common fare in most African American magazines. Many of these articles continued to criticize the reluctance of white America to recognize the beauty of black women and decried the difficulties black women faced finding lead acting roles and "mainstream" modeling jobs. Others, particularly in the 1960s, hailed the successes of African American models and modeling agencies and reported on black winners of interracial beauty contests and black homecoming queens at predominantly white colleges. Black media had sought to celebrate black beauty earlier in the twentieth century, but within the context of segregation. When black celebrities, socialites, and winners of black beauty contests were pictured in African American magazines and newspapers in the 1920s and 1930s, the stories represented efforts to recognize and celebrate beautiful black women within black communities, outside the mainstream beauty and entertainment industry that ignored and denied black beauty. Writers in African American magazines continued their efforts after World War II, but they were also now calling for the success of black beauty in a white world. They demanded that Hollywood, Madison Avenue, and Atlantic City recognize gorgeous and glamorous black women. Essentially, these writers were promoting the desegregation of American beauty standards and institutions.[20]

Little had changed in terms of modeling opportunities for African American women by the early 1960s. Few non-Caucasian faces graced the pages of popular fashion magazines like *Vogue*, *Glamour*, and *Mademoiselle*. A black model might appear in the odd fashion spread, but it was a rare occurrence. The first black fashion magazine cover girl appeared in *Glamour* in 1968, and it was not until 1974 that Beverly Johnson became the first black woman on the cover of *Vogue*. In May 1970, *Essence* became the first fashion magazine for African American women, offering at least one such publication where black models would be in constant demand. In spite of the continuing segregation of the American beauty industry, people involved in black women's modeling observed small gains throughout the 1960s. In December 1962, the *Pittsburgh Courier* reported that black models would be used to advertise Artra bleaching cream during the national television show *Gospel Time*. A 1963 cover story in *Jet* claimed that the white-controlled branch of the industry had begun to open up to African American models. Precola Devore, owner of a Washington, D.C., charm school, commented in 1964, "The demand for trained Negro models is growing. . . . Their various tones of color are in demand. They are like a beautiful bouquet of flowers, with various undertones. We tell our students they should be proud of their color; that is their greatest asset." Devore might have exaggerated the demand for models of all hues, but she accurately expressed the new pride in African American beauty that echoed the ideals of the civil rights movement in its later phases. The first fashion show in which African American models wore natural hair and African-inspired clothing was held quite early in the decade, in 1963. At the time, observers viewed it as a quirky fad, one that would have little impact on the beauty industry at large. But the show was in fact a harbinger of things to come.[21]

In 1970, *Ebony* addressed the continuing problems African American models faced. Asking "Have Black Models Really Made It?" the magazine pointed out that beautiful, dark-complexioned black models were in demand for designer fashion shoots, as well as in the new, "hip" advertising, where Afro-wearing models proclaimed that a particular brand of cigarette was "where it's at." At the same time, *Ebony* warned, "beautiful though black is, and despite the fact that it seems to be 'busting out all over,' . . . there are still only two or three black models who command top rates." Ophelia DeVore, head of a top African American modeling firm, observed that, although "the black model had come a long way since I started 23 years ago," she had far to go before gaining equity with white models. "Black is now a fad," DeVore commented shrewdly; "let's make sure that black remains a part of the American scene." Commented Gerard Ford, head of the famous Ford modeling agency, "There is no boom in black modeling. There is a happy trickle. It's a happy trickle that wasn't there five years ago. . . . But I wouldn't be overly optimistic to suggest that the problem is being solved." Top black models Naomi Simms and Dorotala Simms expressed hope that the long neglect of African American models would soon be over. Indeed, by the late 1960s, models wearing Afros and with a range of skin complexions were much more common in fashion spreads and in product advertising. This was especially true in African American publications, but the trend had begun to influence the look of white-run magazines as well. Social and political transformations in African American society repeatedly helped to broaden beauty ideals and, albeit slowly and haltingly, engender changes in the beauty and modeling industries themselves.[22]

Another topic of media discussions of African American beauty was black beauty contests, which were still popular in the postwar years. Maxine Craig has examined extensively the political overtones of black beauty contests, but the subject bears revisiting here. Earlier contests, as we have seen, functioned as public relations vehicles for cosmetics manufacturers, publishers, and entertainers. At the same time, however, they offered African American women the chance to compete in beauty contests at a time when white-run pageants excluded them. This did not change much between World War II and the late 1960s. Local groups held small, exclusively black contests, such as the 1946 Queen for a Day competition staged by the fraternal organization Delta Sigma Theta in Jefferson City, Missouri. Designed as a promotion for local black-owned businesses, the event featured contestants who were sponsored by these businesses and who modeled fashions from local stores. The winner, Vatchye Winston, sponsored by Turner's Grocery, won prizes donated by participating businesses, including clothing, jewelry, perfume, theater tickets, and a dinner party for twenty. African American magazines continued, as they had in earlier decades, to invite readers to send in pictures of beautiful black women for consideration in contests. For several months in 1950 and 1951, *Our World* conducted a "Search for Beauty," promising that "rich rewards and fame await the most beautiful Negro woman discovered in [this] nation-wide hunt." Meanwhile, African Americans in cities across the country staged pageants that mirrored the preliminary city and state contests that led up to the Miss America Pageant. Such pageants included Miss Quaker City and Miss Sepia in Philadelphia and Miss Bronze Chicago. In Windsor, Ontario, the local black community ran a Miss Sepia International contest every year in celebration of Emancipation Day.[23]

In addition, a few African American women were entering, and winning, white-run beauty contests. The African American press followed this increasing integration of white-run beauty contests, which began with small contests early in the 1950s, such as Miss Detroit Street Railway in 1950 and Miss DeSoto in 1951. Later in the decade, *Ebony* recognized the "hand-writing on the wall" when it reported on Caroline Smith's success at the Miss San Francisco pageant in 1958. Smith made the finals and received honors as Miss Congeniality and Miss Grand Talent. In "Beauty Queens of 1959," *Ebony* profiled five African American winners of beauty contests, hailing these victories as signs of racial progress. "Negro beauty," *Ebony* declared, "long neglected in national competitions, reared its pretty head as never before this year, with girls of hues ranging from dark brown to near-white winning contests from California to France." Among the winners were Miss Empire State and International Queen of the Cannes Festival Cecelia Cooper, Miss Sacramento Patricia Ann Williams, and Miss Indiana University Nancy Williams. Williams, *Ebony* observed, faced criticism from some whites for being chosen, even though she "had white relations on both sides and [was] frequently mistaken for a white girl herself." Nevertheless, *Ebony* concluded, the 1959 victories "held out one great hope to all Negro beauty contest aspirants: that the day is not too far off when one of them will be in Atlantic City, a candidate for the top title of them all, Miss America."[24]

In the 1960s, however, African American beauty contestants still appeared to be making slow progress in white-run pageants. The African American press described the prospects of black women's competing in white-run beauty contests hopefully, but wins were still scattered and small in scale. At the 1962 International Freedom Festival, an interracial event put on jointly by the cities of Detroit and Windsor, an African American woman won an interracial beauty contest over the blond competition. In 1965, Sarah Pener became Miss Rochester, raising hopes that she might win the title of Miss New York State and become the first black woman to compete in the Miss America Pageant. She did not make it that far. In 1966, *Ebony* hailed Tampa native Cheryl Pride as a "Brown Beauty with Courage" for being the first black woman from the Deep South to compete in a beauty contest leading up to the Miss America Pageant. Pride did not become Miss Tampa, but *Ebony* applauded her as a path-breaker nevertheless, as evidenced by her contest statement that she entered to show that "all individuals in this great city of Tampa have an equal opportunity to prove themselves acceptable in the community. I am part of Tampa and Tampa is part of me." In 1967, *Jet* ran a five-page story on the increasing number of African American homecoming queens elected at white colleges and universities, including the University of Chicago, the Chicago Teachers College, Los Angeles State College, Case Western Reserve, and Canada's McGill University. Nevertheless, most observers admitted that these were relatively small victories, given the overwhelming "whiteness" of most of the national beauty contests.[25]

In 1967, *Ebony* addressed the perennial problem of integrating beauty contests while evaluating the "New Trend Toward Black Beauties." "For the Negro woman, who has been as much a captive of the white man's beauty standards as his economy, the very idea of competing for a national beauty crown is a touchy proposition." The author pointed out that, in recent years, African American women had won some white-sponsored beauty contests but warned that "progress has been gradual" and added that the real measure of progress should "be measured by the extent to which successful entrants have looked Negroid instead of merely resembling sun-tanned white girls." Whereas the 1950s, according to *Ebony*, were dominated by African American beauty contestants who "could pass," the 1960s witnessed greater varieties of skin color among the new generation of black female beauties. In particular, although the Miss America Pageant remained difficult for black women to crack, *Ebony* pointed out that the Miss USA contest, the precursor to Miss Universe, provided better opportunities. Indeed, the photographs accompanying the *Ebony* article confirmed that Miss USA contestants from Michigan, Idaho, and New York possessed darker complexions than earlier African American beauty contestants had.[26]

Despite such positive stories, the mantra "black is beautiful" was slow to penetrate the beauty contest industry. Still, small, black-run contests sometimes expressed this ideal. In 1961, *Muhammad Speaks* published a small picture of the winner of a Miss Africa contest held in New York. Terri Malone, the caption read, "typifies the dignified beauty of black women. The Negro race has millions like her, all the more reason for black men to be proud of and to exalt their own women." In 1966, Robyn Gregory made news when she beat her "processed" rivals to become Howard University's first Afro-wearing homecoming queen. On a conservative campus, where only three hundred of eleven thousand students were said to wear naturals, Gregory's victorious campaign stressed black pride and offered a new image of the beauty queen. In 1970, an Afro-wearing woman became the first black Cherry Blossom Festival Princess in Washington, D.C. Crowned "Miss Washington D.C." in 1969 (with straightened hair), Linda Smythe, *Ebony* observed, "is a young woman who has wrestled with that problem of 'identity' and has emerged *black* . . . and proud." These examples suggest engagement by some beauty contestants with the political context and fashion trends that were transforming definitions of African American beauty in the 1960s. Nevertheless, darker-skinned, Afro-wearing beauty contestants could not expect great success in beauty contests, white- or black-sponsored, in this decade or even in the next one. Contestants in the Miss Black America Pageant, which began in 1968, favored processed hair, although stylized Afros were fashionable for a few years. The first African American Miss America contestant was Cheryl Browne, a university student who won Miss Iowa in 1970. The first African American winner of the Miss America Pageant, Vanessa Williams of New York, was then still thirteen years away.[27]

African American women's beauty culture reached new heights of commercialization and economic prominence in urban black communities during the twenty years following World War II. Ironically, this status reflected both the successes and the limitations of black people's struggles for political, economic, and social justice during these years. On one hand, the growth of the beauty culture industry, in which salon owners, manufacturers, advertisers, and the media all participated, reflected the growing economic power of African American consumers. On the other hand, the continuing segregation of American beauty culture paralleled continuing racial divisions in the United States. The existence of salons like Harlem's House of Beauty indicated the success of black female entrepreneurs and the growing affluence of black female consumers. But it was the intransigence of de facto segregation in northern cities that had created both the economic niche and the social need for such salons.

The black beauty culture industry constantly demonstrated this paradox. Black hairdressers were clearly proud of their achievements and of their roles in their communities. They strove to provide black women with the same luxury services and up-to-date methods white women enjoyed while remaining sensitive to the particular beauty preferences and requirements of black women. Some fought to secure an African American presence on state beauty culture regulatory boards, in part to counter segregation in the industry. Meanwhile, many manufacturers of beauty products rhetorically desegregated their branches of the beauty industry with interracial advertising. Hairdressers, black beauty experts, and writers for mass market black magazines constantly focused on the beauty of African American women and insisted that American beauty standards themselves be desegregated. They did this, however, within a limited aesthetic context: hair straightening was still the centerpiece of black beauty culture, and the "beautiful" black models and entertainers featured in magazines generally had lighter complexions. Black beauty culture was as politically charged as ever, but there were few direct challenges to the beauty standard itself as it was presented by African American stylists and product manufacturers.

Chapter 6

"Black Is Beautiful"

Redefining Beauty in the 1960s and 1970s

In a 1998 article, the black activist and scholar Angela Davis complained that the Afro had recently been reduced to a merely nostalgic hairdo. This development, she argued, served to reduce "a politics of liberation to a politics of fashion." Davis cited, for example, a 1994 fashion spread from the urban music and lifestyle magazine *Vibe* that featured an actress dressed as a "revolutionary" Angela Davis, circa 1969. Davis decried the use of her image as a "commodified backdrop for advertising" without reference to the historical and political context that gave wearing an Afro meaning and power in the 1960s. The phenomenon Davis describes, however, is nothing new. The revival of the Afro as "retro-chic" is only the latest development in a commodification process that began a few years after the style emerged as a symbol of black pride and rejection of white beauty standards. In the late 1960s and early 1970s, at the height of the Black Power era, the Afro was as fashionable as it was political. Many black women, as well as the African American beauty industry, embraced the natural look in these years, but not all of those who liked the new style completely rejected hair straightening. Nor did they necessarily explicitly recognize that their hairstyle choices could be politically charged. Nevertheless, the popularity of the Afro and the commercial responses to that popularity contributed to a redefinition of black female beauty in the United States. Afros were part of a beauty standard that emerged out of political struggle whether or not hairstylists, cosmetics producers, and trend followers acknowledged it.[1]

The commodification of the Afro is in many ways emblematic of changes that occurred in African American consumer culture and beauty culture from the mid-1960s to the mid-1970s. Black hairdressers, beauty product manufacturers, and other beauty experts had long celebrated the beauty of black women, but they recognized a very narrow range of skin tones and hair textures as beautiful. Aside from declaring that black women could be beautiful in the first place, aesthetic discussions of beauty in black women rarely offered a diverse vision of African American beauty standards in the years leading up to the 1960s. Few African Americans, inside or outside the beauty industry, challenged the ideal of shiny, long hair and light brown skin in the 1950s and early 1960s. African American beauty professionals did, however, during these decades, articulate an integrationist vision of how their industry ought to be run. This coincided with efforts by black businesspeople in the post–World War II and civil rights years to gain increased respect and recognition for black consumers. The appearance in black magazines and newspapers of advertisements that used black models to tout national-brand-name companies, such as Pepsi, RCA Victor, Ford, and United Airlines, represented real social progress to black publishing and marketing professionals, for whom the achievement of black consumer citizenship was a significant part of the civil rights agenda.

By the mid- to late 1960s, national corporations of all kinds were courting African American consumers. Continuing urbanization, along with civil rights victories, contributed to the unprecedented attention white companies paid to black people in these years. Surprisingly, the Black Power movement, with its outspoken denunciations of corporate white America, did not slow this trend, although it did influence the rhetoric of advertising directed at African Americans. White and black corporations began to incorporate the language and images of black identity politics into advertising campaigns starting in the late 1960s. Advertising firms and product manufacturers rushed to find marketing strategies that might capture what they referred to as the "soul" market. Nowhere was this more clearly demonstrated than in the black beauty culture industry. Black Power advocates declared that black was beautiful and encouraged black women to stop wearing makeup and straightening their hair as a way of rejecting commercially promoted "white" beauty standards. It was not too long, though, before manufacturers of beauty products embraced the Afro as a youthful, "hip" style that they could promote as easily as they could the new, gentler hair relaxers coming onto the market in the 1960s. African American companies like Johnson Products and Supreme Beauty Products were first to do this, but white companies like Avon, Clairol, even hair relaxer producer Perma-Strate and skin bleaching cream maker Nadinola were soon promoting the "black is beautiful" idea. Cosmetics producers developed new lines of lipsticks, powders, and eye colors particularly suited to black women's complexions. All these companies incorporated soul and black pride rhetoric into their marketing campaigns. Such advertisements helped to expand definitions of beauty in American society generally, and they gave black women a broader and more realistic range of looks to choose from. This was an important achievement, but the African American beauty industry, not surprisingly, promoted the new definitions of black beauty in commercial ways that often blunted or ignored debates over the politics of black women's appearance. It did, in fact, reduce "a politics of liberation to a politics of fashion." The transformation in African American beauty culture in these years further illuminates how ambiguous a victory the achievement of consumer citizenship was for black women.

Selling Black Power

The integrationist agenda of the early civil rights movement had meshed well with black marketing experts' efforts to get white advertisers to court African Americans. Boycotts and lunch counter sit-ins, however, represented a more radical challenge to discrimination against black consumers than did cries for more national advertising in black publications or demands for an end to racial stereotypes in advertisements. Nevertheless, these goals were not antithetical. As Robert Weems explains, liberal white advertising executives sympathized with the larger goals of the civil rights movement, and they accepted claims that African Americans wanted only to consume on equal terms with whites. Black Power, on the other hand, seemed to reject integration altogether. The Black Power slogan came to public attention in 1966 in the context of conflicts that emerged between Dr. Martin Luther King Jr. and the

Student Nonviolent Coordinating Committee (SNCC) over the efficacy of continuing a 220-mile march through rural Mississippi as a demonstration for voting rights. James Meredith, who had begun the march on his own, was shot to death one day after starting out from Memphis. Disagreements had occurred for several years between King's Southern Christian Leadership Conference and the SNCC over several ideological and strategic issues, including the wisdom of nonviolent methods in the face of unrelenting white brutality, particularly in the small, rural towns where the student activists operated. SNCC chairman Stokely Carmichael agreed to the march but, much to King's dismay, made nightly speeches critiquing the goals and rhetoric that had shaped the movement up to that point. Grassroots activists in the South had been talking about Black Power for some time, but Carmichael helped transform the phrase into the famous rallying cry it became: "The only way we gonna stop them white men from whuppin' us is to take over. We been saying freedom for six years—and we ain't got nothing. What we gonna start saying now is 'Black Power.'" Although the divisions that emerged in Mississippi had been simmering within the movement for years, the emergence of Black Power as an explicit ideological principle publicly signaled a rift in the civil rights movement and encouraged the emergence of new initiatives and organizations that were skeptical about the goals of integration, disenchanted with nonviolent tactics, and less open to building coalitions with whites. At the same time, African Americans in northern cities, facing the limits of liberal reform, growing poverty, police harassment, and urban violence, were receptive to Black Power activists' cries for economic and political independence and "community control." In terms of economic ideology, Black Power activists ranged from black economic nationalists, who stressed the need to establish black-owned and black-run enterprises, to more radical nationalists, such as the Black Panthers, who rejected capitalism and denounced consumer culture. From the perspective of white potential advertisers, neither economic perspective could have seemed that welcoming. The key for those who hoped to appeal to the changing urban black market was to find a way to invoke popular new assertions of black pride in advertising without putting emphasis on the black economic nationalist or Marxist dimension of the Black Power movement. By the late 1960s, many white-owned companies were learning to do just that.[2]

Black Power must have initially seemed a barrier to white market-ers, particularly since its political ideology encouraged African Americans to reject white-controlled consumer culture altogether. Nevertheless, the urban black market could not easily be ignored. By 1970, 81 percent of African Americans lived in cities, and white advertisers, with the help of black advertising executives like Caroline Jones, had discovered the "soul" market. Ignoring the political ideology of Black Power, white marketing executives latched on to dynamic changes in black urban style to market their products in a new way. The trend attracted the attention of independent filmmaker Robert Downey Sr., whose 1969 film *Putney Swope* satirized the new vogue of "selling soul." In the film, the title character, a "token" black executive at an all-white advertising firm, unexpectedly becomes the firm's president when the current pres-ident drops dead in the middle of a board meeting. Swope renames the agency "Truth and Soul" and replaces the staff with young, urban blacks who develop hip, streetwise campaigns for white companies. Swope's new team hopes to bring "the revolution" to Madison Avenue while, of course, making a fortune along the way. In the real world of advertising, marketing magazines like *Sales Management* acknowledged that black-owned companies had the inside track on the "soul" market but prom-ised that savvy white companies could use soul to attract young black and white consumers alike. "What's happening is pride," one 1969 ar-ticle observed. "It cuts across the color barrier to give youth an identity and plugged-in marketers a whole new scene." The article went on to offer a helpful glossary of "soul" vocabulary (e.g., "boss," "fox," "jive") and an excerpt from Eldridge Cleaver's *Soul on Ice* that described soul food. The year 1969 also witnessed the creation of Zebra Associates, an integrated advertising firm that touted both the racial diversity and the extensive marketing experience of its staff. Zebra, which counted Caroline Jones, onetime J. Walter Thompson ad executive, among its employees, claimed an extensive understanding of minority and low-income markets, as well as the combined knowledge of the top advertis-ing firms in the country. The creation of the "soul" market by advertisers and the emergence of advertising companies like Zebra changed the look of advertising aimed at African Americans. Advertisements for all manner of products routinely invoked themes of black pride, solidarity, and "soul" style. Although the images and rhetoric in these ads implic-itly invoked Black Power's aesthetics, they virtually never referred to the economic or political ideals of black nationalism. The advertisements seemed to offer merely an alternative version of consumer citizenship; cultural pluralism replaced assimilation.[3]

Black Is Profitable

Beauty product advertising vividly illustrates this commodification of "soul" during the late 1960s and early 1970s. White- and black-owned companies used black pride, and particularly the "black is beautiful" ideal, to sell everything from soaps and lotions to shampoos, hair dressings, and cosmetics. Again, African American–owned companies were first with these kinds of appeals, but white-owned companies were no more than a few years behind. In 1965, while at J. Walter Thompson, Caroline Jones was asked to develop a hypothetical advertising campaign for a black women's cosmetics line. Downplaying the nationalist angle but still referring to black pride, Jones explained that earlier generations of African American women had eschewed makeup as "a proud but basically unconscious protest against the insufficient colors offered to them." Now, though, the younger woman wanted "to be accepted by the white populace and yet retain a distinctive beauty of her own." Jones proposed a product line and advertising campaign for an existing cosmetics company, Aziza, stressing that appeals should focus more on telling women they could wear cosmetics and still look "natural" and "less on the blatant, 'you're different approach.'" Television commercials would feature black women of various skin tones touting Aziza's "new Bronze Beauty cosmetics . . . specially perfected and blended to enhance the beauty of deep-toned complexions." Later, at the Zebra Agency, Jones made a similar hypothetical proposal for "the most complete line of hair care products yet designed especially for black consumers who wear their hair in its natural state," intended for an established company such as Clairol. Jones suggested a new name and marketing concept based on the idea of freedom: freedom to wear natural hair, freedom from trips to the beauty salon, and the freedom "that comes from no longer trying to emulate white beauty standards." In this way, Jones encouraged white-owned companies to play on racial pride's political consciousness in their advertising.[4]

Although many white-owned hair product companies had produced lines for black women for years, white cosmetics manufacturers were just beginning to recognize this market. An overview of the black cosmetics market in *American Druggist* cited black pride, growth in African American population and income, and technological innovations (translucent bases for foundations, powders, and blushes that allowed for greater shade ranges) as factors that had created better makeup choices for black women. The trade magazine *Drug and Cosmetics Industry* reported in 1969 that more than half a dozen new cosmetics lines for black women had been launched in the previous five years. By 1971, two celebrity lines had entered this expanding market: Nancy Wilson's Cosmetics for Beautiful Ladies of Colour and Barbara Walden Cosmetics. Libra, a white-run manufacturer of luxury cosmetics for African American women, used black saleswomen, black demonstrators, and racially focused advertising to attract customers. Black women who attended product demonstrations in 1969 were treated to a promotional movie titled *Sense of Beauty, Source of Pride.* Flori Roberts, white owner of an African American cosmetics company, spoke to company executives and advertising representatives at an industry seminar in 1969. She told them that the history of neglect of black women's cosmetics needs required established white companies to develop separate product lines with different brand names. In the context of the Black Power movement, it was very likely that the advertising for these new cosmetics lines would use words and images evocative of black pride.[5]

Posner, a white manufacturer of beauty products throughout the twentieth century, began making its Custom Blends line of cosmetics for African American complexions in 1969. Advertising strategies included a beauty advice column, Afro-wearing models, and "hip" advertising copy. Echoing Timothy Leary's famous slogan from the psychedelic drug scene, one 1971 ad read, "To tune in and turn on your complexion beauty, wear CUSTOM BLENDS COSMETICS. . . . They harmonize with *your* skin tones." Slick-On Glow sheer face glisteners put "a black woman's face in a beautiful new light," according to another Custom Blends ad, and a third echoed Black Power by proclaiming, "Posner is Beauty Power." Despite such appeals, Karl Heinze, white owner of Posner, perhaps hoping to deflect a racial backlash or accusations that he was pandering to identity politics in the beauty industry, downplayed race as a selling point in one 1969 interview. According to Heinze, Posner marketed its products based on the assumption that black hair and skin were "different." However, future marketing would emphasize not the "ethnic identity" of a product but its effectiveness. "People will use anything that works for them," Heinze observed.[6]

Avon began to use black models in *Ebony* advertising as early as 1961, and by 1969 the company was using Afro-wearing models in ads designed to appeal to a youth audience. At first, these ads did not make specific reference to race. A typical advertisement for Patterns fragrance and lipstick was published in a black version and a white version, using the same background and text but changing the race of the model. Nevertheless, the picture of a dark-complexioned, natural-haired black woman along with the text "A new kind of world . . . happening all around you" subtly, perhaps unintentionally, referred to late-1960s race consciousness. Certainly it was meant to invoke 1960s American youth culture more generally. By the early to mid-1970s, Avon was marketing cosmetics and hair products designed exclusively for African American women. The company launched its Shades of Beauty line in 1975, using print ads as well as television and radio commercials. One television advertisement proclaimed that the Shades of Beauty makeup line had been created "especially for black women. . . . Sheer earthy liquid foundation in Umber, Sienna, Sable, Mocha and Cafe," as well as blush in "just right colors, just right for you." An actress in a 1975 Shades of Beauty advertisement observed, "It's not every day you find makeup in just the right colors . . . especially if you're Black." Avon's print ads, both for Shades of Beauty cosmetics and for Natural Sheen hair products, contained similar appeals.[7]

Fashion Fair Cosmetics, manufactured by Johnson's Publishing (publisher of *Ebony* and *Jet*), did not stress politics in its advertising. Stylish ads for Noir fragrance notwithstanding, Fashion Fair ads tended to mimic the celebrity-studded articles common in the parent company's magazines. Some ads offered before-and-after makeover stories. Others featured profiles of celebrities, models, or "regular girls" who owed their careers, beauty, or success in finding a husband to *Ebony*, *Jet*, and Fashion Fair Cosmetics. For example, "I'm just a soul singer from Detroit" was the headline over an advertisement starring Aretha Franklin, and an "ex-RN from Lenox Hill" credited Fashion Fair with helping her "catch an M.D." for a husband. Not only were these ads decidedly apolitical in tone, but they also often offered a very traditional, and by 1975 decidedly outdated, version of femininity. Nevertheless, this

Nadinola advertisement, 1968: "Black is beautiful" (*Ebony*)

advertising continued a longstanding tradition in the African American beauty industry of using language that glorified black womanhood, and it is important that more companies, black and white, were producing makeup in colors black women could use.[8]

Ironically, the most overtly political cosmetics advertisement from this era promoted one of black beauty culture's most controversial products. In 1968 Nadinola ran a full-page ad for its bleaching cream in *Ebony*. It featured a simple, full-face close-up of a black woman with an Afro and the caption "Black is beautiful." The company, which for more than sixty years had declared in ads that fairer skin was more beautiful, and offered to lighten black women's skin by several shades, now exclaimed that black skin was "naturally beautiful." Nadinola claimed, as bleaching cream ads in the past had done, that its cream could eliminate blotches and blemishes, bring out "the natural beauty of your complexion," and create "a smooth, glowing skin tone that's even all over." This ad, though, made no mention of "brighter" skin. The advertisement represented a shrewd attempt to retain a market for a product that, given the political climate at the time, seemed doomed. It was by far the most radical of the ads for facial cosmetics in terms of its overt reference to racial pride. Still, even more striking was the use of black pride to sell hair products during the late 1960s and early 1970s. The commodification of the Afro in the social, political, and historical context in which Afros became popular provides one of the most powerful examples of advertisers' exploitation of the "soul" market.[9]

The Afro as a Case Study in Selling "Soul"

The Afro originated in the United States as a style worn by a tiny minority of cosmopolitan black women and developed into a prominent symbol of racial pride during the mid-1960s. Responding to the Afro's grassroots popularity, the African American beauty culture industry mounted a largely successful effort to transform the style from political statement to fashion commodity. Black beauty businesses responded differently to the Afro depending on timing, the nature of the business, and the demands of customers. Some beauty salon owners complained that the Afro would ruin their businesses, whereas others rushed to accommodate patrons who desired the new style. Hair-product manufacturers produced and marketed with equal enthusiasm both hair-straightening and Afro-enhancing preparations. Advertisements for Afro products, particularly those manufactured by African American–owned companies, frequently invoked black pride. The commodification of the Afro was not exclusively a cynical exploitation of a political symbol. Rather, the selling of the Afro often entailed a complex blending of ideals, goals, and motivations based, to varying degrees, on considerations of fashion, politics, and the bottom line. By the early 1970s, the Afro had been thoroughly commodified. It is worth considering, however, whether it had been completely depoliticized.

As scholars such as Robin Kelley and Maxine Craig have observed, the Afro, or the natural, as it was called early on, appeared as an American hairstyle years before Black Power became prominent. The earliest female Afro wearers came from the fringes of African American society. Avant-garde artists and intellectuals, as well as elite urban trendsetters, began wearing their hair short and unprocessed as early as the late 1950s. Black men at this time commonly wore their hair closely cropped and unstraightened. (The longer, chemically straightened conk was a controversial style, often associated, according to Craig, with musicians, young hipsters, and the "criminal element.") Black women, on the other hand, were rarely seen in public with hair that had not undergone the press-and-curl treatment. As late as 1966, *Ebony* quoted a Frenchman who exclaimed, perhaps facetiously, upon seeing an African American woman with a natural, "I thought only Negro *men* had kinky hair!" Women who went natural before 1965 offered a range of personal explanations for their decision to stop straightening. Some stressed a desire to celebrate African beauty and recognize African anticolonial movements, but others cited merely the convenience and comfort of the new style. Unlike men and women who would wear the style in the late 1960s, they had few examples to follow. Many experienced disapproval from friends, family, and community members. Regardless of why a black woman chose to wear an Afro, the style was hardly commercially popular when it emerged, and it represented a radical break from norms of African American femininity.[10]

In 1943 Hampton Institute art student Annabelle Baker decided to let her hair go natural as part of her growing "regard for bone structure, skin tone, and hair texture." The reaction of the community at the African American college was immediate and almost universally unsympathetic. Dean of Women Flemmie Kittrell told her that her hair made her "unacceptable" to represent Hampton at a conference she had been invited to at Wellesley College in Massachusetts. After considerable wrangling, Baker went to the conference, only to be confronted in her dorm room by "two strikingly beautiful Negro co-eds . . . well-dressed with hair that flowed into long pageboys." Baker recalled, "They told me that I should be ashamed to be seen with my hair in its natural state." Once back at Hampton, she became the subject of repeated disciplinary actions, for breaking curfew and other infractions, but Baker contended it was her hair that caused her to be targeted, and the problems slowed the completion of her degree. Early natural wearers operated outside of and, to a great extent, in opposition to both the African American beauty industry and dominant beauty standards in African American society. Nevertheless, these women were not, for the most part, challenging the beauty industry as deliberately or openly as later Afro wearers would. Women who stopped processing their hair before the mid-1960s did so on their own or within very small groups of like-minded individuals. Mostly students, writers, and musicians, they could afford eccentricity in their appearance. The popular black press viewed early Afro wearers as exotic anomalies, and the African American beauty culture industry ignored the trend in these years.[11]

African American dancers Ruth Beckford, Katherine Dunham, and Pearl Primus were some of the first prominent female Afro wearers. Beckford, for example, claimed to have worn the style as early as 1952. These women chose to wear their hair short and unstraightened so they could dance and perspire without having to worry about pressed hair reverting to kinkiness after every performance or rehearsal. In addition, these dancers incorporated traditional African dance movements into their routines, and natural hair was therefore part of their image as performers. Maxine Craig notes that women like Dunham and Primus had artistic license to wear a hairstyle few black women would have felt comfortable with at the time. Other artists, such as the American blues singer Odetta and South African folk singer Miriam Makeba, garnered attention for their unprocessed heads and inspired some of the earliest noncelebrity natural wearers. Andrea Benton Rushing recalls admiring Odetta's "short kinky halo" at a performance at the Village Gate in the early 1960s, but whereas Odetta was a "famous entertainer,' she herself was a "square student encased in braces and eyeglasses," and such styles were not, she thought at the time, appropriate for her. At Howard University, a few young women involved in the civil rights movement, especially those involved in the SNCC's community organizing campaigns, began wearing their hair natural in 1961, despite loud disapproval from the conservative Howard community. One of the first of these women was Mary O'Neal, whose boyfriend at the time, Stokely Carmichael, had encouraged her to stop straightening her hair. As Craig's oral interviews with O'Neal and others show, the decision to stop straightening was to these women a natural outgrowth of their political commitment. For other black women—those who were not student activists or artists, or living lives that otherwise challenged mainstream middle-class black mores—wearing a natural could be a more problematic choice.[12]

Many women who decided to go natural early in the 1960s experienced personal conflict and faced considerable opposition from more conservative segments of African American society. Michelle Wallace recalls first wearing an Afro to school in 1964, a time when few women wore the style. Wallace received a few compliments from people in her building, but, she writes, "others, the older permanent fixtures in the lobby, gaped at me in horror." On the streets of Harlem, the thirteen-year-old faced catcalls from men on corners; she was later told that it was because her wild hair made her look, to some, like a prostitute. Wallace decided to fix her hair back to "normal" and did not wear an Afro again until 1968. She explained in retrospect that, although the natural look "appealed to my proclivity for rebellion, . . . having people think I was not a 'nice girl' was The War already and I was not prepared for it." In her attempt to counter white standards of beauty and look unconventionally attractive, Wallace had unwittingly challenged African American conventions of feminine respectability.[13]

Other women who began wearing natural hair in the early 1960s may not have received quite the negative reaction Wallace did, but they often described their decision as a difficult one. *Jet* associate editor Helen Hays King withstood "disapproving stares" in her Chicago South Side neighborhood and "have you gone crazy" looks from coworkers when she decided to stop straightening in 1963. Describing herself as a "terribly conventional woman," King wrote that she wore the new style because it looked and felt better, not out of any desire, in the context of post–World War II decolonization, to celebrate the "neo-African aspects of the 'au naturelle.'" Writer Margaret Burroughs described her rejection of the straightening comb in 1961 as a "revolt" that "came about as a result of five or more years of pondering and wondering about the state of my hair." It took her that long to overcome her own hair insecurities, ignore the disapproval of family, friends, and coworkers, and believe finally that kinky hair could be beautiful. "My search for a type of hair conditioning particular to me was in essence an effort to reject adherence to white standards of beauty in the grooming of hair," she wrote. "Mine was a determination to become aware of myself and to aid other Negroes to become aware of themselves as a beautiful contribution to the human race." For Burroughs, as for King, wearing a natural was initially a personal choice, one that suited her better than straightening. But unlike King, Burroughs came to appreciate the political dimension of her choice, embracing the natural in the end as a symbol of racial consciousness as well as a comfortable and attractive hairstyle.[14]

Although the style was not widely popular in the 1960s, a few prominent women were trying to encourage African American women to give up the straightening comb. One of the most famous wearers of the natural in these years was jazz singer Abbey Lincoln, who explained that media depictions of her as a glamour girl rather than a serious singer led her to change her image. She declared in 1961, "I have viewpoints, outlook, and values. . . . I'm not anybody's symbol." But Lincoln's new look was not simply a personal choice; she hoped to use her image and music to celebrate black womanhood. "I think now that the black woman is most beautiful and perfectly wonderful," she said. "I am proud of her." Lincoln's efforts to celebrate black womanhood included the Naturally '62 and Naturally '63 fashion shows, which featured the Afro-wearing Grandessa models, who toured cities across the United States and received considerable attention in the black press. The use of a fashion show to promote the natural suggested no one was questioning the idea that it was a woman's ultimate desire and duty to be beautiful, but it did reveal the desire for more diverse beauty standards. "All women want to look beautiful," Lincoln told Muhammad Speaks in 1963. "Now it is up to our men to let our women know that they are beautiful as they are." Show director Cecil Braithwate stressed that the shows were "designed to dignify the Negro image and present racial standards which promote dignity, class and pride." Grandessa model Rose Nelms observed, "Nationalism does go deeper than natural hair . . . but nationalism has to be practiced on many levels."[15]

Black newspapers that covered the Grandessa fashion shows, however, paid little attention to the political dimension its promoters stressed. Although the shows featured much more than natural hair, including African fashions, as well as drama, music, and dance "dedicated to the Dark Continent," media attention focused on and sensationalized the "fuzzy 'au naturelle' coiffure" on the head of each model. Articles speculated extensively on whether the new hairstyle would catch on, but most concluded that it was too controversial to gain widespread acceptance. Typical assessments characterized the natural as a passing fad. In an article headlined "Will 'Natural' Style Be the New Hair-Do?" the *New York Amsterdam News* acknowledged that the women who chose to wear Afros tended to "lean toward the Black Nationalist group." Still, it characterized Afros as "just another style," along with the Jackie Kennedy coifs and blond dye jobs then in vogue among the cutting edge of urban fashionable black women. It was, the paper continued, a fad with little social significance, no different from the "white-shoes-all-year style of the Harvard fellows . . . or a thousand and one styles and fashions that might strike one's fancy." Other newspapers reported on African American women's negative reactions to the style. An Associated Negro Press account of the Naturally '63 show in Chicago highlighted controversy among the three hundred attendees. The article first acknowledged that the models in the show "would have looked good with any kind of hair style . . . or no hair at all" and quoted Braithwate predicting a "lucrative new market" available to hairdressers willing to learn the various natural styles. But then the article quickly moved on to the critics. Alma Pryor, an African American model who attended the show, said, "I think the styles are beautiful, and there are some women who can wear them . . . but in my line of work it is doubtful if they would be acceptable." Bessie Bridey, another show attendee, also liked the styles but said, "It will be some time before the American Negro women in general will accept the natural hair styles." One woman was overheard saying only "It's horrible," and another claimed to have been fired from her Cook County credit bureau job because she wore her hair unstraightened. The mainstream black press treated the style as an anomaly, a fad, appropriate only for daring, artistic types. Although some gave passing acknowledgment to the political message of the Afro, they mostly portrayed it as a rather exotic and obscure fashion statement with doubtful staying power or commercial significance.[16]

By the late 1960s, however, as part of the developing Black Power movement, the natural began to emerge as one of the most familiar symbols of racial pride for male and female activists and was common among civil rights workers, college students, actors, musicians, and even some professionals. That said, it must be noted that the Afro was worn by a minority of African Americans and was favored mostly by young, urban people who were, after all, the strongest advocates of Black Power. Furthermore, the increased popularity of the style did not resolve conflicts black women faced about their hair, beauty, and femininity. Black women could not escape the question, Can one wear an Afro and still be attractive? Although the decision to go natural was no longer rare, it continued to be complicated by the longstanding, commercially promoted standards of beauty. At the same time, the growth of the Afro opened the door to later efforts by the black beauty industry to turn natural hair into a money-making proposition.

In his history of the Black Power movement, William L. Van Deburg points out that at the height of the movement's popularity, only about 10 percent of African Americans supported political separatism, approved of the Black Panthers, or favored figures like Stokely Carmichael and Rap Brown as leaders. Studies of inner cities revealed greater support for Black Power, but even there, the NAACP, Dr. Martin Luther King Jr., and integration were consistently favored. Nevertheless, Van Deburg points out, Black Power's cultural dimension received considerably more support from black Americans than did its political agenda. Promotion of African language, history, and culture, the creation of black studies programs in colleges and high schools, and the adoption of "distinctive hair styles, clothing, cuisine, and music" were broadly popular developments in African American society. The Afro, then, was one of many cultural symbols and practices of the late 1960s that had a powerful political message to convey about racial pride and solidarity. It was much the same message Abbey Lincoln and others had attempted to communicate a few years earlier, but the victories and disappointments of the civil rights movement had created a new racial climate. The same developments that led to the creation of the Black Power movement spurred a much wider acceptance for Black Power's cultural symbols than would have been likely just five years earlier. When Carmichael declared in 1966, "Black is beautiful," African Americans rallied to his words, transforming them into one of the most familiar political slogans of the 1960s.[17]

By the second half of the decade, although natural hair was widely popular with African Americans whether they were politically active or not, the style continued to attract controversy. Readers who responded to a 1966 *Ebony* article about the natural look offered a range of reactions to the style. One man denounced Afro-wearing women as "lazy, nappy-haired females." Another writer gushed over the beauty of the women photographed in the article, proclaiming, "May we all become more natural . . . in every way!" By the end of the decade, the style seemed to enjoy extensive, if not entirely overwhelming, popularity. A 1969 *Newsweek* poll of black Americans revealed strong support for Afros. Although it is not surprising that 75 percent of northern blacks under the age of thirty liked the style, it must be noted that a majority of all northern blacks, and a full 40 percent of all southern blacks, liked "the new natural hair styles." The percentage of people actually wearing Afros was probably much smaller, particularly among those who were not politically active and those who lived outside major cities. For example, in her 1970 ethnography of a Seattle beauty shop, Leatha Chadiha observed that the Afro was not commonly worn in the community or in Washington State. Late in the 1960s, southern civil rights leader Ralph Abernathy expressed approval for the natural not just as a generational marker but also as a symbol of how far the movement had come and how much it had changed. Mentioning his wife's straightened hair, Abernathy declared that his children "wouldn't do that in a million years. They've got their Afros. That's the difference these fifteen years have made for blacks—they look black, they think black, and they want freedom now."[18]

Whether or not a woman chose to wear an Afro for political reasons, unprocessed hair was often perceived as a direct challenge to well-established images of African American femininity. Andrea Benton Rushing recalls feeling "so self-conscious" when she finally decided to wear her hair in an Afro in the late 1960s. Her hairdresser relatives "thought I'd lost my mind," and her teachers at Julliard "stole sideways glances at me and talked about the importance of appearance in auditions and concerts." Rushing took heart from black men "I didn't *even* know" yelling, "Watch out, African Queen," and she became an "evangelist" for unprocessed hair. Maxine Craig relates many similar stories from oral interviews with black women who wore their hair natural in the mid-1960s and ran up against the prevailing African American opinion that straightening was "essential to a dignified and appropriately feminine appearance." Young, politically conscious black women like Craig's interviewees and Rushing often hoped natural hair would help them to escape the commercial beauty industry along with the white beauty ideal. Nevertheless, they frequently felt pressured to accept that it was still their duty as women to be beautiful. Indeed, the beauty industry continued to play an important role in shaping the new beauty standards.[19]

Beauty businesses may have been wary of the Afro at first, but many were quick to recognize the profit potential of the popular new style. Some felt natural hair threatened to close beauty salons and cripple the black beauty culture industry, but the late 1960s, savvy salon owners and cosmetics companies were offering black women an array of products and services to help them achieve the new, racially conscious hairstyle. Whatever else the Afro might have represented, it was youthful and urban and symbolized the questioning of authority, all highly marketable qualities in the 1960s. Advertising copy and beauty culture literature trivialized, downplayed, or ignored the political meaning of the Afro, portraying it as a hip modern style that could be adopted or abandoned at will. By the early 1970s, the Afro was commonly promoted by the beauty industry as just another popular style, another example that rebellion was in. Beauty professionals assumed that, like any fashion trend, the style would inevitably run its course. It might not die out completely, but it would always be one among many hair choices, including straightened ones.

This commercialization of the Afro stood at odds with the ideals of those African American women who had adopted the style for political reasons. For many, natural hair represented an abandonment of commodified beauty culture as much as it expressed a rejection of a white aesthetic. This position paralleled critiques of American capitalism coming from the Black Power movement (particularly from the Black Panthers), but it also echoed challenges to the beauty industry leveled by feminists around the same time. Michelle Wallace, who let her hair go natural for a second time in 1968, lumped her old hairstyle with numerous other commercial and cultural trappings of femininity. In addition to hair straightening, Wallace discarded "makeup, high heels, stockings, garter belts," and supportive underwear in favor of "T-shirts and dungarees, or loose African print dresses." Maxine Craig notes that women who went natural in the mid-1960s were happy to find a new, more "authentic" look that was also beautiful, and that "the brown skin and tightly curled hair that had been black women's 'problems' were suddenly their joys." Although these women saw the Afro as a symbol of political resistance, they also felt a communal sense of pride in themselves as naturally beautiful women. A 1966 *Ebony* article interviewed several women about their decisions to go natural. Suzi Hill, a Southern Christian Leadership Conference field worker, expressed the opinion that African American women "must realize that there is beauty in what we are, without having to make ourselves into something we aren't." Another woman pointed out that the standard of straight hair forced poor women to forego necessities to afford trips to the beauty salon. For many black women, then, embracing the natural meant rejecting not only white beauty standards but also commercially promoted beauty products and services of any kind.[20]

A crucial part of the political ideology behind the Afro, particularly by the mid-1960s, was the indictment of white beauty standards, the embracing of African traditions, and a return to simple, natural hair. People who expressed an opinion on the subject portrayed the Afro as an uncomplicated style that required little maintenance. The Afro was meant also to demonstrate one's political commitment and an appreciation of one's cultural heritage. In a 1962 essay, Eldridge Cleaver declared that black liberation would prove impossible unless African Americans could claim their "crinkly" hair as their own. Not all black nationalists took such a drastic position. In 1963, Eleanor Mason allowed that, although natural hair had "its place," it did not in itself amount to a celebration of black women. She contended that the American mass media would never accept black women as beautiful, and she claimed furthermore that African women had for centuries used irons on their hair and cosmetics on their faces. Given these facts, Mason argued, the issue was not "naturalness" so much as black consciousness. Whether a woman straightened her hair was not the point. "Nationalism," she wrote, "demands only one thing from the black woman—that she think black."[21]

Nevertheless, many advocates of the Afro explicitly connected their chosen hairstyle with authentic blackness, enthusiastically proclaiming that they were abandoning artifice and simply letting their hair do what it was going to do. Lee McDaniel and Joyce Gere, Chicago-based designers of African-inspired clothing, declared that they had stopped "trying to look like Doris Day and Elizabeth Taylor." Saying she "never really liked elaborate curls," an art student interviewed by *Ebony* remarked, "I just feel more black and realistic this way." In response to the assertion that the style was "primitive," Afro barber Ernest X of Los

Angeles retorted, "What's wrong with being primitive? The word primitive simply means primary or original. So, the black man is returning to his original state and is no longer being artificial." In his 1973 book *400 Years without a Comb,* Willie Morrow traces the history of African American hair, claiming that under slavery, African Americans had been robbed of the tools, particularly the wide-toothed comb, they needed to groom their hair. They were made to feel ashamed of their kinky locks and therefore turned to straightening as the only way to keep their hair neat and attractive. Whereas black hair had once been "put to sleep through years of denial," now it was, according to Morrow, "alive and growing freely and naturally on the scalps of black people all over the world." The rejection of old beauty processes and products and the reintroduction of the simple Afro comb were for Morrow promising signs of a return to African traditions.[22]

Still, even as the Afro reached the height of its popularity, some questioned the style's naturalness and its African credentials. In 1970 a group of Africans denounced the Afro as a "cultural invasion from America." African women wore their hair closely cropped or elaborately plaited, commented Tanzanian writer Kadji Konde; the "wild oiled bushes on the skull" popular in the United States were as American as "soul music, jeans, drug trips and cowboy boots." Essentially, Konde was recognizing how much a part of American popular culture the Afro had become. Cultural critic Kobena Mercer makes a similar point, arguing that the Afro was neither African nor natural. Mercer maintains that the style's claims to "naturalness" and "Africanness" were part of a political rhetoric that framed white beauty standards and commercial beauty culture as artificial and antithetical to the project of black liberation. A central element of natural hair, according to its most vocal advocates, was the abandonment of all but the essential commercial hair products. Except for combing, shampooing, and the occasional trim, natural hair was essentially to be left alone.[23]

Not surprisingly, then, a 1969 *Ebony* article observed that hairdressers were initially among the most vocal opponents to the style and that, "perhaps through wishful thinking," they were eager to predict its demise. A "midwestern stylist" was quoted complaining that the natural hair "fad" threatened to weaken one of the bastions of African American economic independence. "People do all this talking about black power and going 'natural,'" she said, "but they don't stop to think that it might all backfire. . . . If they go all the way with this thing, they'll be putting people out of work." One journalist observed in 1965 that New York City hairdressers were in dire straits, primarily because of the "ever increasing legions of black women who are no longer convinced that they must straighten their hair to be beautiful" and who choose to wear their hair "au naturel." In 1970, *Jet* cited a study by the National Beauty Culturists' League that suggested the style was a national trend. The study revealed that there had been a 20 percent decline overall in black beauty shop business in the past year alone, and that the decline was closer to 30 or 35 percent in New York, Chicago, and Los Angeles. Catherine Cardozo Lewis of the Cardozo salon believed the Afro hurt the salon, since "Negroes didn't have to have their hair fixed as much as they did. I think," she added, "that's probably one of the reason [*sic*] why Negro beauty shops went down so quickly at that particular time."[24]

By the late 1960s, the beauty culture industry could no longer ignore the popularity of the Afro, which, as Maxine Craig observes, had become stylish and "socially easy" as well as "practical" and a symbol of racial pride. Beauticians responded to this development by commodifying the natural. Many hairdressers and beauty companies insisted that Afros still required professional care and took pride in offering the most up-to-date hairstyles and treatments to black women. Increasingly, black beauticians' services included creating and maintaining Afros. As the style became more popular, black and white hair care companies quickly developed products designed specifically for the care of Afros. Advertisements for Afro products began to appear in magazines around 1969. These ads, particularly the ones promoting products made by black-owned companies, deliberately invoked themes of racial pride and black beauty. Nevertheless, advertisers and hairdressers alike portrayed the natural as just one among many styles available for sale. Natural hair was promoted as young, hip, and trendy, but representatives of the beauty culture industry did not suggest that all women ought to stop straightening. On the contrary, professional beauticians offered the Afro as a choice—a style that could be worn all the time, sometimes, or not at all. What was important, the beauty culture industry continued to insist, was that regardless of the hairstyle a black woman chose, she needed to be beautiful, and she required commercial products and services to achieve that beauty.[25]

It is not altogether correct to conclude, however, that the black beauty culture industry was merely trying to protect itself from the threat of business lost to Afro wearers without sincerely embracing the style's ideological dimension, that it was cynically co-opting a powerful political symbol for its own economic gain. The motivations of salon owners were often different from those of cosmetics companies, and black-owned companies often promoted Afro products differently than white companies did. Beauticians were fiercely protective of their businesses, but this came at least in part from the sincere belief that they performed an essential service for black women, and not merely from fear over lost revenue. Beauticians countered the idea that natural hair could simply be washed, combed, and left to "do its thing." They argued that black women who wore Afros still needed to visit the beauty shop and follow a careful maintenance process at home. Failure to do so would result in damaged, unhealthy hair. These beauticians continued to echo the message that had undoubtedly been drilled into them through beauty school, apprenticeship, and trade literature: that black women's hair, because it was so curly, was prone to dryness and breakage and therefore required special care. Many beauticians represented their trade as a health service. Like going to the doctor or dentist, going to the beauty shop was, according to one barber, "not a luxury but a necessity." A Chicago beautician observed that her business had decreased because "many people misunderstand the natural and think they don't have to keep it groomed." Beauty culturists maintained that combing out Afros potentially caused hair breakage and argued that people could not maintain scalp health at home. "When a person shampoos at home, he can never get to the scalp properly," a New York salon owner told *Jet* in 1970. The "constant picking of the Afro," particularly the bigger versions of the style, was blamed for breaking hair shafts and causing early baldness.[26]

Once hairstylists succumbed to the trend, then, they found the Afro could be seamlessly adopted into the world of commercial beauty culture after all. In the words of a prominent black male stylist, "Women who came to the salon every week to have their hair styled still do so, after they've gone 'natural.'" "It's not simply a matter of looking nice," said Mr. Paul, owner of a salon in Chicago's Hyde Park, where a quarter of the middle-class clientele had gone natural by 1969. "Women like to be pampered, to have someone do something for them instead of having to do for others all the time." Beauty advice columnist Marie Cooke rec-

ommended periodic trims, frequent shampooing, and deep conditioning to protect natural hair. In a 1969 editorial in the African American
trade magazine *Beauty Trade*, industry leader Marjorie Stewart Joyner
assured beauticians that they could weather the Afro trend. "This Virgin
hair must be kept clean, cut and styled," she wrote. "The scalp needs
treatments before and after a shampoo—then the hair shows its Natural
Beauty." Joyner added that beauticians could get "$5 and up to sham-
poo, cut and dress a Natural." Older, established beauty shop owners
may not have liked the Afro, but most were happy to accommodate the
women in their communities who wanted the style. Prominent beauticians Rose Morgan and Margaret Cardozo Holmes expressed no distaste
for the look that diverged so sharply from the glossy, waved coiffeurs
they had spent their careers refining and promoting. Reflecting upon
1960s criticisms of hair straightening, Morgan said that the natural did
not hurt her business at all because women still needed to have their
hair shampooed, cut, and treated. Margaret Holmes agreed: when the
natural came along, the hairdressers in her shop "got busy right quick
and learned how to do that."[27]

The difference between women like Morgan and Holmes and
women who wore Afros to reject commercial beauty and express black
identity was perhaps more generational than political. Beauty culturists had always placed themselves at the forefront of African American
struggles for racial equality and advancement. Beauty culture pioneers
Madam C. J. Walker, Annie Turnbo Malone, and Sara Washington were
famous for their philanthropic endeavors and their support of political causes. African American beauty culturists always emphasized their
role as entrepreneurs who did not have to rely on whites for business
or income. As we have seen, it was this economic independence that
allowed many southern black beauty parlor owners to participate actively in the civil rights movement. Black beauty professionals saw no
conflict between supporting racial causes and making money caring for
black women's hair, no matter what style they chose. In contrast, black
nationalists rejected straightened hair outright and often criticized the
middle-class, capitalist, and integrationist proclivities of pro–civil rights
entrepreneurs. African American consumers of beauty culture typically
fell somewhere in the middle of this continuum. Most African American women continued to get their hair done professionally. At the same
time, increasing numbers of black women admired Afros and appreciated

"black is beautiful" both as a political idea and as a fashion statement. These women were not necessarily ready to give up trips to the beauty parlor and were prime targets for commercial marketers of the "radical" new style.[28]

By the late 1960s, a wide array of goods and services were available to the woman who wanted to go natural. Even the venerable Madam C. J. Walker Company was getting in on the "black is beautiful" theme. A promotional circular sent to grocery store owners declared, "Yes—Black is Beautiful . . . and so is brown, and so is white, and red, and yellow. . . . That is, they are all beautiful *if* they buy products suited for them—for *their* color tones and *their* complexion needs." The letter went on to remind readers why the Walker Company was particularly well suited to supply the African American market: "We've got the products that helped produce Black Beauty for many years—in fact, we were the first company in the field—and our founder Madam C. J. Walker, *more than any one person, actually created* the Black Beauty Industry." Early female Afro wearers had had to go to men's barbershops to get their hair done, but by the late 1960s, beauty parlors that catered exclusively to persons who wanted the natural look sprang up in major cities, including New York, Los Angeles, Washington, D.C., and Chicago. These establishments did not merely accommodate the Afro; they celebrated it and deliberately emphasized the style's political significance. At the same time, Afro stylists frankly played up the fashion angle. Barber Ernest X expressed the opinion that black people should abandon "artificial" hair straightening and be proud of their natural appearance. Still, he saw a role for professional beauty experts like himself, promising that "in the future there will be better and more beautiful natural hair styles."[29]

Advertisements for Afro hair care products began to appear in African American magazines around 1969. Among the most prominent producers and advertisers of these new products were black-owned companies. Murray's Superior Products Company, for example, marketed Natural Sheen hair conditioner as "New for the Natural," while promoting the same pomade it had produced for decades as perfect for enhancing the look of the new Afro styles. The black-owned Johnson Products Company was a top seller of African American hair products in these years. While continuing to promote the Ultra Sheen line of straightening products, the company also marketed the popular Afro Sheen line of conditioners, shampoos, and sprays. Advertising cam-

Johnson advertisement, 1971: "Kama mama, kama binti" (*Ebony*)

paigns featured explicit appeals to racial pride. "Natural Hair hangs out. Beautiful!" declared a 1969 Afro Sheen advertisement that featured a large photo of a man and woman wearing impeccably groomed Afros. Other advertisements touted Afro Sheen as "A Beautiful New Hair Product For A Beautiful People" and "soul food for the natural." One Afro Sheen advertisement pictured a woman and girl above the Swahili caption "Kama mama, kama binti (Like mother, like daughter)." Black-owned companies like Murray's Superior Products, Johnson Products, and Supreme Beauty Products enthusiastically used the politicized image of the Afro to sell Afro products. At the same time, these companies did not abandon the hair-straightening products of their businesses, nor did they shy away from producing mass-market hair relaxers, which were gaining a significant foothold in the women's beauty culture market. Obviously these companies wanted to make money whether they were selling hair straighteners or Afro enhancers. The use of black pride as a selling tool was nothing new for the African American beauty culture industry, which had consistently invoked themes of economic independence and the celebration of black female beauty in its advertising. That black-owned companies played a role in commodifying the Afro represents a continuation of this trend—with the recognition that popular images and definitions of black pride had changed by the late 1960s.[30]

Many white beauty companies also promoted products for use on Afros and depicted models with natural hair in their advertisements. Clairol used Afro-wearing models in advertisements for hair coloring in the early 1970s. The company had been courting African American women since the early 1960s, placing ads for its hair coloring in *Ebony*, conducting research on potential markets for their African American–targeted products, and sending representatives and demonstrators to black hair shows. Drawing from a longstanding relationship with black female consumers, Clairol was well prepared to take advantage of the Afro trend. Although the company did not develop new products specifically for Afros, it did promote established items for use on natural hair. For example, the company marketed its Hair So New cream rinse in African American magazines using a picture of a black woman with a huge Afro and the caption "Don't beat around the bush. Get *Hair So New*." ("Bush" was popular slang for the Afro. A Washington, D.C., Afro barber, Nathaniel Mathis, promoted himself as Nat the Bush Doctor.) The Hair So New advertisement promised that the spray would make "life easy for your pick, your hair, and your head. It's a fine mist of creme rinse that lets you spray away snarls and tangles. So you can pick out your hair as fast and full as you like. Without all that ripping or breaking . . . or leaving a lot of it in the sink." Avon was another white-owned company with established ties to the black cosmetics market. Avon ads began appearing in *Ebony* in the early 1960s, and African American Avon representatives had been working in black neighborhoods at least since the 1940s. In 1974, rather late in the game, Avon began to offer Natural Sheen products specifically for Afros. The company used the African American firm Uniworld to develop print and radio advertising campaigns aimed at the black consumer.[31]

Promotion of the Afro differed across gender lines. Magazine articles that discussed women and the Afro often broached the issue of the style's running counter to established standards of female beauty.

A 1966 *Ebony* article observed that, "like all women, those who wear naturals are concerned about male response and recognize that short hair might detract from their femininity." Earrings and makeup were cited as essential accessories for those who did not want to be mistaken for teenage boys, which was, according to Maxine Craig, a frequent occurrence for women who wore Afros in the mid-1960s. In 1969, *Ebony* noted the social significance of natural hair for black men and women but maintained that, "all along, the 'change' has been a more drastic step" for black women "due to the greater emphasis placed on women as sexual objects" and women's innate desire to "look good." Advertisements for Afro products frequently stressed the glamour of the style. One company in particular, black-owned Supreme Beauty Products, offered separate product lines for men and women, with highly gendered sales pitches. Duke Natural products were for men, and related

Supreme Beauty Products advertisements, 1969: "The Beautiful" and "The Bold" (*Ebony*)

advertising portrayed the Afro as an appropriate symbol of masculine strength and independence. Raveen Au Naturelle products were designed for the "natural woman, free, at last, from rollers, hot combs, sticky dressings." Although the actual products, conditioning spray and a spray for "sheen," were identical, the advertising copy expressed different meanings for the Afro according to gender. A pair of advertisements that usually appeared facing each other in a two-page spread juxtaposed the "bold" (male) and the "beautiful" (female) Afro wearer, and another declared simply, "Sisters are different from brothers." In this way, Afros were gendered as symbols of masculinity for black men and, when long and properly accessorized, as symbols of a new, beautiful femininity for black women.[32]

The more "feminine" Afros sold to women were generally larger and more complex in shape and required more maintenance than those men wore. Beauticians, once they had become adjusted to the popularity of the Afro for women, devised ever-more-complicated "natural" styles. The earliest naturals had been simple—unprocessed hair, trimmed about two or three inches from the head. By the late 1960s, hair designers were promoting elaborate versions of the style. Afros that were almost impossibly large and domelike continued the popular African American ideal of long hair for women. Afros with multiple puffs and braids, and Afros with decorative attachments, were offered as examples of how chic and elegant natural hair could be. In the late 1960s and early 1970s, *Beauty Trade* regularly featured Afro styles in its pages. The magazine featured the first-ever Natural Competition at the African American beauty culturists' and barbers' trade show in 1970. The winning style was a high, round Afro with a sculpted widow's peak at the forehead. Styles were said to have lost points with judges if "proportions were out of balance for the face." The designer of the winning style remarked that he was concerned with "form more than anything else," although he did admit that his mission was to express "the beauty in 'Blackness.'" The second prize winner created a big "African Queen" Afro, which might be worn, for evening, with a jewel at the forehead, and which was designed to "fit the facial features and contour of the heads of black women." The Afro category became a regular part of hair trade show contests in the early 1970s, and the pages of *Beauty Trade* were full of suggestions for creating beautiful, intricate, and high-maintenance "natural" hairstyles.[33]

A 1971 book, *All About the Natural*, by hairdresser Lois Liberty Jones and journalist John Henry Jones, featured a stunning array of Afro styles from which to choose. The book was published by Clairol and endorsed Clairol shampoos, conditioners, and coloring products. The text of the book traced the history of African and African American hair traditions and criticized hair-straightening methods as damaging to black women's hair. Although the writers took the perspective that natural hair was a symbol of black pride, they also reassured readers that the style was trendy. They stated, for example, that "Afro-American is in" and that pressing and processing were on their way "out." "Fortunately," they declared, "the 'fashion of the moment' is the natural hair style." The Joneses asserted that the natural was for everybody but that it was not a "do it yourself thing. There is the 'primitive' Natural and there's the well groomed coiffure." The remainder of the book featured multiple high-fashion Afro styles, including the Delta Magic with a medium Afro above a band of braids, the demure Teen Twist, the Miss Zanzie (described as a "burst of Natural beauty"), the Soul Love, and the Freedom Burst.[34]

In this way, beauty culturists constructed the Afro as a fashion statement. This was not entirely new, of course; among the earliest promotions of the natural style were Abbey Lincoln's fashion shows. Nevertheless, these early shows always put the hairstyle in a distinctly political context and featured relatively simple versions of the style. Afro stylists in the late 1960s and early 1970s were certainly promoting the "black is beautiful" ideal, and in this way they were at the forefront of creating a new and elegant beauty standard for black women. The difference between them and earlier Afro advocates was that they insisted that black beauty could include straightened as well as natural hair. Also, the complicated Afro styles that came into vogue by the late 1960s left the notion of simplicity and the freedom to let one's hair "do its thing" by the wayside. Women, in particular, were faced with new images of black beauty that were probably as difficult to achieve and maintain as straightened hair. By 1968 Michelle Wallace had embraced natural hair as a symbol of her commitment to "Blackness" and her emancipation from commercial beauty standards. Nevertheless, within a few years she found herself in a new femininity trap. "No I wasn't to wear makeup but yes I had to wear skirts that I could hardly walk in," Wallace writes. "No I wasn't to go to the beauty parlor, but yes I was to spend countless hours cornrolling my hair." Wallace observes that even black women who were part of "The Movement" were expected to be beautiful, "whatever that was." "So I was again obsessed with my appearance," Wallace recalls, "worried about the rain again—the Black women's nightmare—for fear that my huge, full Afro would shrivel up to my head." Parenthetically, she adds, "Despite Blackness, Black men still didn't like short hair." Whether one felt compelled to wear the big, full Afro of feminine black consciousness or to follow the latest spectacular Afro trends promoted by the beauty industry, natural hair seemed to offer little escape from the admonition that black women needed to work hard—and spend money—to be beautiful.[35]

Like black beauticians, manufacturers of hair products insisted that black women who went natural would have to continue to spend money on their hair. Magazine advertising and articles about the Afro paid particular attention to women and the "dilemma" of wearing one's hair natural and still being feminine and beautiful. Advertisers and hairdressers took special care, as well, not to alienate the majority of women who chose to continue straightening their hair. As we have seen, advertising for black hair products frequently portrayed the Afro as merely one choice among many, downplaying its political significance. Typical were advertisements such as that for Raveen conditioner, which featured one woman with straightened hair and one woman with an Afro: "Whatever Hairstyle You Choose, NEW RAVEEN Is the Hair Conditioner to Use." Posner, a white-owned company, exhorted black women to "Go smooth. Go curly. Be a 'natural.'" But use Posner's conditioner for "smooth and pretty hair." An advertisement for Tintz hair color asked, "Natural or Straight? . . . Color It Black, Baby, But By All Means Color It." The copy further observed that the natural looked good on those who could wear it, thus highlighting the commercial characterization of the style as primarily a fashion choice. Some companies exhorted black women to use chemical relaxers to achieve a bigger, better natural. An advertisement for Perma-Strate's hair relaxer told women that whether they wanted "smoothly straight hair, soft curls . . . or a sweeping Afro . . . [hairstyles will] look their best only if you *first straighten, then style!*" An Ultra Sheen advertisement that pictured one woman with an Afro and two others with straight hair told female readers, "You can change your hair style as easily as you change your mind—with Ultra Sheen Permanent Creme Relaxer." Like some advertisers, *Beauty Trade* promoted the use of relaxers to "improve" the Afro and suggested women alternate between straight and "kinky" styles. The March 1969 issue featured a method allowing "the patron who wants both permanent and natural" to "have her cake and eat it too." "There's no need for you to lose important revenue," the article stressed. Hair could be permanently straightened, then cold waved on small rods to achieve a "tight frizzy curl." Such a process, in theory, allowed hair to be blown straight or set in tiny curlers for the "Curly 'Fro' look." The blow-out involved using a hair drier to create the bigger Afro look, and *Beauty Trade* advocated the use of a relaxer cream before drying to create an even bigger Afro. In this commercialized context, the natural was not natural at all. It was

NATURAL OR STRAIGHT?

Color It Black, Baby, But By All Means Color It

NATURAL...

not everyone can wear it, so it looks all the more smashing on those who can. But watch out for the "burnt" look... use TINTZ CREME COLOR SHAMPOO to penetrate and condition each hair strand, add deep-down lustre and sheen. Jet Black, Black or Dark Ash Brown shades recommended for the Natural Look.

STRAIGHT...

to give hair an "invisible tint" that's natural-like and won't interfere with straightening treatments, use TINTZ CREME COLOR SHAMPOO. In only 17 minutes drab off-color hair takes on a lustrous, natural-looking color that won't wash out or rub off. Only occasional touch-ups needed. Jet black, black or brown shades very life-like!

Ask for Tintz at Drug Counters Everywhere

Tintz advertisement, 1969: "Natural or Straight?" (*Ebony*)

promoted as a bold new look, albeit a look virtually devoid of its original political meaning.[36]

By the late 1960s, black women could easily have an Afro without going natural in any sense of the word. Advertisements for Afro wigs crowded the pages of black magazines. In 1971, the Summit Company launched its Afrylic line of wigs "created to make the black woman even more beautiful." The Brown Skin Baby wigs, which featured "scalps" tinted to match African American skin tones, were touted as the only wigs with "brown skin, baby!" In obvious conflict with the original goal of the Afro, one Afrylic advertisement promised that the wigs were "so natural" they would "make you hate your own hair." Beauty culturists embraced the Afro wig, which had long made up a part of their business, as a way of recouping the loss of business that resulted from the natural trend. Salon owners could conceivably straighten and style a woman's hair *and* sell that same woman an Afro wig for when she felt like going a little "wild." Rose Morgan maintained that the popularity of the Afro created an entirely new market for her line of wigs. *Beauty Trade* championed the Afro wig as a revenue maker compatible with established black beauty processes. Model Cynthia Archer, featured in an Afro wig on the December 1968 cover of *Beauty Trade*, said that she straightened her hair but wore the wig as a "change of pace." "This is the way us Professionals like our Customers," commented *Beauty Trade*. "We endorse Afro Wigs. But we also endorse Professional Care at all times." The designer of Archer's wig was a prominent New York salon owner, who touted the Afro wig as ideal for black women "who don't want to cut their hair for the natural because then they are stuck with it" and for beauticians, who could both sell the wigs and provide care for the hair under them. Another New York salon owner commented in 1969, "Naturally, we push the Afro Wigs to try to protect the Permanent business. One can help the other, if it's sold correctly." By the late 1960s and early 1970s, then, the black beauty culture industry was actively endorsing the Afro as a fashion that was easy to put on and just as easy to take off. It was no longer recognized as a permanent lifestyle choice that denoted racial consciousness or as an outright rejection of hair straightening, either for the sake of convenience or as a political statement. From the perspective of black beauty professionals—if not politically active black women—the Afro truly seemed to be just another style to be bought and sold.[37]

By 1975, few would have argued that the Afro was rebellious or revolutionary; the prominence of the commercialized version of the style had helped blunt the militant edge of the natural look. Nevertheless, hairdressers and hair product manufacturers who promoted the Afro very likely saw supporting images of Black Power and making a profit as complementary rather than antithetical goals. Commodification was certainly not the sole reason for the popularity of the natural look. Widespread acceptance of the Afro in black communities developed *before* efforts to sell the style were in full swing. Into the 1970s, the Afro continued to be viewed as a symbol of pride and an assertion that black was indeed beautiful. As late as 1973, magazine articles portrayed it as a controversial style. Indeed, African American women who wore natural hair potentially faced real threats to their livelihoods. Late 1960s reports on the Afro trend noted that some women wore wigs over their naturals when at work to avoid trouble with white employers. In 1971, *Jet* observed that the Philadelphia Commission on Human Rights had received several complaints from black women who had been sent home from work, or even fired, for wearing Afros. Even though the Afro had gained prominence as a chic and daring new look in fashion circles, wearing the style could be problematic for ordinary black women.[38]

By the mid-1970s, the Afro was featured less frequently in magazines like *Beauty Trade* and *Ebony*, and advertising for Afro products in black magazines was waning. Like any successful fashion commodity, the style had been heavily promoted and elaborately developed, and then it quickly faded from prominence. By the end of the decade, the Afro was quite likely seen by the style-conscious as passé. Meanwhile, chemical relaxers, once eschewed by most black women, had become the preferred method of salon and at-home hair straightening. Nevertheless, the natural look remained a choice for black women throughout the 1970s. Indeed, as the style became less fashionable toward the end of the decade, the Afro may have regained some of its political significance for the few who continued to wear it. In 1973, *Encore*, a short-lived African American news and arts magazine, featured a "Point/ Counterpoint" article in which one writer criticized the political message of natural hair as "nonsense," while another writer affirmed the political significance of hair.[39]

The Afro was part of an effort by a generation of African Americans to carve out new definitions of freedom and racial identity that better suited their times and circumstances. It was merely the first of several "natural" hairstyles to gain prominence after 1960. At the height of the Afro's popularity in the late 1960s and early 1970s, cornrows, braids, and other African-inspired hairstyling methods emerged as attractive alternatives for women who felt Afros were too commercial and not authentically African. Although the bigger versions of the Afro were out of style by the mid- to late 1970s, unprocessed hair remained popular among black women, whether they wanted to denote racial pride, show political consciousness, make a fashion statement, or achieve some combination of the three. In fact these more recent additions to the array of hairstyle choices available to black women followed a similar path to the Afro, evolving from styles chosen by a handful of politically conscious women, to "hip" fashion popularity, to something close to mainstream acceptance. Thus the Afro leaves us with an important legacy: a consistent use of hairstyle by many African American men and women to signify political loyalties and commitments. It is not true that there was no political meaning in African American hair before the Afro, but the deliberate use of hair to make a social or political statement became much more conscious and explicit as a result of the Black Power movement and the popularity of the Afro in the 1960s. Whether or not they were motivated by racial consciousness, the hairdressers and beauty product manufacturers who provided goods and services for natural hair played a vital role in supporting the "black is beautiful" principle. Thus the black beauty culture industry did not rob the Afro entirely of its political meaning. Ultimately the Afro had a symbolic power and a material influence on African American women's style and beauty standards that went beyond the narrow meanings commodification gave it.[40]

Conclusion

Why African American Beauty Culture Is Still Contested

In a 1987 speech at her alma mater, Spelman College, Alice Walker told a part of her own hair history. Placing the story in the context of her spiritual and intellectual growth as she reached forty, Walker told her audience that it took considerable contemplation and soul searching before she realized "in my physical self there remained one last barrier to my spiritual liberation, at least in the present phase: my hair." It was, she asserted, her "oppressed hair" that was holding her back. Walker recalled her hair's beleaguered history: "I remembered years of enduring hairdressers—from my mother onward—doing missionary work on my hair. They dominated, suppressed, controlled." After "experimenting" with long braid extensions while allowing her "short, mildly processed (oppressed) hair" to grow out, Walker reveled in letting her hair do what it pleased. "Eventually," she said, "I knew precisely what my hair wanted: it wanted to grow, to be itself, to attract lint, if that was its destiny, but to be left alone by anyone, including me, who did not love it as it was." As a result, Walker concluded, "the ceiling at the top of my brain lifted; once again my mind (and spirit) could get outside myself."[1]

Like so many intellectual and politically active black women since the mid-1960s, Walker connected her hair, particularly her unprocessed hair, to her racial identity and to notions of personal liberation.

Walker's individual story illustrates the central ideas about the larger social significance of African American women's hair and beauty ideals that this study has explored. Letting one's hair "be itself," to the extent that it was supposed to represent an expression of liberation from oppressive beauty ideals, was an important rhetorical tool after 1960 for many black people to collectively and individually define ideas about racial freedom. Still, it was not the first time African American women's hair and appearance were made to take on social and political meaning within black communities. Walker's reference to hair straightening as "missionary work" is an apt one, and not only in the negative sense that beauty culturists sought to "control" and "suppress" black women's hair. African American hairdressers in the twentieth century saw themselves as missionaries of sorts. In the 1920s and 1930s, beauty culture was part of a program of racial uplift; it promised to free black women from labor oppression and poverty. From the 1940s through the mid-1960s, hairdressers, in their rhetoric and actions, took up the ideals and objectives of the civil rights movement, maintaining that their profession, and the appearance of African American women, could represent and promote both black economic independence and interracial harmony. In fact, the rise of natural hair as a statement of black pride was only one in a series of examples of how hair was political for black women in the United States in the twentieth century.

It is important to place African American women's beauty culture in its cultural, economic, political, and historical context to understand the social origins and development of beauty standards for black women from the 1920s to the 1970s. The beauty standards sold by the African American beauty industry and promoted by beauticians and entertainers and in the mass media were, of course, heavily influenced by white America, but there was a more complex process at work than simple emulation of white beauty ideals. Much of the time, African American beauty standards were shaped within black society as much as they were formed in reaction to (let alone imposed by) the majority culture. It is important, therefore, to understand the influence of such factors as migration and urbanization, class dynamics, and the rise of mass consumer culture on the history of African American commercial beauty culture and commercialized beauty ideals. In addition, one must pay close attention to the connections between African American beauty culture and black consumerism in general, linking both to twentieth-century racial politics. African American advertising and marketing boosters throughout the period examined here viewed beauty culture as a special kind of business that exemplified both black consumer power and the potential for successful black entrepreneurship. People like Claude Barnett and David Sullivan called for greater recognition of black consumerism by white advertisers, using beauty culture as proof that African Americans were eager to buy luxury goods and services while also criticizing white companies that entered the business and advertised their products in black publications. This apparently contradictory mix of integrationism and black economic nationalism actually represented a practical response to the economic and social realities that African American business owners and consumers faced both before and during the civil rights era. Barnett, for example, portrayed black consumers as deserving of the same attention white consumers got, but he also argued that segregation in the 1920s and 1930s necessitated advertising directed specifically at African Americans. Decades later, as legal segregation was being dismantled and white advertisers, more than ever before, were recognizing the value of targeting black consumers, African American marketing experts insisted that continuing cultural differences necessitated continuing race-based advertising strategies. Such arguments, for instance, drove advertisers' creation of the "soul" market in the late 1960s and early 1970s. Thus marketing professionals argued both for inclusion of African Americans as consumer citizens and for special treatment of African Americans as a separate market, all the while perceiving a need to protect independent and successful black enterprises and markets, such as black beauty culture, from too much attention from white corporations.

This position is clarified when placed in the context of black activism in other political arenas during the same period, particularly during the civil rights and Black Power eras. In *Up South: Civil Rights and Black Power in Philadelphia*, Matthew Countryman observes that, during the 1940s and 1950s, black politicians embraced the Democratic liberal coalition that endorsed an integrationist stance on race relations, but that liberalism's limited achievement of racial justice in economic and public institutions in Philadelphia prompted increasing numbers of African American activists to align themselves with Black Power goals and ideologies. But this was not, Countryman argues, always a clear-cut division. Many black political leaders in the city developed a political ideology that effectively meshed liberal components, such as demanding fair access to jobs and a voice in municipal policymaking, with nationalist efforts to control the political and economic futures of African American communities.[2] Similarly, in the case of beauty culture, African American marketing experts could push for more attention from white advertisers and, especially after World War II, racial justice for African American consumers, while maintaining that the survival of black-owned businesses was essential to the growth of black communities.

This was all the more important when black-owned businesses, like those in the beauty culture industry, catered exclusively to an African American clientele. In fact, this component provides an additional explanation for why African American business advocates were so protective of beauty culture in particular. For decades, and for many diverse reasons, the beauty product industry and professional beauticians were sources of pride in African American communities. Entrepreneurs like Madam C. J. Walker and Sara Washington were lauded for their financial success, for their philanthropy, and for providing employment to black men and women. Beauticians were often respected community leaders. All of these people engaged in work that celebrated the beauty of black women within a broader American society that denied it. But this economic and cultural independence rested on the precarious ground of African Americans' financial power to sustain it. This situation was certainly not unique in the history of black entrepreneurial and cultural enterprises. Writing about Motown Record Corporation and racial politics in postwar Detroit, Suzanne Smith observes that African Americans in the Motor City were proud that this music company and musical style, which had originated in black Detroit, were so successful across racial lines and throughout the world. Still, although Motown's integrationist appeal has endured to this day, the economic prosperity and independence for many black Detroiters that initially came with it was short-lived, primarily because of the interrelated factors of Detroit's deindustrialization, Motown's move to Los Angeles, and the label's subsequent sale to a white media corporation. Smith concludes that "Motown's business history proves how difficult it is for black capitalism to survive in the global economy, let alone thrive enough to be able to address or promote the needs of black America."[3]

This crucial idea is well illustrated by the beauty industry. Beauty culturists and product manufacturers often stressed their expertise in working with black women's specific hair and complexion needs, and they frequently deployed this argument to discredit white businesses that entered the African American beauty business. But enter it they did. In the 1920s and 1930s, white companies dramatically increased their presence in this market just as the Depression made it more difficult for African American beauty product companies to compete. This trend intensified after World War II. Even as black-owned beauty parlors experienced considerable success in the immediate postwar years, black-owned beauty product companies continued to be challenged for market share by white ones. In recent years, white corporations have bought out many surviving African American beauty product companies, retaining the names and product lines in a modern version of white companies' earlier attempts to pass as black-owned. L'Oreal bought Chicago-based Soft Sheen in 1998 and in 2000 purchased Carson, the white-owned creator of the Dark and Lovely line (which had acquired Johnson Products, of Afro Sheen fame, two years before). In 2002, L'Oreal went so far as to move its entire "ethnic personal care division" into the old Johnson Products Company building on the South Side of Chicago. A 2002 report in the *Chicago Tribune* reported that remaining small black companies were struggling to maintain market share, some banking on direct sales to salons rather than fighting for shelf space in chain drugstores. In 2006, the *Village Voice* ran interviews of two prominent African American celebrity makeup artists. Both complained that, though white companies were making a big show of offering products to black women and, in the phrase of an old Madam C. J. Walker ad, of "glorifying our womanhood" by using megastars like Halle Barry (for Revlon) as spokespeople, most had yet to effectively tap the market for black women's cosmetics. In many cases these companies still failed, especially in the area of foundations and concealers, to manufacture products that worked. Yet the makeup artists deemed black companies' products too old fashioned, in terms of packaging or shade choices (Fashion Fair was cited an example), or too difficult to find in major department stores. Even MAC Cosmetics, the upscale company famous for deliberately creating genuinely multiracial makeup colors and product lines, was blasted in the article for marketing foundations that looked wrong on the dark complexions they had supposedly been designed for. "Most companies fall short in all areas," commented makeup artist Sam Fine. "Having worked for virtually every major cosmetic brand, I've realized that satisfying the needs of women of color is not a priority."[4]

Thus the limits of black capitalism that Suzanne Smith identifies also apply to the history of African American beauty culture. Promotional rhetoric always exaggerated the power of black-owned beauty businesses to provide economic independence for African American women and their communities, but they certainly did more on that score than any national (or global) white corporation ever could. As with Motown, independent African American–owned beauty businesses experienced their apex of success in the period after World War II, an era of affluence for black Americans, especially in the urban-industrial North and West. Smith cites Detroit's economic decline as one important reason that Motown left—the company followed the money to Hollywood—and points out that this move helped pave the way for the sale of the label to MCA, a white-owned corporation. Similar economic forces since the late 1960s have contributed to the recent entry of companies like L'Oreal and Revlon to the African American beauty market through buyouts of black-owned companies. This trend, of course, makes it less likely than ever before that the beauty business will be a vehicle for African American economic power, but that particular problem is an old one. As the *Village Voice* article cited above suggests, these recent developments also put into question whether the beauty demands of black women will be met any more satisfactorily in the future than they were in the past. Just as important, they prompt one to wonder just how (and by whom) those beauty demands will be defined and promoted in the years to come.

Notes

Abbreviations

AC/HML	Avon Collection, Hagley Museum and Library, Wilmington, Delaware
CBC/CHS	Claude A. Barnett Collection, Chicago Historical Society, Chicago, Illinois
CJC/NMAH	Caroline Jones Collection, Archives Center, National Museum of American History, Smithsonian Institution, Washington, D.C.
MJP/CPL	Marjorie Stewart Joyner Papers, Vivian G. Harsh Research Collection, Chicago Public Library, Chicago, Illinois
MWC/IHS	Madam C. J. Walker Collection, Indiana Historical Society, Indianapolis, Indiana
NMC/NMAH	Nathaniel Mathis Collection, Archives Center, National Museum of American History, Smithsonian Institution, Washington, D.C.
RBC/NYPL	Rare Books Collection, Schomburg Center for Research in Black Culture, New York Public Library, New York
WB/NA	Women's Bureau, U.S. Department of Labor, RG 86, National Archives, Washington, D.C.
WCBA/NMAH	Warshaw Collection of Business Americana, Archives Center, National Museum of American History, Smithsonian Institution, Washington, D.C.

Introduction: Why Hair Is Political

1. Andrea Benton Rushing, "Hair Raising," *Feminist Studies* 14, no. 2 (Summer 1988): 328–30, 335.

2. Lisa Jones, "Hair Always and Forever," in *Bulletproof Diva: Tales of Race, Sex and Hair* (New York: Anchor Books, 1995), 11–12; Ingrid Banks, *Hair Matters: Beauty, Power, and Black Women's Consciousness* (New York: New York University Press, 2000), 38. On non-blacks in the African American beauty trade, see Lisa Jones, "The Hair Trade," in Jones, *Bulletproof Diva*, 278–97. On black women being punished for the hairstyles they choose, see Ayana D. Byrd and Lori Tharps, *Hair Story: Untangling the Roots of Black Hair in America* (New York: St. Martin's Press, 2001), 177–79, and Banks, *Hair Matters*, 16. On the

continuing resonance of "good" and "bad" hair for black women, see Banks, *Hair Matters*, 28–31.

3. One of the earliest historical studies of beauty standards in the United States is Lois Banner, *American Beauty* (New York: Knopf, 1983). The most comprehensive work on the topic of commercial beauty culture is Kathy Piess, *Hope in a Jar: The Making of America's Beauty Culture* (New York: Holt, 1998). On black and white women's beauty shops, see Julie Willett, *Permanent Waves: The Making of the American Beauty Shop* (New York: New York University Press, 1998). On African American beauty culture, see Noliwe Rooks, *Hair Raising: Beauty, Culture, and African American Women* (New Brunswick, N.J.: Rutgers University Press, 1996), and Gwendolyn Robinson, "Class, Race, and Gender: A Transcultural, Theoretical, and Sociohistorical Analysis of Cosmetic Institutions and Practices to 1920" (Ph.D. diss., University of Illinois at Chicago, 1984). On African American beauty schools, see Julia Kirk Blackwelder, *Styling Jim Crow: African American Beauty Training During Segregation* (College Station: Texas A&M University Press, 2003). Another important contribution to this emerging scholarship is Maxine Craig's study of black beauty contests and the politics of African American beauty standards in the twentieth century, *Ain't I a Beauty Queen? Black Women, Beauty, and the Politics of Race* (New York: Oxford University Press, 2002).

4. Evelyn Brooks Higginbotham, "African American Women's History and the Metalanguage of Race," *Signs* 17 (Winter 1992): 251–74; Robin D. G. Kelley, *Race Rebels: Culture, Politics, and the Black Working Class* (New York: Free Press, 1994); Shane White and Graham White, *Stylin': African American Expressive Culture from Its Beginnings to the Zoot Suit* (Ithaca, N.Y.: Cornell University Press, 1998).

5. Roland Marchand, *Advertising the American Dream: Making Way for Modernity, 1920–1940* (Berkeley: University of California Press, 1985), 64.

6. On the history of African Americans and marketing, see Robert Weems, *Desegregating the Dollar* (New York: New York University Press, 1998). For a good, recent study of post-WWII consumerism and the concept of consumer citizenship, see Lizabeth Cohen, *A Consumers' Republic: The Politics of Mass Consumption in Postwar America* (New York: Knopf, 2003). For more on the history of American consumer culture, see Stuart Ewen, *Captains of Consciousness: Advertising and the Social Roots of the Consumer Culture* (New York: McGraw-Hill, 1976); Richard Wightman Fox and T. J. Jackson Lears, eds., *The Culture of Consumption: Critical Essays in American History, 1880–1980* (New York: Pantheon Books, 1983); Lawrence B. Glickman, ed., *Consumer Society in American History: A Reader* (Ithaca, N.Y.: Cornell University Press, 1999); and Gary Cross, *An All-Consuming Century: Why Commercialism Won in Modern America* (New York: Columbia University Press, 2000).

7. Jackson Lears, *Fables of Abundance: A Cultural History of Advertising in America* (New York: Basic Books, 1994), esp. chap. 6; Susan Bordo, "'Material Girl': The Effacements of Postmodern Culture," in *Unbearable Weight: Feminism, Western Culture, and the Body* (Berkeley: University of California Press, 1993), 245–75; Peiss, *Hope in a Jar*, 151.

1. "The Beauty Industry Is Ours"

1. Claude A. Barnett to F. B. Ransom, 24 January 1929, box 262, CBC/CHS; Claude A. Barnett to Annie Malone, 8 February 1929, box 262, CBC/CHS.

2. Marchand, *Advertising the American Dream*, 64

3. H. A. Haring, "The Negro as Consumer: How to Sell to a Race That, for the First Time in Its History, Has Money to Spend," *Advertising and Selling*, 3 September 1930, 20; H. A. Haring, "Selling to Harlem," *Advertising and Selling*, 31 October 1928, 17–18.

4. Joe W. Trotter and Earl Lewis, *African Americans in the Industrial Age: A Documentary History, 1915–1945* (Boston: Northeastern University Press, 1996), 1, 105, 169.

5. Claude A. Barnett to Robert R. Morton, 22 September 1930, box 11, CBC/CHS; Guy B. Johnson, "Newspaper Advertisements and Negro Culture," *Journal of Social Forces* 3 (1925): 706; Paul K. Edwards, *The Southern Urban Negro as a Consumer* (New York: Prentice-Hall, 1932), 185–87.

6. Claude A. Barnett to Associated Publishers representative, form letter, [1930], box 131, CBC/CHS.

7. Claude A. Barnett to A. L. Holsey, 29 October 1930, box 261, CBC/CHS; Barnett to Morton, 22 September 1930.

8. Edwards, *Southern Urban Negro*, 56, 243, 251, 159; Lizabeth Cohen, *Making a New Deal: Industrial Workers in Chicago, 1919–1939* (New York: Cambridge University Press, 1990), 52–54. Paul Edwards received an MBA from Harvard in 1922 and a PhD in commercial science in 1936. He was at Fisk from 1928 to 1934. He worked as a market researcher for Crossley Radio Company, Simmons Mattress Company, and Daniel Stach's advertising firm. *New York Times*, "Paul K. Edwards of Rutgers Dead," 8 December 1959.

9. Interracial Council, news release, 25 April 1928, box 131, CBC/CHS; W. B. Ziff Co., *The Negro Market*, 1932, box 131, CBC/CHS.

10. Ziff, *Negro Market*.

11. Claude A. Barnett "The Negro Market" (letter to advertisers and manufacturers), 2 April 1932, box 132, CBC/CHS; Claude A. Barnett to Paul Edwards, 13 June 1931, box 132, CBC/CHS; Claude A. Barnett to Paul Edwards, 18 October 1932, box 132, CBC/CHS; Paul Edwards to Claude A. Barnett, 15 December 1933, box 132, CBC/CHS.

12. Trotter and Lewis, *African Americans in the Industrial Age*, 169.

13. Robinson, "Class, Race, and Gender," 523.

14. F. B. Ransom to Kashmir Chemical Company, 18 March 1920, box 262, CBC/CHS; Kashmir Chemical Company to F. B. Ransom, 19 March 1920, box 262, CBC/CHS; F. B. Ransom to Kashmir Chemical Company, 20 March 1920, box 262, CBC/CHS.

15. Barnett to Malone, 8 February 1929; Claude A. Barnett to Annie Malone, 21 September 1934, box 262, CBC/CHS.

16. Frank Linn, "Ethiopian Invasion in America," *Apex News*, November–December 1935, 4; Nannie Burroughs, "Address at Apex Commencement,"

Apex News, January–February–March 1938, 27; Claude A. Barnett to A. L. Holsey, 4 March 1933, box 261, CBC/CHS; "Table of Product Sales, 1918–1936," box 10, MWC/IHS.

17. Linda J. Evans, "Claude A. Barnett and the Associated Negro Press," *Chicago History* 12, no. 1 (1983): 53. I found white-owned companies' cosmetics advertising to be equally prominent in all the newspapers I examined, including the *Chicago Defender*, the *Pittsburgh Courier*, the *New York Amsterdam News*, the *California Eagle*, and the *Norfolk (Va.) Journal and Guide*.

18. Linn, "Ethiopian Invasion," 4; Barnett to Holsey, 4 March 1933; Rooks, *Hair Raising*, 30–35; Peiss, *Hope in a Jar*, 42.

19. Plough's advertisements, *Chicago Defender*, 20 October 1923, 20 March 1926; Hi-Ja advertisement, *Pittsburgh Courier*, 11 October 1924.

20. Barnett to Holsey, 29 October 1930; Golden Brown advertisement, *New York Amsterdam News*, 14 April 1926; Golden Brown advertisements, *Chicago Defender*, 6 September 1923, 5 May 1923; Golden Brown advertisement, *Pittsburgh Courier*, 10 October 1925; Peiss, *Hope in a Jar*, 117; Barnett to Holsey, 29 October 1930. Kathy Peiss observes that African American newspapers believed Golden Brown was black-owned. Peiss, *Hope in a Jar*, 117.

21. Claude A. Barnett, "Fly out of Darkness" (unpublished manuscript, [1966]), box 406, CBC/CHS; Poro advertisements, *Pittsburgh Courier*, 26 June 1926, 11 October 1924.

22. Barnett to Malone, 8 February 1929.

23. Poro advertisement, *Pittsburgh Courier*, 7 December 1929; Poro advertisement, *Baltimore Afro-American*, 29 August 1931; Poro advertisement, *Pittsburgh Courier*, 11 April 1931.

24. Correspondence between Barnett and Poro from 1932 to 1935 is dominated by Barnett's proposing advertising campaigns and Poro's declining because of financial reasons. Box 262, CBC/CHS.

25. Peiss, *Hope in a Jar*, esp. chap. 5. Also see Kathy Peiss, "Making Faces: The Cosmetics Industry and the Cultural Construction of Gender, 1890–1930," in *Unequal Sisters: A Multicultural Reader in U.S. Women's History*, 2nd ed., ed. Vicki L. Ruiz and Ellen Carol DuBois (New York: Routledge, 1994), 372–94.

26. Susan Porter Benson, *Counter Cultures: Saleswomen, Managers, and Customers in American Department Stores, 1890–1940* (Urbana: Illinois University Press, 1988), 273.

27. Sabra Waldfogel, "The Body Beautiful, the Body Hateful: Feminine Body Image and the Culture of Consumption in Twentieth Century America" (Ph.D. diss., University of Minnesota, 1986), 1. The idea that women were encouraged to use consumption to achieve beauty is explored by many scholars. See Banner, *American Beauty*, 274; Ewen, *Captains of Consciousness*, 47; and Fox and Lears, *Culture of Consumption*, 19–27.

28. On African American consumer culture, see Weems, *Desegregating the Dollar*, and Ted Ownsby, *American Dreams in Mississippi: Consumers, Poverty, and Culture, 1830–1998* (Chapel Hill: University of North Carolina Press, 1999).

29. Marchand, *Advertising the American Dream*, 9; Peiss, "Making Faces," 376; Peiss, *Hope in a Jar*, 7. For more on white women's roles as workers, con-

sumers, and participants in leisure at the turn of the century, see Kathy Peiss, *Cheap Amusements: Working Women and Leisure in Turn-of-the-Century New York* (Philadelphia: Temple University Press, 1986); Nan Enstad, *Ladies of Labor, Girls of Adventure: Working Women, Popular Culture, and Labor Politics* (New York: Columbia University Press, 1999); and Tera Hunter, *To 'joy My Freedom: Southern Black Women's Lives and Labor after the Civil War* (Cambridge, Mass.: Harvard University Press, 1997), esp. chaps. 7 and 8.

30. Darlene Clark Hine, "Rape and the Inner Lives of Black Women in the Middle West: Preliminary Thoughts on the Culture of Dissemblance," *Signs* 14 (Summer 1989): 912–20; Robinson, "Class, Race, and Gender," 282; Hazel Carby, "'It Jus Be's Dat Way Sometime': The Sexual Politics of Women's Blues," *Radical America* 20, no. 4 (1986): 9–22; Hazel Carby, "Policing the Black Woman's Body in an Urban Context," *Critical Inquiry* 18 (Summer 1992): 739–55; Evelyn Brooks Higginbotham, *Righteous Discontent: The Women's Movement in the Black Baptist Church, 1880–1920* (Cambridge, Mass.: Harvard University Press, 1993), 191.

31. Madam C. J. Walker advertisement, *Chicago Defender*, 4 July 1931; Plough's advertisement, *Chicago Defender*, 11 July 1931.

32. *Half-Century Magazine,* "Rouge and Progress," May–June 1921; Rose Doggett, "Make Me Beautiful," *Apex News*, April–May–June 1938, 8; Burroughs, "Address at Apex Commencement," 26. According to Kathy Peiss, modernity was also a common motif in cosmetics advertising for white women by the 1920s. Peiss, "Making Faces," 381.

33. Madam C. J. Walker advertisement, *Chicago Defender*, 7 November 1925; White and White, *Stylin'*, 57–58.

34. Plough's advertisement, *Chicago Defender*, 11 July 1931; Nadinola advertisement, *Pittsburgh Courier*, 9 April 1927; Kashmir Nile Queen pamphlet, 1919, box 261, CBC/CHS. One example of white companies' using Egyptian motifs is Palmolive facial soap advertisements, which appeared frequently in *Ladies' Home Journal* in the 1920s. Egypt is also featured prominently in a pamphlet on the history of beauty put out by Elizabeth Arden, *A Pageant of Beauty*, 1937, box 1, WCBA/NMAH.

35. Kashmir Nile Queen pamphlet, 1919; Goldie M. Walden, "Beauty," *Abbott's Monthly*, January 1933; Aimee Torriani, "The Business of Becoming Beautiful," *Abbott's Monthly*, February 1931; Dr. Fred Palmer advertisement, *Pittsburgh Courier*, 11 April 1931; Plough's advertisement, *Pittsburgh Courier*, 7 December 1929; Plough's advertisement, *Chicago Defender*, 21 September 1929; Hi-Ja advertisement, *Chicago Defender*, 25 February 1928.

36. Burroughs, "Address at Apex Commencement," 26–27; Hi-Ja advertisement, *Chicago Defender*, 5 May 1923; Madam C. J. Walker advertisement, *Pittsburgh Courier*, 11 April 1925; Plough's advertisement, *Chicago Defender*, 20 February 1926.

37. Dr. Fred Palmer advertisements, *Chicago Defender*, [1929], 19 November 1932; Nadinola advertisement, *Baltimore Afro-American*, 23 May 1931; Golden Peacock advertisement, *Pittsburgh Courier*, 29 August 1931; Hi-Ja advertisement, *Pittsburgh Courier*, 8 April 1928; Plough's advertisement, *Pittsburgh*

Courier, 4 July 1931; Plough's advertisement, *Pittsburgh Courier*, 2 December 1933; Zura Kinkout advertisement, *Negro World*, 2 June 1923.

38. Peiss, *Hope in a Jar*, 149.

39. Madam C. J. Walker newspaper advertisement, [1920s], box 262, CBC/CHS; Madam C. J. Walker advertisement, 1925, MWC/IHS; Madam C. J. Walker Beauty Shoppe advertisement, *New York Amsterdam News*, 17 June 1925; Apex advertisement, *Apex News*, November–December 1935; Plough's advertisement, *Chicago Defender*, 13 March 1926; Golden Brown advertisements, *New York Amsterdam News*, 11 August 1923, 10 June 1925.

40. Madam C. J. Walker advertisement, *Pittsburgh Courier*, 1 December 1923; Golden Brown advertisement, *Chicago Defender*, 10 June 1925; Edwards, *Southern Urban Negro*, 251.

41. Golden Brown advertisement, *Chicago Defender*, 11 August 1923; McBrady and Company advertisement, early twentieth century, cosmetics box 3, WCBA/NMAH; Plough's advertisement, *Chicago Defender*, 25 August 1923.

2. "Everyone Admires the Woman Who Has Beautiful Hair"

1. Madam C. J. Walker advertisement, [1920], box 11, MWC/IHS; *New York Interstate Tattler*, Lonesome Hearts, 26 April 1929, 1 February 1929.

2. *Poro Hair and Beauty Culture*, 1922, box 262, CBC/CHS. For an extensive biography of Malone and the Poro Company, see Robinson, "Class, Race, and Gender."

3. Madam C. J. Walker advertisement, 1928, box 11, MWC/IHS; Madam C. J. Walker newspaper advertisement, [1920s], box 262, CBC/CHS. Much has been written on Walker and her company. See esp. Robinson, "Class, Race, and Gender"; A'Lelia Bundles, *On Her Own Ground: The Life and Times of Madam C. J. Walker* (New York: Scribner, 2001); Rooks, *Hair Raising*; and Blackwelder, *Styling Jim Crow*.

4. Walker newspaper advertisement, [1920s], box 262, CBC/CHS. On advertising and the middle-class obsession with hygiene and personal appearance, see Lears, *Fables of Abundance*, chap. 6. On the efforts of the urban black middle class to impose its standards of grooming on African American migrants, see Carby, "Policing the Black Woman's Body," 739–55.

5. Marjorie Joyner, interview, *Two Dollars and a Dream*, directed by Stanley Nelson (New York: Diversity Video Project, 1980); Marjorie Joyner, Violet Reynolds, and southern beauty culturists, interviews, *Nine Leaves on a Sprig*, directed by Tom Alvarez (Indianapolis: WRTV, 1980).

6. Overton Hygienic advertisement, *Half-Century Magazine*, November–December 1922; Kashmir promotional letter, [1919], box 262, CBC/CHS; "Sarah Washington" in *Notable Black American Women*, vol. 1, ed. Jessie Carney Smith (Detroit: Gale Research, 1992), 1224.

7. Poro advertisement, *Chicago Defender*, 14 June 1924.

8. U.S. Bureau of the Census, *Census of Population: Occupations* (Washington, D.C.: GPO, 1920, 1930, 1940).

9. Madam C. J. Walker Manufacturing Company, news release, 1917, box 12, MWC/IHC; C. J. Walker to F. B. Ransom, 6 March 1918, box 1, MWC/HIS; *The Madam C. J. Walker Beauty Manual: A Thorough Treatise Covering All Branches of Beauty Culture* (Indianapolis: Walker, 1928), foreword; Madam C. J. Walker advertisement, *Chicago Defender*, 23 January 1926; Marjorie Stewart Joyner, interview by Toni Costonie, 1983–1984, box 28, MJP/CPL.

10. Madam C. J. Walker Company pamphlet, 1928, box 13, MWC/IHS; Poro advertisement, *Pittsburgh Courier*, 26 June 1926; *Poro Hair and Beauty Culture*, 1924; Apex advertisement, *Apex News*, March 1929; *Apex News*, December 1929, January–February 1930.

11. *Apex News*, "What the Rambling Grads Are Doing," January–February–March 1938, 32, 34, Summer 1938, 34, June 1929, 4.

12. Ethel Erickson, *Employment Conditions in Beauty Shops: A Study of Four Cities*, U.S. Department of Labor Women's Bureau, Bulletin no. 133 (Washington, D.C.: GPO, 1935), 37–45; Vivian Morris, "Harlem Beauty Shops," American Life Histories: Manuscripts from the Federal Writers' Project, 1936–1940, available from http://lcweb2.loc.gov/ammem/wpaintro/wpahome.html.

13. Madam C. J. Walker Company pamphlet, 1928, box 13, MWC/IHS

14. LeRoy Jeffries, "The Decay of the Beauty Parlor Industry in Harlem," *Opportunity*, February 1938, 52.

15. Erickson, *Employment Conditions in Beauty Shops*, 39–43; Willett, *Permanent Waves*, 105; Jeffries, "Decay of the Beauty Parlor Industry," 52; "Preliminary Report on a Survey of Negro Beauty Shops in the District of Columbia," November 1939, unpublished studies and materials, 1919–1972, WB/NA.

16. *Negro World*, "I Am a Negro—And Beautiful," 10 July 1926; *Negro World*, "Are We Proud of Our Black Skins and Curly Hair?" 1 August 1925.

17. Marjorie Stewart Joyner, interview by Michael Flug, 4 May 1993, MJP/CPL; Bundles, *On Her Own Ground*, 92, 153, 195; Rooks, *Hair Raising*, 87; Higginbotham, *Righteous Discontent*, 195–96, 200.

18. Peiss, *Hope in a Jar*, 113; Rooks, *Hair Raising*, 63; Madam C. J. Walker Company pamphlet, 1928, box 13, MWC/IHS; *Walker News*, "The Newest in Beauty Culture Language," September 1928; Joyner, interview by Flug; Joyner quoted in *Two Dollars and a Dream*.

19. Elizabeth Cardozo Barker, interview by Marcia Greenlee, 8 December 1976, in *The Black Women Oral History Project: From the Arthur and Elizabeth Schlesinger Library on the History of Women in America, Radcliffe College*, ed. Ruth Edmonds Hill (Westport, Conn.: Meckler, 1991), 108–9; Catherine Cardozo Lewis, interview by Marcia Greenlee, 12 September 1980, in Hill, *Black Women Oral History Project*, 259.

20. Rooks, *Hair Raising*, 34, 45.

21. Golden Peacock advertisement, *Chicago Defender*, 6 March 1926; Nadinola advertisement, *Pittsburgh Courier*, 7 May 1927; Plough's advertisements, *Chicago Defender*, 11 July 1931, 4 July 1931; Rooks, *Hair Raising*, 29–30.

22. Plough's advertisement, *Chicago Defender*, 2 December 1933; Golden Brown advertisement, *Chicago Defender*, 4 September 1928; Plough's advertisement, *Chicago Defender*, 4 July 1931.

23. Madam C. J. Walker advertisements, *Chicago Defender*, 14 April 1928, 23 January 1926, 17 October 1930; Barker, interview by Greenlee, 98.

24. Murray's Superior Products advertisement, *Abbott's Monthly*, March 1931; *Poro Hair and Beauty Culture*, 1922; Apex advertisements, *Apex News*, August–September 1931, November–December 1935.

25. Langston Hughes and Milton Meltzer, *Black Magic: A Pictorial History of the Negro in American Entertainment* (New York: Pantheon, 1968), 97–103; Phyllis Rose, *Jazz Cleopatra: Josephine Baker in Her Time* (New York: Vintage, 1991), 53–57; Daphne Duval Harrison, *Black Pearls: Blues Queens of the 1920s* (New Brunswick: Rutgers University Press, 1988), 182. On the role of chorus girls in helping to set more sexualized beauty standards for American women in general, see Angela Latham, *Posing a Threat: Flappers, Chorus Girls, and Other Brazen Performers of the American 1920s* (Hanover, N.H.: University Press of New England, 2000).

26. Rose, *Jazz Cleopatra*, 53; Linda Mizejewski, *Ziegfeld Girl: Image and Icon in Culture and Cinema* (Durham, N.C.: Duke University Press, 1999), 123–31.

27. Peiss, *Hope in a Jar*, 124, 126; White and White, *Stylin'*, 208.

28. Plough's advertisements, *Chicago Defender*, 20 March 1926, 6 February 1926.

29. Golden Brown advertisement, *Chicago Defender*, 11 August 1923; Plough's advertisement, *Chicago Defender*, 27 February 1926; Hi-Ja advertisements, *Chicago Defender*, 5 May 1923, 12 June 1926.

30. Hi-Ja advertisement, *Chicago Defender*, 12 June 1926; Plough's advertisement, *Chicago Defender*, 6 February 1926; Hi-Ja advertisement, *Chicago Defender*, 5 May 1923; Plough's advertisement, *Pittsburgh Courier*, 26 June 1926; Plough's advertisement, *Chicago Defender*, 27 February 1926; Golden Brown advertisement, *Chicago Defender*, 4 September 1928.

31. White and White, *Stylin'*, 198–201; Craig, *Ain't I a Beauty Queen*, 47–59; Apex beauty contest advertisement, *Apex News*, November 1929.

32. Craig, *Ain't I a Beauty Queen*, 47; *Half-Century Magazine*, "Who Is the Prettiest Colored Girl in the United States?" November 1921; *Half-Century Magazine*, "Who Is the Prettiest Colored Girl in the United States?" September 1921.

33. *Half-Century Magazine*, "Types of Racial Beauty," June 1919, 7; Craig, *Ain't I a Beauty Queen*, 40–42.

34. Craig, *Ain't I a Beauty Queen*, 39–40; Smith song in Angela Y. Davis, *Blues Legacies and Black Feminism: Gertrude "Ma" Rainey, Bessie Smith, and Billie Holiday* (New York: Pantheon, 1998), 356; Maya Angelou, *I Know Why the Caged Bird Sings* (New York: Bantam, 1971), 49, 58.

35. Annabelle Baker, "Severed," in *Tenderheaded: A Comb-Bending Collection of Hair Stories*, ed. Juliette Harris and Pamela Johnson (New York: Pocket Books, 2001), 16–17; Morris, "Harlem Beauty Shops." The translations are Morris's.

36. Madam C. J. Walker Manufacturing Company, closing entries, 31 December 1920, box 31, MWC/IHS; Walker advertisement, *Norfolk (Va.) Journal and Guide*, 3 January 1925; *Walker News*, Agent News, September 1928, Febru-

ary 1930; *Walker News*, "Practical Hints," July 1930; Morris, "Harlem Beauty Shops."

37. *New York Interstate Tattler*, Lonesome Hearts, 8 February 1929, 29 March 1929, 26 April 1929, 2 August 1929, 1 February 1929, 22 November 1929.

38. Ibid., 26 April 1929, 2 August 1929, 19 July 1929, 1 February 1929.

39. Poro advertisement, *Pittsburgh Courier*, 2 June 1923; Evelyn Northington, "The Care of the Hair," *Half-Century Magazine*, November 1920, 18; Overton Hygienic advertisement, *Half-Century Magazine*, November 1921; Poro advertisement, *Pittsburgh Courier*, 11 April 1931; Marguerita Ward advertisement, *Abbott's Monthly*, October 1932.

40. Lelia Walker to F. B. Ransom, 15 March 1927, box 4, MWC/IHS.

41. For an overview of the influence of skin color on social status in African American society, see Craig, *Ain't I a Beauty Queen*, and Kathy Russell, Midge Wilson, and Ronald Hall, *The Color Complex: The Politics of Skin Color among African Americans* (New York: Harcourt Brace Jovanovich, 1992). For a discussion of mulattos during slavery, see Eugene D. Genovese, "Miscegenation," in *Roll, Jordan, Roll: The World the Slaves Made* (New York: Vintage Books, 1972), 413–31, and Willard B. Gatewood, *Aristocrats of Color: The Black Elite, 1880–1920* (Bloomington: Indiana University Press, 1990), 150–54. For more on the significance of color in African American culture, see Winthrop Jordan, *White over Black: American Attitudes toward the Negro, 1550–1812* (Chapel Hill: University of North Carolina Press, 1968); George M. Fredrickson, *The Black Image in the White Mind: The Debate on Afro-American Character and Destiny, 1817–1914* (New York: Harper and Row, 1971); and Mia Bay, *The White Image in the Black Mind* (New York: Oxford University Press, 2000).

42. Robinson, "Class, Race, and Gender," 526.

43. White and White, *Stylin'*, 169–71; Barnett to Malone, 8 February 1929, box 262, CBC/CHS; Morris, "Harlem Beauty Shops."

3. "An 'Export' Market at Home"

1. Jacqueline Jones, *Labor of Love, Labor of Sorrow: Black Women, Work, and the Family from Slavery to the Present* (New York: Random House, 1985), 237. On consumerism in the immediate postwar period, see Cohen, *Consumers' Republic*, chap. 3. On African American migration and economic opportunities during World War II, see Kenneth L. Kusmer, "African Americans in the City since World War II: From the Industrial to the Post-Industrial Era," *Journal of Urban History* 21, no. 4 (1995): 458–504.

2. Weems, *Desegregating the Dollar*, 34, 39, 41–42.

3. David J. Sullivan, "The American Negro—an 'Export' Market at Home!" *Printer's Ink*, 21 July 1944, 90. Of the few prominent white companies that advertised in black newspapers in the 1920s and 1930s, most were based in cities with large black populations. For example, Chicago-based Colgate-Palmolive and Wrigley's advertised in the *Chicago Defender* in these years.

4. Weems, *Desegregating the Dollar*, 35–36.

5. Negro Market Organization pamphlet, 1945, box 131, CBC/CHS; *Publishers Weekly*, "National Negro Market Survey Shows $12 Billion Expenditures," 5 July 1947, 34; Research Company of America, *Washington's 28% Plus Market* (Research Company of America, 1945).

6. Sullivan, "American Negro," 90; *Tide*, "Negro Markets," 15 March 1946, 86, 88; Negro Market Organization pamphlet, 1945; Research Company of America, *Washington's 28% Plus Market*.

7. *Tide*, "The Negro Market: An Appraisal," 7 March 1947, 15.

8. Ibid., 16; Eddie Ellis, "Is EBONY a Negro Magazine?" pts. 1 and 2, *Liberator*, October 1965, 4–5, November 1965, 18–19; Jones, *Labor of Love*, 269–70.

9. Weems, *Desegregating the Dollar*, 70–74.

10. J. Walter Thompson Company records, box 10, CJC/NMAH; D. Parke Gibson, "Creating Products for Negro Consumers," *Marketing Magazine*, 1 May 1969, 61–65; Weems, *Desegregating the Dollar*, 76.

11. David Sullivan to Madam C. J. Walker Company, 1945, box 10, MWC/IHS; Madam C. J. Walker Company sales records, box 31, MWC/IHS. A Lucky Heart cosmetic product catalogue from 1946 offered a range of hair pomades and dressings, soaps, lotion, skin bleaches, and face powders. Lucky Heart Company, *Lucky Heart Agent's Catalogue and Beauty Book* (Memphis, [1940]), RBC/NYPL.

12. Barnett's correspondence with beauty culture businesses is full of encouragements to invest in his advertising and press release services. The correspondence suggests spotty results. See, for example, Claude A. Barnett to Robert L. Brokenburr, Madam C. J. Walker Company, 29 December 1948; Claude A. Barnett to Marjorie Joyner, United Beauty Shop Owners and Teachers Association, 15 October 1955; and Claude A. Barnett to Constance Curtis, Rose-Meta Beauty Products Company, 20 July 1954, all in box 262, CBC/CHS.

13. *Sales Management*, 1943, quoted in Sullivan to Madam C. J. Walker Company, 1945; Snow White advertisement, *Ebony*, August 1947; Royal Crown advertisements, *Ebony*, October 1958, May 1956; Dixie Peach advertisements, *Ebony*, May 1957, September 1961. Although the examples I cite in this chapter are from *Ebony*, these advertisements also appeared in other African American magazines.

14. Posner advertisement, *Ebony*, August 1960; Supreme Beauty Products advertisement, *Ebony*, August 1960; Johnson Products advertisements, *Ebony*, November 1959, March 1962, February 1963; Apex advertisements, *Ebony*, May 1960, July 1957.

15. White and White, *Stylin'*, chaps. 6, 8; Hunter, *To 'joy My Freedom*, chap. 8; Kelley, *Race Rebels*, chap. 2.

16. White and White, *Stylin'*, 185. For a detailed comparative analysis of the male conk and the female press-and-style during the 1940s and 1950s, see Maxine Craig, "The Decline and Fall of the Conk; or, How to Read a Process," *Fashion Theory* 1, no. 4 (December 1997): 399–419.

17. Silky Strate advertisement, *Jet*, 12 May 1955; Perma-Strate advertisements, *Ebony*, May 1957, November 1949; Craig, "Decline and Fall of the Conk," 404–9.

18. *Our World*, May 1946, 36; *Our World*, "Color, Milady, Color," April 1949, 53.

19. Artra advertisement, *Ebony*, May 1962; Golden Peacock advertisements, *Ebony*, April 1957, June 1957; Dr Fred Palmer advertisement, *Ebony*, June 1962; Bleach and Glow advertisements, *Ebony*, May 1963, November 1963; Posner advertisements, *Ebony*, December 1960, June 1961; Nadinola advertisements, *Ebony*, November 1963, May 1959, December 1961, August 1953, June 1963, May 1953.

20. W. B. Ransom to Mark Gross, 11 September 1953, box 9, MWC/IHS; Lustrasilk advertisement, *Ebony*, December 1953. Several advertisements for Madam C. J. Walker products throughout the early 1950s used the "natural beauty" theme. See, for example, Madam C. J. Walker advertisements, *Ebony*, November 1952, July 1954, October 1953.

21. Murray's Superior Products advertisement, *Ebony*, May 1946; Apex advertisements, *Ebony*, December 1956, April 1957, July 1957, May 1964.

22. Thyra Edwards, "What Shall I Do with My Hair?" *Our World*, April 1946, 31; Peiss, *Hope in a Jar*, 10–12, 23–24, 152–54.

4. "Beauty Services Offered from Head to Toe"

1. *Ebony*, "House of Beauty: Rose-Meta Salon Is Biggest Negro Beauty Parlor in the World," May 1946, 25; Rose Morgan, interview by James Murray, Morgan's salon, New York City, 1988, RBC/NYPL; Woody Taylor, "Here's a $31,000 Beauty Enterprise," *Baltimore Afro-American*, 15 November 1947, magazine section; Blackwelder, *Styling Jim Crow*, 31–32.

2. Arnold C. de Mille, "For New Glamour Today," *Pulse*, April 1943, 17; *Ebony*, "Rose-Meta Salon," 25; Taylor, "Here's a $31,000 Beauty Enterprise"; Bob Queen, "Thriving Beauty Shops Prove Women Pay for Glamour," *Baltimore Afro-American*, 18 October 1947, magazine section; Ruby Smith, "Modern Beauticians Replace 'Hairdressers,'" *Baltimore Afro-American*, 18 October 1947, magazine section; Betty Granger, "Houses That Beauty Built," *New York Age*, 28 May 1949, 18; *Ebony*, "Harlem's New House of Beauty," June 1955, 62; *Ebony*, "Detroit House of Beauty," December 1951, 117.

3. Willett, *Permanent Waves*, 126, 135; Barker, interview by Greenlee, 102; Morgan, interview by Murray; Taylor, "Here's a $31,000 Beauty Enterprise"; Queen, "Thriving Beauty Shops."

4. de Mille, "For New Glamour Today," 17; *Ebony*, "Detroit House of Beauty," 117; Lewis, interview by Greenlee, 259; Granger, "Houses That Beauty Built," 18.

5. de Mille, "For New Glamour Today," 17; *Ebony*, "Harlem's New House of Beauty," 62; *Ebony*, "Detroit House of Beauty," 117; Taylor, "Here's a $31,000 Beauty Enterprise."

6. Trotter and Lewis, *African Americans in the Industrial Age*, 251.

7. Morgan, interview by Murray; Barker, interview by Greenlee, 114.

8. Morris, "Harlem Beauty Shops"; Alice Murray, "Reader Talk: Compassion, Determination, and Hardwork," *Shoptalk*, Spring 1988, 10–12, quoted in Willett, *Permanent Waves*, 147.

9. Barker, interview by Greenlee, 102–3, 114.

10. Barker, interview by Greenlee, 118; *Poro Hair and Beauty Culture*, 1924, box 262, CBC/CHS; Barker, interview by Greenlee, 114.

11. Barker, interview by Greenlee, 128. Apprentices were approved by most state cosmetology boards in 1956. Mary-Elizabeth Pidgeon and Agness W. Mitchell, *Employment Opportunities for Women in Beauty Service*, U.S. Department of Labor Women's Bureau, Bulletin no. 260 (Washington, D.C.: GPO, 1956), 24.

12. Barker, interview by Greenlee, 108.

13. Ibid., 108, 110; Morgan, interview by Murray; *Ebony*, "Detroit House of Beauty," 121.

14. Holmes quoted in Taylor, "Here's a $31,000 Beauty Enterprise"; Wood endorsement enclosed in W. B. Ransom to Mark Gross, 7 July 1953, box 9, MWC/IHS; *Walker Newsletter*, March 1949, March 1955, box 12, MWC/IHS.

15. Robert Brokenburr to Marjorie Joyner, 18 October 1949, box 8, MJP/CPL; *Beauty Trade*, "Integrated Beauty Salon Prospers in Detroit's Federal Department Store," December 1966, 27; *Chicago Defender*, 1949, box 90, MJP/CPL; Rushing, "Hair Raising," 330.

16. See, for example, *Muhammad Speaks*, 31 August 1962, 15 September 1962, 30 September 1962, 30 November 1962, 30 December 1962, and 15 January 1963.

17. Deborah E. McDowell, *Leaving Pipe Shop: Memories of Kin* (New York: Scribner, 1996), 52–53; Henry Louis Gates Jr., "It All Comes Down to the Kitchen," in Harris and Johnson, *Tenderheaded*, 24; bell hooks, "Straightening Our Hair," in Harris and Johnson, *Tenderheaded*, 111.

18. Ed Brandford, "What Is Negro Beauty?" *Our World*, November 1947, 35.

19. *Jet*, "The World's Best-Dressed Woman," 29 November 1951, 32; Rose, *Jazz Cleopatra*, 211, 167–75.

20. Donald Bogle, *Toms, Coons, Mulattos, Mammies, and Bucks: An Interpretive History of Blacks in American Films*, 3rd ed. (New York: Continuum, 1994), 125–27.

21. *Our World*, "What Is Sex Appeal?" July 1952, 59; E. Sims Campbell, "The Perfect Negro Beauty," *Jet*, 13 March 1957, 6.

22. *Our World*, "How Evil Is Eartha?" September 1954, 10; *Our World*, "Can Dandridge Outshine Lena Horne?" June 1952, 29; *Jet*, "Hollywood's Unknown Negro Beauties," 22 November 1951, 58–61; Bogle, *Toms, Coons, Mulattos, Mammies, and Bucks*, 161.

23. *Our World*, "Lena Horne: *Our World's* First Cover Girl," April 1950, 11–13. Also see James Haskins, *Lena: A Personal and Political Biography* (New York: Stein and Day, 1984).

24. *Jet*, "Why Brownskin Girls Get the Best Movie Roles," 16 October 1952, 56–59; Haskins, *Lena*, 51; Jim Goodrich and A. S. Young, "Why Hollywood Won't Glamorize Negro Girls," *Jet*, 17 September 1953, 56–59.

25. *Our World*, "What Happened to the Brandford Models?" February 1954, 30–31; Peiss, *Hope in a Jar*, 256; *Color*, "Is Beauty a Curse?" February 1953, 23.

26. White and White, *Stylin'*, 209; Claude A. Barnett to Edgar McDaniel, 28 April 1925, box 262, CBC/CHS.

27. Raveen advertisement, *Ebony*, December 1960; Lustrasilk advertisement, *Ebony*, December 1955; June Taylor to Madam C. J. Walker Company, 1959, box 9, MWC/IHS; Silky Strate advertisements, *Ebony*, March 1957, April 1957, November 1957.

28. *Ebony*, "Model School: First Interracial Charm School Runs Hit West Coast Fashion Show," July 1948, 36; *Our World*, "The Glamazons: Beauty by the Ton," November 1954, 71–74.

29. *Ebony*, "Model Schools: Racket or Business?" September 1950, 73–76.

30. *Ebony*, "Is It True What They Say about Models?" November 1951, 60–64.

31. "What Makes a Model?" *Our World*, October 1953, 34, 36; *Ebony*, "Can Negro Models Make the Bigtime?" September 1954; 100–102; *Our World*, "Glamazons," 71–74.

32. *Ebony*, "Paris Model: Los Angeles Girl Gets Schiaparelli Job to Become Only Negro in Fashion Capital of the World," February 1950, 51–57; *Our World*, "Dorothea Towles: Paris' Fabulous Negro Model," August 1952, 44; *Sepia*, "The Private Life of Dorothea Towles," November 1959, 8–9.

33. Kobena Mercer, "Black Hair/Style Politics," in *Out There: Marginalization and Contemporary Cultures*, ed. Russell Ferguson, Martha Gever, Trinh T. Minh-ha, and Cornel West (New York: New Museum of Contemporary Art, 1990), 259; *Jet*, "Brown Blondes of Show Business," 23 July 1953, 30–31; *Jet*, "News Bulletin," 31 March 1955, 58.

5. "All Hair Is Good Hair"

1. On civil rights and consumerism, see Weems, *Desegregating the Dollar*, 61–69; Cohen, *Consumers' Republic*, 166–91; Eric Foner, *The Story of American Freedom* (New York: Norton, 1998), 278.

2. Taylor Branch, *Parting the Waters: American in the King Years, 1954–1964* (New York: Simon and Schuster, 1988), 273; Kelley, *Race Rebels*, 87–88.

3. Anne Moody, *Coming of Age in Mississippi* (1968; repr., New York: Dell, 1976), 267–68.

4. Michelle Wallace, "A Black Woman's Search for Sisterhood," in *All the Women Are White, All the Blacks Are Men, but Some of Us Are Brave: Black Women's Studies*, ed. Gloria T. Hull, Patricia Bell Scott, and Barbara Smith (Old Westbury, N.Y.: Feminist Press, 1982), 5.

5. Gladys L. Porter, *Three Negro Pioneers in Beauty Culture* (New York: Vantage Press, 1966), 18. Julia Kirk Blackwelder, whose study of African American beauty training focuses in large part on Texas, observes that Texas regulations for training were also segregated, which does not mesh with Porter's memory of having to learn methods for "white" hair while her white friend had to learn methods for "black" hair. Blackwelder does mention that Texas law did not prevent a beauty student from learning to do "the other race's" hair, but she

would have to take two certification exams to qualify to work on women of both races. Blackwelder, *Styling Jim Crow*, 85–86.

6. Porter, *Three Negro Pioneers*, 19.

7. *Ebony*, "Harlem's New House of Beauty," 62–68; Morgan, interview by Murray; Barker, interview by Greenlee, 259; *Ebony*, "Rose-Meta Campaigns against Idea Negro Hair Inferior," May 1946, 27; Taylor, "Here's a $31,000 Beauty Enterprise."

8. *Our World*, "Beauty Is His World," March 1955, 59; Barker, interview by Greenlee, 98, 106.

9. Barker, interview by Greenlee, 99, 104–5.

10. Joyner, interview by Costonie, 1983–1984, box 28, MJP/CPL.

11. *Beauty Trade*, "Integrated Beauty Salon Prospers," 25–27; *Beauty Trade*, "Coiffure Show," February 1965, 8–11; Peiss, *Hope in a Jar*, 257.

12. Associated Negro Press, news release, 26 April 1950, box 261, CBC/CHS; *Jet*, "119 Beauticians to Study in France," 3 December 1953, 22; *Our World*, "Beauty Train to Paris," August 1954, 62; Joyner, interview by Costonie.

13. Tiffany Melissa Gill, "'I Had My Own Business . . . So I Didn't Have to Worry': Beauty Salons, Beauty Culturists, and the Politics of African American Female Entrepreneurship," in *Beauty and Business: Commerce, Gender, and Culture in Modern America*, ed. Philip Scranton (New York: Routledge, 2001), 188; Morgan, interview by Murray; *Jet*, "Named 1st Negro Woman to Florida State Post," 30 June 1955, 7; *Ebony*, "Integration Comes to the Beauty Business," August 1966, 143.

14. Barker, interview by Greenlee, 106; Gill, "'I Had My Own Business,'" 188, 190; United Beauty School Owners and Teachers Association, news release, 25 January 1958, box 5, MJP/CPL.

15. Peter Bart, "Advertising: Role of Negroes Is Discussed," *New York Times*, 6 October 1963; Claude H. Hall, "The Negro Market: White Models in Negro Media," *Pittsburgh Courier*, 9 February 1963; Madam C. J. Walker flyer, [1960], box 11, MWC/IHS; Apex advertisement, *Ebony*, November 1967; Supreme Beauty Products advertisement, *Ebony*, October 1972; Nadinola advertisement, *Ebony*, February 1970; Artra advertisement, *Ebony*, September 1964.

16. Apex advertisement, *Ebony*, May 1963.

17. *Jet*, "Hollywood's Unknown Negro Beauties," 59; Goodrich and Young, "Why Hollywood Won't Glamorize Negro Girls," 58–59.

18. *Jet*, "Paris Model Has Dazzling Wardrobe," 6 December 1951; *Our World*, "Paris' Fabulous Negro Model"; *Our World*, "What Makes a Model?"; *Our World*, "What Happened to the Brandford Models"; *Ebony*, "Can Negro Models Make the Bigtime"; E. Simms Campbell, "Are Black Women Beautiful?" *Negro Digest*, June 1951; *Ebony*, "Are Negro Girls Getting Prettier?" February 1966; *Hue*, "Are Whites Accepting Brown Beauties?" July 1954.

19. A. S. Young, "Beauty in Negro Women," *Sepia*, September 1963, 42, 47.

20. See, for example, ibid., 42–48; *Ebony*, "Detroit Beauty Queen," September 1962, 23–24; and *Ebony*, "New Trend toward Black Beauties," December 1967, 164–70. Also see White and White, *Stylin'*, 180–218.

21. *Pittsburgh Courier*, "Artra Sponsors Negro Models on T.V. 'Gospel Time,'"

8 December 1962; *Jet*, "Industry Makes Room for Negro Models," 19 December 1963, 46–49; *Sepia*, "Precola Devore's Charm School," December 1964, 39; *Muhammad Speaks*, "Many Negro Women Favor New African-Type Hairdos," April 1963, 17.

22. *Ebony*, "Have Black Models Really Made It?" May 1970, 152–53.

23. Craig, *Ain't I a Beauty Queen*, 59–77; *Eyes*, "Cinderella Show," August 1946, 39–41; *Our World*, Search for Beauty, December 1950, 6, February 1951, 6–7, March 1951, 58–60; *Jet*, "What Happens to Beauty Queens?" 20 March 1952, 32–37; *Our World*, "Miss Bronze Los Angeles," August 1952, 25; *Our World*, "Philadelphia's Miss Sepia," January 1953, 61; *Sepia*, "Will There Ever Be a Black Miss America?" February 1975, 28–35.

24. *Jet*, "What Happens to Beauty Queens," 35, 37; *Ebony*, "Beauty Queens of 1959," September 1959, 116.

25. *Ebony*, "Detroit Beauty Queen," 23; *Ebony*, "Negro Girl in Miss America Race," July 1965, 70; *Ebony*, "Brown Beauty with Courage," October 1966; *Jet*, "Beauty Queens at White Schools," 30 November 1967.

26. *Ebony*, "New Trend toward Black Beauties," 164–70.

27. *Muhammad Speaks*, December 1961, 24; Fannie E. Granton, "Pride in Blackness and Natural Hairdo Led to Spirited Campaign," *Jet*, 10 November 1966, 48–53; *Ebony*, "Capital's Proud Black Princess," July 1970, 105; *New York Times*, "Miss Iowa, 19, First Negro in Miss America Contest," 16 June 1970.

6. "Black Is Beautiful"

Portions of the material in this chapter appeared, in an earlier version, in "Black Is Profitable: The Commodification of the Afro, 1960–1975," in *Beauty and Business: Commerce, Gender, and Culture in Modern America*, ed. Philip Scranton (New York: Routledge, 2001), 254–77.

1. Angela Y. Davis, "Afro Images: Politics, Fashion, and Nostalgia," in *Soul: Black Power, Politics, and Pleasure*, ed. Monique Guillory and Richard C. Green (New York: New York University Press, 1998), 23, 28.

2. Weems, *Desegregating the Dollar*, 76. For an excellent case study of the practical interplay between civil rights liberalism and Black Power separatism among black activists seeking political power in their northern urban communities, see Matthew J. Countryman, *Up South: Civil Rights and Black Power in Philadelphia* (Philadelphia: University of Pennsylvania Press, 2006).

3. Weems, *Desegregating the Dollar*, 80; *Sales Management*, "The Soul Market in Black and White," 1 June 1969, 37; Zebra Associates, news release, 1969, Zebra Associates records, box 11, CJC/NMAH.

4. Copywriters workshop, 1964–1965, box 10, CJC/NMAH; "Hair," [1969–1970], Zebra Associates records, box 11, CJC/NMAH.

5. Ethel Malvik, "The Black Cosmetics Market," *American Druggist*, 21 September 1970, 66; *Drug and Cosmetics Industry*, "Now It's Nancy Wilson with a New Cosmetic Line!" March 1971, 66; *Drug and Cosmetics Industry*, "A Celebrity for Negro Cosmetics," February 1971, 43; *Drug and Cosmetics Industry*, "Libra: New Line of Negro Cosmetics," December 1969, 44–46; *Drug*

and Cosmetics Industry, "Negro Cosmetics: Seminar Assesses Special Needs," October 1969, 66.

6. Posner advertisements, *Ebony*, March 1971, December 1970, May 1970; Malvik, "Black Cosmetics Market," 67.

7. Avon advertisement, 1969, National Black Advertising, AC/HML; Avon television storyboards and radio scripts, 1975, National Black Advertising, AC/HML. The use of countercultural images and language in 1960s advertising was a broad trend that crossed racial boundaries. For a good study of this phenomenon (though it does not discuss the "soul" market), see Thomas Frank, *The Conquest of Cool: Business Culture, Counterculture, and the Rise of Hip Consumerism* (Chicago: University of Chicago Press, 1997).

8. Fashion Fair advertisements, *Ebony*, December 1974, September 1975.

9. Nadinola advertisement, *Ebony*, October 1968.

10. Robin D. G. Kelley, "Nap Time: Historicizing the Afro," *Fashion Theory* 1, no. 4 (December 1997): 341; Craig, *Ain't I a Beauty Queen*, 78; Craig, "Decline and Fall of the Conk," 404–9; Phyl Garland, "The Natural Look," *Ebony*, June 1966, 143.

11. Baker, "Severed," 15, 18.

12. Rushing, *Hair Raising*, 234; Craig, *Ain't I a Beauty Queen*, 79–84.

13. Wallace, "Black Woman's Search," 5–6.

14. Helen Hays King, "Should Women Straighten Their Hair?—No!" *Negro Digest*, August 1963, 65, 68–71; Margaret Burroughs, "Down the Straight and Narrow," *Urbanite*, May 1961, 15.

15. June Lirhue, "The New Abbey Lincoln: A Voice of Protest," *Pittsburgh Courier*, 27 May 1961; *Muhammad Speaks*, "The Natural Look Is Reborn in Brilliant New Show," 9 February 1963, 12; Associated Negro Press, "Many Women Favor New African-Type Hairdos," *Muhammad Speaks*, April 1963, 17; Rose Nelms, "Natural Hair Yes, Hot Irons No," *Liberator*, July 1963, 13. For more on Abbey Lincoln, the Grandessa models, and other early attempts to make the natural fashionable, see Craig, *Ain't I a Beauty Queen*, 87–88.

16. *New York Amsterdam News*, "Will 'Natural' Style Be the New Hair-Do?" 10 March 1962; Associated Negro Press, "'Au Naturelle' Revue Sparks Controversy," *Pittsburgh Courier*, 9 March 1963. *Muhammad Speaks* ran most of the same Associated Negro Press article under quite a different headline: "Many Negro Women Favor New African-Type Hairdos."

17. Van Deburg, *New Day in Babylon*, 17; Maxine B. Craig, "Black Is Beautiful: Personal Transformation and Political Change" (Ph.D. diss., University of California, Berkeley, 1996), 96–101.

18. *Ebony*, letters to the editor, August 1966; Leatha Chadiha, "A Study of Black Beauty Culture and Values About Beauty in Black Society" (master's thesis, Washington State University, 1970), 13; Abernathy quoted in Peter Goldman, *Report from Black America* (New York: Simon and Schuster, 1969), 157.

19. Rushing, "Hair Raising," 334; Craig, *Ain't I a Beauty Queen*, 122.

20. Wallace, "Black Woman's Search," 6; Craig, *Ain't I a Beauty Queen*, 92; Garland, "Natural Look," 143.

21. Eldridge Cleaver, "As Crinkly as Yours," *Negro History Bulletin* 30 (March 1962): 127–32; Eleanor Mason, "Hot Irons and Black Nationalism," *Liberator*, May 1963, 22.

22. Garland, "Natural Look," 144; *Sepia*, "Los Angeles Goes 'Natural,'" January 1967, 60; Willie L. Morrow, *400 Years without a Comb: The Untold Story* (San Diego: Black Publishers of America, 1973), 19, 86.

23. *Jet*, "Afro Hairdo Upsets African Writer," 15 October 1970, 45; Mercer, "Black Hair/Style Politics," 247–64.

24. *Ebony*, "The Natural Look—Is It Here To Stay?" January 1969, 108; Sylvester Leak, "The Revolution in Hair Grooming—Is the Black Beautician Losing Fight for Life?" *Muhammad Speaks*, 26 February 1965, 21; *Jet*, "Beauty Shop Business Suffers 20% Decline," 26 March 1970, 49, 50; Lewis, interview by Greenlee, 261.

25. Craig, *Ain't I a Beauty Queen*, 101, 104.

26. *Jet*, "What Are Naturals Doing to Beauty and Barber Shops?" 26 March 1970, 46–51; *Jet*, "The Afro: A Natural Groove or a Natural Mess?" 13 July 1972, 16.

27. *Ebony*, "Natural Look—Is It Here To Stay?" 109; Marie Cooke, "Wear Your Natural Beautifully and Proudly," *Dawn Magazine*, 25 May 1974, 12; Marjorie Joyner, "Naturals Paying Off!" *Beauty Trade*, May 1969, 12; Morgan, interview by Murray; Margaret Cardozo Holmes, interview by Marcia Greenlee, 9 November 1977, in Hill, *Black Women Oral History Project*, 112.

28. Gill, "'I Had My Own Business,'" 188–90.

29. W. B. Ransom to grocery store managers, [1960s], box 11, MWC/IHS; Garland, "Natural Look," 146; *Sepia*, "Los Angeles Goes 'Natural,'" 60.

30. Murray's Superior Products advertisement, *Ebony*, February 1970, March 1971; James F. Forkan, "Who's Who in $350,000,000 Black Grooming Market," *Advertising Age*, 20 November 1972, 96; Murray's Superior Products advertisements, *Tuesday Magazine*, April 1969, June 1968; Murray's Superior Products advertisements, *Ebony*, June 1971, April 1971.

31. Raymond Oladipupo, "All-out Marketing Keeps Clairol Ahead with Negro Women," *Media-Scope*, September 1969, 18; Clairol advertisement, *Tuesday Magazine*, October 1972; offprints of print advertisements and radio advertisement scripts, 1961–1980, Record Group I, boxes OS-37, OS-38, and OS-39, National Black Advertising, AC/HML. Mrs. Willie Miller, a black woman who started with Avon in 1947, was profiled in *Outlook*, Avon's promotional magazine for representatives. *Outlook*, 1970, AC/HML.

32. Garland, "Natural Look," 146; Craig, *Ain't I a Beauty Queen*, 123, 124–25; *Ebony*, "Natural Look—Is It Here to Stay?" 104; Supreme Beauty Products advertisements, *Ebony*, December 1969. The model in the Supreme Beauty Products advertisement "The Bold" is Richard Roundtree, who would star in *Shaft* two years later.

33. *Beauty Trade*, "Big Show—Natural Competition," December 1970, 12–14.

34. Lois Liberty Jones and John Henry Jones, *All about the Natural* (Clairol, 1971).

35. Wallace, "Black Woman's Search," 6–7.

36. Supreme Beauty Products advertisement, *Jet*, 2 March 1967; Posner advertisement, *Ebony*, May 1971; Tintz advertisement, *Ebony*, April 1969; Perma-Strate advertisement, *Ebony*, July 1972; *Beauty Trade*, "From Permanent to Natural the Easy Way," March 1969, 24; Edward Clay, "Blow-Out Technique for Men and Women," *Beauty Trade*, July 1972, 22–23.

37. News release, 1973, box 2, CJC/NMAH; Kenyon and Eckhardt records, box 13, CJC/NMAH; Afrilyc Wig advertisement, *Ebony*, September 1971; Afrilyc Wig advertisement, *Jet*, 11 May 1972; Morgan, interview by Murray; *Beauty Trade*, "Cover Description," December 1968, 9; "Afro Wigs Are Good Money-Makers," *Beauty Trade*, December 1968, 19; Minnie Easley, "The Natural Will Be Around for Awhile," *Beauty Trade*, April 1969, 16.

38. Garland, "Natural Look," 146; *Sepia*, "Los Angeles Goes 'Natural,'" 60; *Jet*, "Afro Hair Styles, Attire Cause Bias Complaints," 7 January 1971, 25.

39. Carl Rowan, "Hair Ain't Where It's At," and Lillian Benbow, "Hair *Is* Where It's At," *Encore*, 4 October 1973, 38–39.

40. Phyl Garland, "Is the Afro on Its Way Out?" *Ebony*, February 1973, 128–36.

Conclusion

1. Alice Walker, "Oppressed Hair Puts a Ceiling on the Brain," in *Living by The Word: Selected Writings, 1973–1987* (San Diego: Harcourt Brace Jovanovich, 1988), 69–74.

2. Countryman, *Up South*, esp. chap. 3.

3. Suzanne E. Smith, *Dancing in the Street: Motown and the Cultural Politics of Detroit* (Cambridge, Mass.: Harvard University Press, 1999), 248.

4. T. Shawn Taylor, "Buying into the Ethnic Beauty Sector," *Chicago Tribune*, 9 June 2002; Corina Zappia, "Why Women of Color Can't Find Good Cosmetics," *Village Voice*, 26 May 2006.

Selected Bibliography

Archival Collections

Avon Collection, Hagley Museum and Library, Wilmington, Delaware

Claude A. Barnett Collection, Chicago Historical Society, Chicago, Illinois

Caroline Jones Collection, Archives Center, National Museum of American History, Smithsonian Institution, Washington, D.C.

Madam C. J. Walker Collection, Indiana Historical Society, Indianapolis, Indiana

Marjorie Stewart Joyner Papers, Vivian G. Harsh Research Collection, Chicago Public Library, Chicago, Illinois

Nathaniel Mathis Collection, Archives Center, National Museum of American History, Smithsonian Institution, Washington, D.C.

Warshaw Collection of Business Americana, Archives Center, National Museum of American History, Smithsonian Institution, Washington, D.C.

Women's Bureau, U.S. Department of Labor, National Archives, RG 86, Washington, D.C.

Books and Dissertations

Anderson, Lisa M. *Mammies No More: The Changing Image of Black Women on the Stage and Screen.* Lanham, Md.: Rowman and Littlefield, 1997.

Banks, Ingrid. *Hair Matters: Beauty, Power, and Black Women's Consciousness.* New York: New York University Press, 2000.

Banner, Lois. *American Beauty.* New York: Knopf, 1983.

Bay, Mia. *The White Image in the Black Mind.* New York: Oxford University Press, 2000.

Benson, Susan Porter. *Counter Cultures: Saleswomen, Managers, and Customers in American Department Stores, 1890–1940.* Urbana: University of Illinois Press, 1988.

Blackwelder, Julia Kirk. *Styling Jim Crow: African American Beauty Training during Segregation.* College Station: Texas A&M University Press, 2003.

Bogle, Donald. *Toms, Coons, Mulattoes, Mammies, and Bucks: An Interpretive History of Blacks in American Films.* 3rd ed. New York: Continuum, 1994.

Bordo, Susan. *Unbearable Weight: Feminism, Western Culture, and the Body.* Berkeley: University of California Press, 1993.

Branch, Taylor. *Parting the Waters: America in the King Years, 1954–1964.* New York: Simon and Schuster, 1988.

Bundles, A'Lelia. *On Her Own Ground: The Life and Times of Madam C. J. Walker.* New York: Scribner, 2001.

Byrd, Ayana D., and Lori Tharps. *Hair Story: Untangling the Roots of Black Hair in America.* New York: St. Martin's Press, 2001.

Chadiha, Leatha. "A Study of Black Beauty Culture and Values about Beauty in Black Society." Master's thesis, Washington State University, 1970.

Cohen, Lizabeth. *A Consumers' Republic: The Politics of Mass Consumption in Postwar America.* New York: Knopf, 2003.

———. *Making a New Deal: Industrial Workers in Chicago, 1919–1939.* New York: Cambridge University Press, 1990.

Countryman, Matthew J. *Up South: Civil Rights and Black Power in Philadelphia.* Philadelphia: University of Pennsylvania Press, 2006.

Craig, Maxine B. *Ain't I a Beauty Queen?: Black Women, Beauty, and the Politics of Race.* New York: Oxford University Press, 2002.

———. "Black Is Beautiful: Personal Transformation and Political Change." Ph.D. dissertation, University of California, Berkeley, 1996.

Cross, Gary. *An All-Consuming Century: Why Commercialism Won in Modern America.* New York: Columbia University Press, 2000.

Davis, Angela Y. *Blues Legacies and Black Feminism: Gertrude "Ma" Rainey, Bessie Smith, and Billie Holiday.* New York: Pantheon, 1998.

Edsforth, Ronald. *Class Conflict and Cultural Consensus: The Making of a Mass Consumer Society in Flint, Michigan.* New Brunswick, N.J.: Rutgers University Press, 1987.

Edwards, Paul K. *The Southern Urban Negro as a Consumer.* New York: Prentice-Hall, 1932.

Employment Opportunities for Women in Beauty Shops. U.S. Department of Labor, Women's Bureau, Bulletin no. 260. Washington, D.C.: GPO, 1956.

Enstad, Nan. *Ladies of Labor, Girls of Adventure: Working Women, Popular Culture, and Labor Politics.* New York: Columbia University Press, 1999.

Erickson, Ethel. *Employment Conditions in Beauty Shops: A Study of Four Cities.* U.S. Department of Labor, Women's Bureau, Bulletin no. 133. Washington, D.C.: GPO, 1935.

Ewen, Stuart. *Captains of Consciousness: Advertising and the Social Roots of the Consumer Culture.* New York: McGraw-Hill, 1976.

Fass, Paula. *The Damned and the Beautiful: American Youth in the 1920s.* New York: Oxford University Press, 1977.

Foner, Eric. *The Story of American Freedom.* New York: Norton, 1998.

Fox, Richard Wightman, and T. J. Jackson Lears, eds. *The Culture of Consumption: Critical Essays in American History, 1880–1980.* New York: Pantheon Books, 1983.

Frank, Thomas. *The Conquest of Cool: Business Culture, Counterculture, and the Rise of Hip Consumerism.* Chicago: University of Chicago Press, 1997.

Fredrickson, George M. *The Black Image in the White Mind: The Debate on Afro-American Character and Destiny, 1817–1914.* New York: Harper and Row, 1971.

Gatewood, Willard B. *Aristocrats of Color: The Black Elite, 1880–1920.* Bloomington: Indiana University Press, 1990.

Glickman, Lawrence B., ed. *Consumer Society in American History: A Reader.* Ithaca, N.Y.: Cornell University Press, 1999.

Goldman, Peter. *Report from Black America.* New York: Simon and Schuster, 1969.

Gottlieb, Peter. *Making Their Own Way: Southern Blacks' Migration to Pittsburgh, 1916–1930.* Urbana: University of Illinois Press, 1987.

Grossman, James. *Land of Hope: Chicago, Black Southerners, and the Great Migration.* Chicago: University of Chicago Press, 1990.

Harris, Juliette, and Pamela Johnson, eds. *Tenderheaded: A Comb-Bending Collection of Hair Stories.* New York: Pocket Books, 2001.

Harrison, Daphne Duval. *Black Pearls: Blues Queens of the 1920s.* New Brunswick, N.J.: Rutgers University Press, 1988.

Haskins, James. *Lena: A Personal and Political Biography.* New York: Stein and Day, 1984.

Higginbotham, Evelyn Brooks. *Righteous Discontent: The Women's Movement in the Black Baptist Church, 1880–1920.* Cambridge, Mass.: Harvard University Press, 1993.

Hill, Ruth Edmonds, ed. *The Black Women's Oral History Project: From the Arthur and Elizabeth Schlesinger Library on the History of Women in America, Radcliffe College.* Westport, Conn.: Meckler, 1991.

Hine, Darlene Clark. *Hine Sight: Black Women and the Reconstruction of America.* Bloomington: Indiana University Press, 1994.

Hughes, Langston, and Milton Meltzer. *Black Magic: A Pictorial History of the Negro in American Entertainment.* New York: Pantheon, 1968.

Hunter, Tera. *To 'joy My Freedom: Southern Black Women's Lives and Labor after the Civil War.* Cambridge, Mass.: Harvard University Press, 1997.

Jones, Jaqueline. *Labor of Love, Labor of Sorrow: Black Women, Work, and the Family from Slavery to the Present.* New York: Random House, 1985.

Jones, Lisa. *Bulletproof Diva: Tales of Race, Sex, and Hair.* New York: Anchor Books, 1995.

Jordan, Winthrop. *White over Black: American Attitudes toward the Negro, 1550–1812.* Chapel Hill: University of North Carolina Press, 1968.

Kelley, Robin D. G. *Race Rebels: Culture, Politics, and the Black Working Class.* New York: Free Press, 1994.

Kusmer, Kenneth L., ed. *Depression, War, and the New Migration, 1930–1960.* Vol. 6 of *Black Communities and Urban Development in America, 1720–1990.* New York: Garland Publishing, 1991.

Latham, Angela. *Posing a Threat: Flappers, Chorus Girls, and Other Brazen Performers of the American 1920s.* Hanover, N.H.: University Press of New England, 2000.

Lears, Jackson. *Fables of Abundance: A Cultural History of Advertising in America.* New York: Basic Books, 1994.

Marchand, Roland. *Advertising the American Dream: Making Way for Modernity, 1920–1940.* Berkeley: University of California Press, 1985.

McDowell, Deborah E. *Leaving Pipe Shop: Memories of Kin.* New York: Scribner, 1996.

Mizejewski, Linda. *Ziegfeld Girl: Image and Icon in Culture and Cinema*. Durham, N.C.: Duke University Press, 1999.

Moody, Anne. *Coming of Age in Mississippi*. 1968. Reprint, New York: Dell, 1976.

Morrow, Willie L. *400 Years without a Comb: The Untold Story*. San Diego: Black Publishers of America, 1973.

North, J. A. *Beauty Culture as an Occupation*. U.S. National Youth Administration, 1937.

Ownsby, Ted. *American Dreams in Mississippi: Consumers, Poverty, and Culture, 1830–1998*. Chapel Hill: University of North Carolina Press, 1999.

Peiss, Kathy. *Cheap Amusements: Working Women and Leisure in Turn-of-the-Century New York*. Philadelphia: Temple University Press, 1986

————. *Hope in a Jar: The Making of America's Beauty Culture*. New York: Holt, 1998.

Porter, Gladys L. *Three Negro Pioneers in Beauty Culture*. New York, Vantage Press, 1966.

Research Company of America. *Washington's 28% Plus Market*. Research Company of America, 1945.

Robinson, Gwendolyn. "Class, Race, and Gender: A Transcultural, Theoretical, and Sociohistorical Analysis of Cosmetic Institutions and Practices to 1920." Ph.D. dissertation, University of Illinois at Chicago, 1984.

Rooks, Noliwe. *Hair Raising: Beauty, Culture, and African American Women*. New Brunswick, N.J.: Rutgers University Press, 1996.

Rose, Phyllis. *Jazz Cleopatra: Josephine Baker in Her Time*. New York: Vintage, 1991.

Russell, Kathy, Midge Wilson, and Ronald Hall. *The Color Complex: The Politics of Skin Color among African Americans*. New York: Harcourt Brace Jovanovich, 1992.

Smith, Jessie Carney. *Notable Black American Women*. 3 vols. Detroit: Gale Research, 1992–2003.

Sochen, June. *From Mae to Madonna: Women Entertainers in Twentieth Century America*. Lexington: University Press of Kentucky, 1999.

Trotter, Joe W., and Earl Lewis. *African Americans in the Industrial Age: A Documentary History, 1915–1945*. Boston: Northeastern University Press, 1996.

Turner, Patricia. *Ceramic Uncles and Celluloid Mammies: Black Images and Their Influence on Culture*. New York: Anchor Books, 1994.

Van Deburg, William L. *New Day in Babylon: The Black Power Movement and American Culture, 1965–1975*. Chicago: University of Chicago Press, 1992.

Waldfogel, Sabra. "The Body Beautiful, The Body Hateful: Feminine Body Image and the Culture of Consumption in Twentieth Century America." Ph.D. dissertation, University of Minnesota, 1986.

Weems, Robert. *Desegregating the Dollar*. New York: New York University Press, 1998.

Weisbrot, Robert. *Freedom Bound: A Narrative History of America's Civil Rights Movement*. New York: Plume, 1991.

Willett, Julie A. *Permanent Waves: The Making of the American Beauty Shop*. New York: New York University Press, 1998.

White, Shane, and Graham White. *Stylin': African American Expressive Culture from Its Beginnings to the Zoot Suit*. Ithaca, N.Y.: Cornell University Press, 1998.

Book Chapters, Journal Articles, and Magazine Articles

Apex News. "Anatomy as It Affects the Beautician." October 1929.
————. "Apex Convention." August–September 1929.
————. "The Pot of Gold." December 1929.
Associated Negro Press. "Many Women Favor New African-Type Hairdos." *Muhammad Speaks*, April 1963.
Ballard, Earl. "Apex Agents Endorse Huge Welfare Program," *Apex News* (January 1940).
Beauty Trade. "Afro Wigs Are Good Money Makers." December 1968.
————. "Big Show—Natural Competition." December 1970.
————. "Coiffure Show." February 1965.
————. "Integrated Beauty Salon Prospers in Detroit's Federal Department Store." December 1966.
Benbow, Lillian. "Hair Is Where It's At." *Encore Magazine*, 4 October 1973.
Brandford, Ed. "What is Negro Beauty?" *Our World*, November 1947.
Brown, Elsa Barkley. "Womanist Consciousness: Maggie Lena Walker and the Independent Order of St. Luke." *Signs* 14 (Spring 1989): 610–633.
Burroughs, Margaret. "Down the Straight and Narrow." *Urbanite*, May 1961.
Burroughs, Nannie. "Address at Apex Commencement." *Apex News*, January–February–March 1938.
Campbell, E. Simms. "Are Black Women Beautiful?" *Negro Digest*, June 1951.
————. "The Perfect Negro Beauty." *Jet*, 13 March 1957.
Carby, Hazel. "'It Jus Be's Dat Way Sometime': The Sexual Politics of Women's Blues." *Radical America* 20, no. 4 (1986): 9–22.
————. "Policing the Black Woman's Body in an Urban Context." *Critical Inquiry* 18 (Summer 1992): 739–55.
Cleaver, Eldridge. "As Crinkly as Yours." *Negro History Bulletin* 30 (March 1962): 127–32.
Color. "Is Beauty a Curse?" February 1953.
Cooke, Marie. "Wear Your Natural Beautifully and Proudly." *Dawn Magazine*, 25 May 1974.
Craig, Maxine. "The Decline and Fall of the Conk; or, How to Read a Process." *Fashion Theory* 1, no. 4 (December 1997): 399–419.
Davis, Angela Y. "Afro Images: Politics, Fashion, and Nostalgia." In *Soul: Black Power, Politics, and Pleasure*, edited by Monique Guillory and Richard C. Green. New York: New York University Press, 1998.
de Mille, Arnold C. "For New Glamour Today." *Pulse*, April 1943.
Doggett, Rose. "Make Me Beautiful." *Apex News*, April–May–June 1938.
Drug and Cosmetics Industry. "A Celebrity for Negro Cosmetics." February 1971.
————. "Libra: New Line of Negro Cosmetics." December 1969.

————. "Negro Cosmetics: Seminar Assesses Special Needs." October 1969.

————. "Now It's Nancy Wilson with a New Cosmetic Line!" March 1971.

Easley, Minnie. "The Natural Will Be Around for Awhile." *Beauty Trade*, April 1969.

Ebony. "Are Negro Girls Getting Prettier?" February 1966.

————. "Beauty Queens of 1959." September 1959.

————. "Brown Beauty with Courage." October 1966.

————. "Can Negro Models Make the Bigtime?" September 1954.

————. "Capital's Proud Black Princess." July 1970.

————. "Detroit Beauty Queen." September 1962.

————. "Detroit House of Beauty." December 1951.

————. "The Girl in the Marilyn Monroe Dress." June 1957.

————. "Harlem's New House of Beauty." June 1955.

————. "Have Black Models Really Made It?" May 1970.

————. "House of Beauty: Rose-Meta Salon Is Biggest Negro Beauty Parlor in the World." May 1946.

————. "Integration Comes to the Beauty Business." August 1966.

————. "Is It True What They Say about Models?" November 1951.

————. "Model School: First Interracial Charm School Runs Hit West Coast Fashion Show." July 1948.

————. "Model Schools: Racket or Business?" September 1950.

————. "The Natural Look—Is It Here to Stay?" January 1969.

————. "Negro Girl in Miss America Race." July 1965.

————. "New Trend toward Black Beauties." December 1967.

————. "Paris Model: Los Angeles Girl Gets Schiaparelli Job to Become Only Negro in Fashion Capital of the World." February 1950.

————. "The Trend toward Black Beauties." December 1967.

Edwards, Thyra. "What Shall I Do with My Hair?" *Our World*, April 1946.

Ellis, Eddie. "Is EBONY a Negro Magazine?" Pts. 1 and 2. *Liberator*, October 1965, November 1965.

Evans, Linda J. "Claude A. Barnett and the Associated Negro Press." *Chicago History* 12, no. 1 (1983): 44–55.

Eyes. "Cinderella Show." August 1946.

Farrel, Barry. "Farewell, More or Less, to the Supremes." *Life*, 13 February 1970.

Forkan, James F. "Who's Who in $350,000,000 Black Grooming Market." *Advertising Age*, 20 November 1972.

Garland, Phyl. "Is the Afro on Its Way Out?" *Ebony*, February 1973.

————. "The Natural Look." *Ebony*, June 1966.

Gibson, D. Parke. "Creating Products for Negro Consumers." *Marketing Magazine*, 1 May 1969.

Gill, Tiffany Melissa. "'I Had My Own Business . . . So I Didn't Have to Worry': Beauty Salons, Beauty Culturists, and the Politics of African American Female Entrepreneurship." In *Beauty and Business: Commerce, Gender, and Culture in Modern America*, edited by Philip Scranton, 169–94. New York: Routledge, 2001.

Goodrich, Jim, and A. S. Young. "Why Hollywood Won't Glamorize Negro Girls." *Jet*, 17 September 1953.

Granton, Fannie E. "Pride in Blackness and Natural Hairdo Led to Spirited Campaign." *Jet*, 10 November 1966.

Half-Century Magazine. "Rouge and Progress." May–June 1921.

———. "Types of Racial Beauty." June 1919.

Haring, H. A. "The Negro as Consumer: How to Sell to a Race That, for the First Time in Its History, Has Money to Spend." *Advertising and Selling*, 3 September 1930.

———. "Selling to Harlem." *Advertising and Selling*, 31 October 1928.

Higginbotham, Evelyn Brooks. "African American Women's History and the Metalanguage of Race." *Signs* 17 (Winter 1992): 251–74.

Hine, Darlene Clark. "Rape and the Inner Lives of Black Women in the Middle West: Preliminary Thoughts on the Culture of Dissemblance." *Signs* 14 (Summer 1989): 912–20.

Hue. "Are Whites Accepting Brown Beauties?" July 1954.

Jeffries, LeRoy. "The Decay of the Beauty Parlor Industry in Harlem." *Opportunity*, February 1938.

Jet. "The Afro: A Natural Groove or a Natural Mess?" 13 July 1972.

———. "Afro Hair Styles, Attire Cause Bias Complaints." 7 February 1971.

———. "Afro Hairdo Upsets African Writer." 15 October 1970.

———. "Beauty Queens at White Schools." 30 November 1967.

———. "Hollywood's Unknown Negro Beauties." 22 November 1951.

———. "Mme. C. J. Walker Co. Celebrates 60th Anniversary." 22 September 1960.

———. "Named 1st Negro Woman to Florida State Post." 30 June 1955.

———. "119 Beauticians to Study in France." 3 December 1953.

———. "Paris Model Has Dazzling Wardrobe." 6 December 1951.

———. "What Are Naturals Doing to Beauty and Barber Shops?" 26 March 1970.

———. "What Happens to Beauty Queens?" 20 March 1952.

———. "Why Brownskin Girls Get the Best Movie Roles." 16 October 1952.

Johnson, Guy B. "Newspaper Advertisements and Negro Culture." *Journal of Social Forces* 3 (1925): 706–9.

Joyner, Marjorie. "Naturals Paying Off!" *Beauty Trade*, May 1969.

Kelley, Robin D. G. "Nap Time: Historicizing the Afro." *Fashion Theory* 1, no. 4 (December 1997): 339–51.

King, Helen Hays. "Should Women Straighten Their Hair?—No!" *Negro Digest*, August 1963.

Kusmer, Kenneth. "African Americans in the City Since World War II: From the Industrial to the Post-Industrial Era," *Journal of Urban History* 21, no. 4 (1995): 458–504.

Leak, Sylvester. "The Revolution in Hair Grooming—Is the Black Beautician Losing Fight for Life?" *Muhammad Speaks*, 26 February 1965.

Linn, Frank. "Ethiopian Invasion in America." *Apex News*, November–December 1935.

Malvik, Ethel. "The Black Cosmetics Market." *American Druggist*, 21 September 1970.

Mason, Eleanor. "Hot Irons and Black Nationalism." *Liberator*, May 1963.

Mercer, Kobena. "Black Hair/Style Politics." In *Out There: Marginalization and Contemporary Cultures*, edited by Russell Ferguson, Martha Gever, Trinh T. Minh-ha, and Cornel West, 247–64. New York: New Museum of Contemporary Art, 1990.

Muhammad Speaks. "The Natural Look Is Reborn in Brilliant New Show." February 1963.

Nelms, Rose. "Natural Hair Yes, Hot Irons No." *Liberator*, July 1963.

Northington, Evelyn. "The Care of the Hair." *Half-Century Magazine*, November 1920.

Oladipupo, Raymond. "All-out Marketing Keeps Clairol Ahead with Negro Women." *Media-Scope*. September 1969.

Our World. "Beauty Is His World." March 1955.

———. "Beauty Train to Paris." August 1954.

———. "Color, Milady, Color." April 1949.

———. "Dorothea Towles: Paris' Fabulous Negro Model." August 1952.

———. "The Glamazons: Beauty by the Ton." November 1954.

———. "How Evil Is Eartha?" September 1954.

———. "Lena Horne: *Our World's* First Cover Girl." April 1950.

———. "Miss Bronze Los Angeles." August 1952.

———. "Philadelphia's Miss Sepia." January 1953.

———. "What Happened to the Brandford Models?" February 1954.

———. "What Is Sex Appeal?" July 1952.

———. "What Makes a Model?" October 1953.

Peiss, Kathy. "Making Faces: The Cosmetics Industry and the Cultural Construction of Gender, 1890–1930." In *Unequal Sisters: A Multicultural Reader in U.S. Women's History*, 2nd ed., edited by Vicki L. Ruiz and Ellen Carol DuDois, 372–94. New York: Routledge, 1994.

Publishers Weekly. "National Negro Market Survey Shows $12 Billion Expenditures." 5 July 1947.

Rowan, Carl. "Hair Ain't Where It's At." *Encore Magazine*, 4 October 1973.

Rushing, Andrea Benton. "Hair Raising." *Feminist Studies* 14, no. 2 (Summer 1998): 325–35.

Sales Management. "The Soul Market in Black and White." 1 June 1969.

Sepia. "Los Angeles Goes 'Natural.'" January 1967.

———. "Precola Devore's Charm School." December 1964.

———. "The Private Life of Dorothea Towles." November 1959.

———. "Will There Ever Be a Black Miss America?" February 1975.

Sullivan, David J. "The American Negro—an 'Export' Market at Home!" *Printer's Ink*, 21 July 1944.

Tide. "The Negro Market: An Appraisal." 7 March 1947.

———. "Negro Markets." 15 March 1946.

Torriani, Aimee. "The Business of Becoming Beautiful." *Abbott's Monthly*, February 1931.

Walden, Goldie M. "Beauty." *Abbott's Monthly*, January 1933.

Walker, Alice. "Oppressed Hair Puts a Ceiling on the Brain." In *Living by the Word: Selected Writings, 1973–1987*, 69–74. San Diego: Harcourt Brace Jovanovich, 1988.

Walker, Susannah. "Black Is Profitable: The Commodification of the Afro, 1960–1975." In *Beauty and Business: Commerce, Gender, and Culture in Modern America*, edited by Philip Scranton, 254–77. New York: Routledge, 2001.

Wallace, Michelle. "A Black Woman's Search for Sisterhood." In *All the Women Are White, All the Blacks Are Men, but Some of Us Are Brave: Black Women's Studies*, edited by Gloria T. Hull, Patricia Bell Scott, and Barbara Smith, 5–12. Old Westbury, N.Y.: Feminist Press, 1982.

Young, A. S. "Beauty in Negro Women." *Sepia*, September 1963.

Index

Page references for illustrations are in italics.